FACING HELL:
The Story of a Nobody

An autobiography 1913–1996

FACING HELL:
The Story of a Nobody

An autobiography 1913–1996

John Wenham

paternoster
press

First published in the UK 1998 by Paternoster Press

03 02 01 00 99 98   7 6 5 4 3 2 1

Paternoster Press is an imprint of Paternoster Publishing,
P.O. Box 300, Carlisle, Cumbria CA3 0QS
http://www.paternoster-publishing.com

British Library Cataloguing in Publication Data
A catalogue record for this book is available from the British Library.

ISBN 0-85364-871-9

Cover design by Mainstream, Lancaster
Typeset by WestKey Ltd, Falmouth, Cornwall
Printed in Great Britain by Mackays of Chatham PLC, Kent

Contents

Preface

'I believe that endless torment is a hideous and unscriptural doctrine which has been a terrible burden on the mind of the church for many centuries and a terrible blot on her presentation of the gospel. I should indeed be happy if, before I die, I could help in sweeping it away.' So I wrote at the end of a paper which I read at Rutherford House, Edinburgh in 1991. I was therefore inclined to take seriously the urgent request of a publisher that I should expand that paper into a book. It seemed to me that such a book would fit into my series on The Christian View of the Bible.

But the subject of hell has become so intertwined with other aspects of theology – the notion of revelation, the differences between Rome and Reformation, the conflict between liberals and fundamentalists, the tension between evangelical Anglicans and evangelical Free Churchmen – that it seemed necessary to set it in a wider context, and even to see it as the climax to a whole world view. But my serious theological works which require research and documenting have taken me on average about ten years each to write, which puts anything of that sort right out of the question since I am now eighty years of age.

Then a thought came to me from a slightly misremembered passage in C.S. Lewis' *The Pilgrim's Regress*. There he explains how allegory is a means of bringing home the feel of a theological idea without spelling the idea out in detail. The thought came: would that not be true also of autobiography? Could not the progression of thought that has brought me to my present position be sketched out in an interesting way without going into theological detail?

Then the memories began to flood in in a quite extraordinary way. For four weeks I was waking at an unearthly hour with thoughts crowding in too numerous to commit to paper. Certain things became clear:

Firstly, I realized that I had been an adult observer for sixty years of one of the most turbulent periods in the history of the world, and of the church.

Secondly, I realized that I was a person of most limited gifts, a mere nobody. Except for my dedication to the Christian View of the Bible project, I am a very ordinary person. In comparison with the big brains of society I am just third-rate; in no sense can I be regarded as big in brain or energy or personality. For one who is moving about among scholars I have in fact (as my friends will bear me out) a bad memory, except for things in which I am deeply interested.

Thirdly, I realized that there is a blessing in a bad memory – it forces one back again and again to ask: What are the essentials? I found the answer to that question to be: The heart of everything is faith in Christ, who is both our theological teacher and the one who authenticates the scriptures to us. These are the two pillars on which a coherent theology rests. What Christ has to say about his authority as a teacher is not to be sought in a vast mass of Christian literature but in four short gospels, which are easily accessible and which will never change. Similarly his view of Holy Scripture is equally accessible and equally unchanging. These two rocks are set in an ocean of problems which are waiting to be explored more fully.

Fourthly, I came to feel that a theology resting on these two pillars had something useful to say to many schools of thought in the present chaotic state of the intellectual world and of Christian theology.

The autobiographical approach also illustrates the intricate relation between theology and life. Theology is bound to become distorted if it is not lived out in prayer and obedience. It is hoped that references to the joys and pains of sexual life will not seem out of place. Possibly the struggles of a resister may have an interest greater than the yieldings so unceasingly presented to us in the soaps and plays and novels of our permissive society.

One

Background — 1913–27

On the wall of the church of St Peter and St Paul, Chaldon, in Surrey, in the churchyard of which my parents lie buried, is a famous thirteenth-century fresco. In it are shown figures of the damned being pushed back into the flames by demons armed with pitchforks. For some years I worshipped in this church and I have carried that picture in my mind as a typical representation of the medieval notion of hell. It did not fill me with terror as it was supposed to do, for I had long since come to believe that such ideas had been completely outgrown in our advanced civilization. But even within my own family these things had not always been so.

Grandfather, Alfred Ebenezer Wenham, came of a large Christian family. His father, Ebenezer, lived in Highgate and was actuary to one of the big insurance companies. He produced eleven children, one of whom died in infancy, and then proceeded to die himself, leaving his remarkable wife, Mary, to bring up the children. She organized the family into a high-class school in which, with the help of the older children, she educated her own offspring and those of her neighbours. She died in 1907 at the age of 102.

I knew five of the family, my grandfather and Uncle John and three maiden great-aunts who lived not far from us at Limpsfield. The eldest, Aunt Anna, was an excellent water-colourist, two of whose pictures hang today in my rooms. She was very prim and proper and we thought her rather unapproachable (which was understandable at her age). She was just coming to terms with the motor car and expressed herself willing to be taken for a drive, provided the vehicle did not exceed the speed of a good horse and carriage. The story is preserved that Anna at the age of 80 was one day taking her mother, then aged over 100, for her daily outing in the bath chair, when her mother exclaimed, 'You ought not to be out on a day like this at your age.' Aunt Gertrude, a mere ninety or so, I knew rather better; she was a bit starchy but she was kind enough to leave me a set of Rockingham china, which she inherited from her nanny, who inherited it from her mother, who was given it on her wedding day. It gives me great pleasure to serve tea in these cups to my more discerning visitors. Aunt Marion we liked best as she had a nice sense of humour and seemed the most human of the aunts.

But the two we knew best were John and Alfred. When I first knew him – I was born in December, 1913 – my grandfather lived at The Old Rose and Crown amid the Lickey Hills in the village of Rednal on the southern fringe of Birmingham. There were the East Hill and the West Hill, covering a hundred or so acres, with the inn converted into a very comfortable house in the middle. There was an indoor staff of four or five and plenty of room for visitors – a lovely place for our family of six to visit.

My grandfather was unashamedly, almost ostentatiously, devout. His parents before him were Congregationalists in a day when it was quite costly to profess nonconformity, and the children grew up with minds of their own. One joined the Plymouth Brethren; the Limpsfield ladies became diligent (slightly High-Church) Anglicans. The tombstone in Limpsfield churchyard records their ages: Anna 94, Gertrude 96, Marion 98. When Marion died her nephew, J.H. Wenham wrote to *The Times*, saying, 'the ten reached an average age of exactly ninety, the oldest living to within seven weeks of his 102nd birthday. The

centenarian prudently purchased an annuity at the age of eighty!'
No one wrote to cap this record. John (the centenarian nonconformist) at the age of ninety was churchwarden at Combe-Down,
Bath when Canon A.B. Lloyd, missionary to the pygmies, was
vicar. John remained a free churchman and Alfred Ebenezer
developed rather extreme Calvinistic views. He had a mission hall
in the grounds of 'The Lickey' and unfortunately got across the
rector at Rednal. The rector had the reputation of being a saintly
High-Churchman, and my mother (before she met my father) was
friendly with the rector's daughters. This meant that she never
really liked her father-in-law.

Alfred Ebenezer was widowed fairly young and for years had
the bitter experience of every night shutting himself in his lonely
bedroom. He then invited his parlour-maid Leah to marry him.
She, though most devoted to him, was quite shattered by this, not
feeling that she had the sort of love a wife should have. She left
his service and for three years debated the matter in her heart,
amidst the clamour of opposing views within her family and his.
At last she felt that she could not live without him and they
entered upon a marriage which was blissfully happy to both
parties. Such a marriage was hardly the done thing in those days,
so Grandfather sold 'The Lickey' to the Birmingham Corpora-
tion and bought a beautiful house near Oban on the Argyllshire
coast. 'Kilbowie' was a well-built, castellated house, overlooking
the Sound of Kerrera, tucked in between the island of Mull and
the mainland. From now on our summer holiday was always at
Oban which we reached sometimes by night sleeper and sometimes by a leisurely road journey with the two cars, stopping off
at various places on the way.

My grandfather presided over family prayers every morning
after breakfast. We continued sitting at the table, the staff
trooped in and sat in a row on one side of the room, while he
read the Bible feelingly, as if it was indeed the Word of God.
Then we would all kneel down and he would pray in his own

well-chosen words. Though technically extempore it developed a semi-liturgical form, part of which my eldest sister was able to recall verbatim: 'Wilt Thou so guide, direct and overrule all that is passing in our own land, and throughout the world, that Thy purposes may be accomplished, and Thy Kingdom and Thy Coming hastened?' When Sunday came we had the problem of which church to go to. Grandfather had joined the Free Presbyterian Church of Scotland, which was the most traditional of the Scottish Presbyterian churches, and had become an elder. In the Free Presbyterian Church the doctrine of the immortality of the soul and the everlasting torment of the damned was regularly and earnestly preached. We tried this church on our first Sunday. The building was very plain, no musical instruments were allowed or 'uninspired' hymns, but only metrical psalms. These were introduced by a precentor in a tone which (I am afraid) suggested to us children a donkey's braying. Prayers were long and the sermon some fifty minutes or so. We went one Sunday, but that was enough; we could not risk another spell of boredom and possibly of uncontrollable giggles, and we tried other churches.

We shall return to Oban in due course, but first let us look at the home from which we came. Our first home, 'Rednal', was a comfortable detached house with about an acre of well-kept garden at Sanderstead which in those days was just beyond the southern edge of London. Grandfather Wenham had established a very successful firm of chartered accountants in Birmingham, where my two uncles continued to work throughout most of their lives, while Father was dispatched to London to establish a branch there. The firm specialized in the running of manufacturers' associations. Grandfather had a great gift for persuading people to do what he wanted and he would get together manufacturers who were competing with one another and sit them round a table and talk to them. 'There is no point in you all cutting one another's throats,' he would say. 'Meet together once a week in my office and decide who will put in the lowest tender for each advertised job.' The lowest tender would of course give a satisfactory profit and all would get a fair share of such tenders. Though more secretive, this system is in principle no more immoral than collective bargaining by trade unions (there are arguments for and against cut-throat competition), but it is open to abuse, though I am sure that my grandfather always conducted his affairs in the strictest honesty. It was a sure way to making money for owners of rapidly expanding industries. (I was later to spend a good many hours working on the books of The Cable Manufacturers Association.) Grandfather did well out of this and was able in the days when taxes were not cripplingly high to become quite a rich man.

My father was educated at King Edward the Sixth School, Birmingham, and at Pembroke College, Cambridge, where he gained an honours degree in mathematics. He had clearly acquired a Christian faith through his home and continued to say his prayers and attend church all his life. We said grace before meals and we had family prayers after breakfast every day, when he read us a passage from the Bible selected according to some Scripture Union system, then said the collect for the day, finishing up with the Lord's Prayer and the grace. But his own faith was not without difficulty. As far as I know he did not read theological books, but he knew his Bible and Book of Common Prayer well and he was fully acquainted with their more obvious difficulties. His father was a literalist who believed the Bible from cover to cover and in his retirement wrote books, including a commentary on Genesis. This had a section on the genealogies of the patriarchs in which he argued that the 4,004 or so years BC provided ample time for Adam and Eve to populate the world as it was in the time of Christ. But Father was educated by academics abreast of all the latest theories which held sway towards the end of the nineteenth century, which means that they were Darwinists almost to a man. *The Origin of Species* was amongst his books on the shelves in the dining room. To a thoughtful, honest-minded man the odds were overwhelming. Of what value were the amateur views of a pious accountant over against all this expert modern knowledge? Though he did not read theological books, he had a ready ear for Dean Inge of St Paul's, a liberal, philosophical theologian of some distinction, who wrote regularly for one of the London evening papers. It was said of him, 'I don't know whether he is a pillar of the church, but he is certainly two columns of the *Evening Standard.*'

This made my father a dutiful, but unenthusiastic Christian, content to worship at the local parish church. St Mary's, Sanderstead, which was next door to our house, was a corrugated iron building when we first knew it and the members worked hard to raise the money for a permanent church. When the time came, my father was asked to lay the foundation stone. Latterly, at the time of the Anglo-Catholic congresses of 1920–30, the church became very high, which he did not at all like, and was glad when he moved out to Whyteleafe to worship at the more moderate church at Chaldon.

My parents' aim was undoubtedly to give us a sound, all-round Christian upbringing, avoiding extremes. Very little of it I would now disapprove of. The general ethos of the home was fairly unworldly. There were no rigid taboos on drink, dancing, theatre, card-playing, gambling or Sunday games, but such things had a very modest place in our family life – a bottle of port at Christmas and a very occasional visit to a show was about all. Father's home was very much his castle. He had two hobbies, tennis-playing and his cars. During the light summer evenings and at week-ends my parents regularly spent time at the Purley Lawn Tennis Club and in the winter at the hard courts club. Father seldom went out at night, but on the dark evenings we would sit round the fire and he would hold us spellbound with readings from the great authors: Charles Dickens, Robert Louis Stevenson, Charles Kingsley and the like, which gave us a feeling for good literature.

He had a great aversion to affectation and was fond of reading (perhaps at a mealtime) from the article in Fowler's *Modern English Usage* on 'Genteelisms'. He was also particular about our speech, specially disliking the Surrey 'ow'. He had a love-hate relationship with his cars which in those days required a lot of maintenance. He often came out from under the car in a bad temper covered with oil and grease from dealing with the numerous lubrication points.

It was of course a world dominated by the Great War and its aftermath. One of my earliest memories in fact is of an air-raid practice in the kindergarten of Woodford School, Croydon, when we had to hide under the tables. I distinguished myself at that school in the gym. It had a gallery which meant that the ceiling was two storeys up. As a very small boy I amazed the onlookers by climbing the rope which was suspended from the ceiling and ringing the bell which hung at the top. From that day to this I have been happy when I have a good grip with my hands, whereas balancing on a bar has always frightened me. (As will appear, there is a big element of fear in my make-up.) I can also remember a holiday on the Kent coast – I think at Kingsdown – just after the war had ended when we saw minesweepers clearing the Straits of Dover.

Father had bad varicose veins, which he attributed to typhoid fever, and so never had to fight in that terrible war. I am told that he undertook, gratis, to manage the accounts of the munitions industry which used the new ferro-chrome (stainless steel). After the war he was presented with a handsome canteen of silver-plated spoons and forks and of stainless steel knives, which has since come down to me. His exemption from military service meant that our home life was relatively undisturbed. We had a pleasant garden to play in with our own hens producing eggs for us. At one time we also had Ginny the donkey, an obstinate creature who pulled a trap. Unfortunately her braying disturbed the neighbours and she had to be got rid of. Percy Smith the

gardener kept an immaculate tennis court, which was to be a
source of great pleasure as we grew up. In front of the house was
a considerable space and an area of blank wall against which I
was to spend hours practising – even of course dreaming of
playing at Wimbledon.

When quite small, still sleeping in my parents' bedroom, I
showed some precocity at mental arithmetic. In the early morning
I would wake up and ask for a sum and they would keep me
amused with little problems. I also loved maps and would pore
over an atlas of the world. My mother Evelyn was a very lovely
person, though when she died during my student days, I felt sadly
that I had not really got to know her – this I think for two reasons.
First and foremost it was because most of the time I was away
either at boarding school or college. Also, in the early days, it was
because so much of mother's duties were delegated to our nanny.
Miss Evans ('Savvy' was the best we could do) suffered from
asthma, and was doubtless frustrated at having no children of her
own, but she loved us and we loved her. She was a great patriot
and taught us to revere the royal family. I always regarded
George V as 'my king'. She had one habit which annoyed my
three sisters, she liked to call me 'the son and heir'! She had
eventually to transfer her affections to another family, the children of a wealthy Jewish artist. She regarded my mother as her
best friend and never came to like her new mistress in any
comparable way. The two families provided her with a good
pension and she was well cared for. She died virtually without
possessions, but left a mahogany tea caddy to my wife, whom she
had come greatly to like. She died in faith and well loved and I
think fulfilled. Singleness need be no tragedy.

The same applies to my maiden aunts. Aunt Hilda was the
Second Mistress at St Paul's Girls' School, Hammersmith. She
taught mathematics and was well loved. Aunt Mabel turned
Roman Catholic to her father's horror. She would work away at
braille for the blind or bury herself in *The Tablet* or read to us

children. Of her my father said, 'Isn't it curious that those who
need to go to confession least, go most?' Aunt Janet, my god-
mother, was a Church Missionary Society worker in Palestine.
For my fifth birthday she gave me a Bible in which she had
inscribed the text, 'From a child thou hast known the holy
scriptures which are able to make thee wise unto salvation
through faith which is in Christ Jesus.' I particularly liked some
of the Copping pictures with which it was illustrated: David and
Goliath and (my favourite) Daniel in the Lions' Den. The latter
shows the dignified figure with his eyes lifted in prayer to heaven
and a great lion nestled against his legs. We used to sing at
Grandfather's:

> Dare to be a Daniel
> Dare to stand alone
> Dare to have a purpose firm
> Dare to make it known.

Later on I met in Palestine someone who had known Aunt Janet's
missionary work at first hand. She described her as not having
brilliant gifts but as being wonderfully dependable. I am sure I
owed a lot to her prayers. I think I kept up the practice of saying
my prayers at my bedside until I left home for Uppingham.

Though our home was a comfortable one, we were by no
means spoilt. My father was a bit of a Spartan and (like so many
Victorians) started each day with a cold bath, a practice which he
continued until quite aged. We children were expected to do as
we were told. During and after World War I the upper middle
classes which had been used to servants in the home were hard
put to it both to obtain and then to retain any servants. When the
servants went off to make munitions, my mother had to teach
herself cooking and other domestic arts. Most of the time we
maintained with difficulty a staff of two, usually short-term
foreigners. We had a Danish cook who was a Pentecostal, from
whose bedroom came the strange sound of singing in 'tongues'.

She was an excellent worker, whom my father called 'the Incomparable Mary', and she was no doubt a good influence in the home. But the retention of maids was so precarious that at one stage we were absolutely prohibited from entering the kitchen, which was not an ideal way of teaching us domestic skills. However, when things were rather more relaxed, I showed my interest in scientific experiments. Our cook, Mrs Burt, was supposed to be very deaf and I thought this was worth testing out, so I entered the kitchen and fired a blank cartridge pistol behind her. She was vindicated, since she was quite unmoved. In the days before central heating one hardly expected to be warm all over, but warm just on the side nearest the fire. I had a bad circulation and used to suffer from chilblains, wretched itchy things on one's fingers and toes. One of the snags about our holidays in Oban was the cold sea-water. Running shivering up the concrete steps at Kilbowie after bathing, I stumbled and broke my newly acquired front tooth which had to remain unsightly for some years before it could be crowned.

When kindergarten days were over, I was sent aged seven as a weekly boarder to The Limes School, South Croydon. This meant five days at school followed by the week-end at home. On the whole it was a good school, run by Major Atkinson who had gathered round him a staff consisting mainly of ex-service men, most of whom were heavy smokers. These men went off in the General Strike of 1926 as special constables to patrol the streets of West Croydon, four of them together.

On first arrival I shot up the school, being moved up after the first fortnight and again at the end of the first term. All subjects were quite well taught and I enjoyed them. Atkinson had rather grandiose ideas, which got him into some trouble. For instance, at one sports day he got the band of the Grenadier Guards (presumably his old regiment) to come to play for us. He evidently got into difficulties financially, for he took into partnership a wealthy local man, who was academically able (and incidentally taught me my first scraps of Greek), but in his attitude to boys morally suspect. This man had quite a literary gift and wrote an article in the school magazine entitled, 'The Human Boy in a Prep. School'. He said that there was a tendency to depict boys according to types. He roundly denied that they fell into types and then proceeded to describe four boys in the school, one of which was me. I quote this outsider's description with a blush:

> My second boy is genial and polished in looks and in manner. He is well-built, and you would pick him out as an athlete – but he isn't. He much prefers playing the piano to playing games. He does his school work efficiently, but he does not ask masters for extra help; he seems, rather, to think that it is up to him to lend a helping hand occasionally to masters. You see, he likes adults and is almost paternal in his attitude towards them. Sometimes, with a pleasant smile, he will quietly and tactfully press a bar of chocolate into your hand. But he doesn't much care for other boys; he does not quarrel with them, but he appears to regard them as barbarians amongst whom he is forced by circumstances to reside. Am I making him sound horrid? But he isn't. He is generous to a fault, and as straight as a die.
>
> But of what type is he?

I suppose he was more or less right. I didn't enjoy rough games and had no love for the cricket ball – I was afraid of showing fear. Parents and school tried at the same time to protect me and to toughen me up. I learnt boxing ('it's good to be able to defend yourself') and loathed it. Major Atkinson said he would rather see me get my cricket colours than get a scholarship. In the end I was made captain of the second eleven. I tried hard and even on one occasion went in last man for the first eleven against our great rival, Heathfield School. I managed by grim determination to keep the ball out of my wicket long enough to win the match. I did enjoy the piano, though I never had any manual dexterity, and when it came to an exam I was so nervous that my teacher vowed she would never put me in for another. When I left her she gave me a volume of Beethoven Sonatas. I never got any of them up to a presentable standard, except perhaps the first movement of the 'Moonlight', but I did get many hours of pleasure from looking through the book for the easy bits and trying to play them. But I am not really musical, though I enjoy good music if it's not too highbrow, and I squirm if it's really bad. An attempt to protect me which I did not appreciate, was the decision in the winter to take me out of shorts (little boys did not wear long trousers) and put me into knickerbockers and stockings. I would rather have suffered any cold than been the odd boy out. It was no consolation to know (as I was told) that such wear was common amongst the sons of the aristocracy! Though I don't recollect it myself, I am told that this episode was on medical advice because I was suffering acute rheumatic pains.

As to being 'straight as a die', I am certainly not very courageous when it comes to a public stand for what I believe but both by temperament and by training I dislike pretending to what I don't believe. I am very unimpressed by the sway of intellectual fashion and the claims of the current consensus and I find that mere honesty may compel one to stand alone. The temptation to go along with the majority is very real, but it is worse than useless as a way of discovering truth and it gives one no inner satisfaction. I was struck by a saying attributed to Walter Scott of which General Wavell was said to be very fond: 'Without courage there cannot be truth; and without truth there can be no other virtue.'

I got on well enough with my schoolfellows but I was not a good mixer and so was always a bit of a loner. A little bullying went on but not much. I remember being scared by some boys who had an electric-shock machine who were looking for victims to torment. With the rest of them I enjoyed Bulldog Drummond and the motor-racing thrillers which were in vogue. But I had a sense of inferiority and even indulged in some self-punishment, possibly in an attempt to bear pain better. (One never knows what is going on in the head of a normal looking child.) However, I remember lying in bed consoling myself with the thought that it was brains which had raised man above the animals, and that in this respect I was better than most of them! One intellectual interest was chess, and my godfather sent me a copy of Réti's *Modern Ideas in Chess*, which fascinated me. Our local parson had been a Cambridge half-blue, and at the age of eleven I played him one week-end. At our first game I caught him off his guard and beat him, but the game excited me too much and returning to school on the Monday morning I had my one and only bout of homesickness, dissolving into uncontrollable tears. Because of this over-excitement I never took to the game seriously, though I still enjoy running my eye over the chess column in the paper.

One unusual pleasure came my way. We had one of the earliest Baby Austins – just big enough to squeeze two children into the back. This was garaged at the back of the house near where Ginny had been stabled. I was allowed to back it out down the side of the house and round to the front by my tennis wall and then drive it forward to the front gate. Thus, at the age of twelve I became quite an adept driver and was allowed to drive the cars wherever no licence was required, as for instance on the South Downs and down the long drive of Horsley Towers where my eldest sister was at school.

They put me in for a scholarship at Winchester College, for which I was altogether below standard. Then they decided to dispatch me to Uppingham, to the house of my mother's brother, Jack Adkins, where a new era began.

Two

Uppingham and Conversion — 1927–30

It was quite an upheaval at the age of thirteen to be sent away from home up into the Midlands. Uppingham is set in a very pleasant countryside in Rutland, the smallest county in England. It was sad when the county of Rutland was abolished and amalgamated with Leicestershire. That little county was almost crime free. In fact I remember one year when no crime was committed in the whole county. My uncle's house (Highfield) had about forty boys. During my first year I was in a room with three others who were a good deal more able at games than I was. However we got on reasonably well; the sense of being protected by my uncle very quickly wore off and everyone seemed to forget that he and I were related.

When I got to Uppingham I gave up saying my prayers publicly and I did not notice any loss. I enjoyed the academic work. Discipline was good in the school and the teaching was also quite good. I quickly moved up the school and in two years I reached the Science and Maths Sixth. I had become exceedingly interested in science and I loved the books of James Jeans on cosmology and astronomy. I also enjoyed Bertrand Russell's *ABC of Atoms* and *ABC of Relativity*. In the Science Sixth we had to write an essay every week, which I got rather tired of doing. I asked whether instead of doing a weekly essay I could write one long one on the theory of relativity. I had found Einstein's popular book *The Theory of Relativity* to be quite intelligible and extremely interesting. So I worked away at this over a long period and came out with quite a decent understanding at least of the special theory of relativity. The general theory was more difficult and I did not profess to understand it at all well. Also while I was in the Science Sixth I went in for a prize essay on the evolution of life. I got hold of my father's copy of Darwin's *The Origin of Species* and read this with great enjoyment, admiring the lucid and logical exposition of his case.

I owed a lot to the principles of essay-writing which were used in the school. We were told that we must work out a scheme for our essay and hand it in to our housemaster for initialling on Saturday evening, the essay itself to be written up in our own time afterwards. The procedure was as follows: We were given a subject and then told to jot down all ideas which came into our heads. These we would sort out into some sort of coherent order. This would then provide the basis for the scheme. After the scheme was in place it might be necessary to collect some more material to fill the gaps. When all was ready it was comparatively easy to write the essay. I have found this method useful for sermons, articles and for any writing ever since.

My best teacher was V.T. Saunders who taught physics. He had taught at the Naval College at Dartmouth and was something of a martinet. He taught me the value of a little accurate knowledge. He would insist that certain definitions and formulae should be learnt by heart, and woe betide you if you had not got them word perfect. When stumped with a problem, he would say to you something like, 'What is Boyle's Law?' You would quote this back to him, and he would say, 'That's it, isn't it?' and, sure enough, it was usually quite easy to solve the problem. This small amount of knowledge was worth more than mountains of vague recollections. We felt that V.T. did not fit altogether comfortably into the Uppingham scene. To begin with he was rather left-wing and generally somewhat anti-establishment. However when he quoted the collect to us he was quite serious: 'Those old boys knew what they were doing when they wrote, "Read, mark, learn and inwardly digest." Learn, young man, and afterwards inwardly digest.'

Perhaps rather unfortunately they tried to make a mathematician of me. The school had two first-class mathematicians and I suppose they hoped to train up one of their own kind. But I lost interest in maths and, since brilliant mathematicians are not usually good at understanding a learner's difficulties, it resulted in my maths career being an almost total failure.

Games figured prominently in the life of the school; every weekday we did some sort of games or PT, or went for a run. I used to play in the second row of the scrum. I pushed as hard as I could but often had the humiliation of finishing up a game of rugger with my knees still clean. We had an Eton Fives courts with the little pill-boxes from which to serve – I quite enjoyed this game. I even came to enjoy fielding at cricket to some extent; I and a friend used to practise throwing high catches to one another. We used to watch matches on the beautiful 'Upper' cricket ground. One day during an interval we were throwing catches and I caught a ball on the tip of my middle finger. The top joint was bent right backwards. I took it to one of the masters who said, 'Hold on, old thing!' He gave it a pull and put it back in place, but a ligament was permanently damaged and I have had a weak middle finger ever since. I greatly admired good games players even though I could not emulate them myself. I remember seeing one very plucky back who did a tackle and sadly broke his neck. In my own form there was D.A. Kendrew who went on to the army class and eventually became an international rugby player. It was a great sight to see him shake himself loose from the pack and dash away. Later on he became a brigadier in the army and I am told he was renowned more for his energy than for his wisdom.

I quite enjoyed the OTC – the Officers' Training Corps. This was rather despised in my house and anyone who showed himself too keen on the corps was dubbed a 'corps groise'. But I did not mind drill, I was interested in military tactics, in map reading and in the giving of orders to fire. On the miniature range I actually became a first-class shot. I could never quite understand this as I had a very shaky hand and not particularly good eyesight. I used to wait until the sights seemed to have come in line with the bull, then pull the trigger and hope for the best. Because no one else in the house was at all keen on the corps, I became an under-officer and leader of the house squad for one term, wearing the statutory Sam Browne belt and brown boots. I was glad of the experience later on when I got into the Royal Air Force, finding that the whole military business was not entirely strange to me. Military ideas have always stuck with me. Looked at from one angle Christianity is a warfare. It is God and his hosts against Satan and his hosts, and one feels the need for discipline in the Christian life and for good tactics and sound strategy in the Christian Church. We need also the backroom boys who will do the research required for producing the weapons of our warfare.

Another source of humiliation at school was the beatings. Edward Thring, Uppingham's famous headmaster, following of course to some extent biblical precedent, believed in short, sharp punishments. He did not think that boys should be kept in with detentions when they would be better out in the open air. As a result Uppingham saw a fairly free use of the cane. For lesser offences beating would be done by the house praepostors or 'pollys' as they were called, but only with the housemaster's permission. For serious offences the beating would be carried out by the housemaster himself and for the most serious offences by the headmaster. I was twice beaten; once for being caught eating a sweet in the school assembly hall and once I think for 'general inefficiency'. The victim would be bent over in the changing room and each polly in turn would take a run at him and give him a stroke of the cane. I found it extremely painful and one was left with great weals on the backside. I think this would now be actionable in the European

Community. I don't know that it did me any harm but I felt such punishment for such offences was unjust. I have a theory (which it is impossible to test) that some people feel pain much more than others. Certainly some boys seemed to shrug off this sort of punishment much more easily than others.

About the time I went to Uppingham, my eldest sister Eleanor, then aged sixteen, went all religious. We thought she had religious mania. She was a highly-strung girl, the product of a difficult conception and traumatic birth. My mother suffered apparently from vaginismus (spasm of pelvic floor muscles), usually due to psycho-sexual problems, and there was prolonged difficulty in consummating the marriage. When at last after treatment she became pregnant, she had an inordinately long labour. (Why they did not resort to Caesarean section, I do not know.) After surviving this my sister's health was somewhat precarious. She suffered from asthma and her relations with both father and mother were never free and happy. She too was sent away to boarding school. Although she found church services boring and God seemed remote, she felt that God and truth were basic. During one of the holidays she went to stay at Witley Manor with my father's cousin, Jack (later chairman of Surrey County Council and knighted). Jack was attracted to this immature girl and, though there were no amorous approaches, she found herself desperately in love with him. He wrote to her sending a copy of *Daily Light* and inviting her to commit herself to Christ as her personal saviour and friend. This she proceeded to do and peace came to her troubled soul. *Daily Light* has a page for each day of the year consisting of a string of sentences or phrases from the Bible put together to illustrate some topic. These texts came to her with great power and comfort as if from God himself, and she found herself trusting him. The heading for one day was: 'Be still, my daughter, until thou know how the matter will fall.' God was no longer remote but someone near to her to whom she began instinctively to pray.

She was then bundled off to a finishing school in Lausanne for a year, where she fell in with some like-minded Christians who helped her and encouraged her. After this she went to Ridgelands Bible College in Wimbledon to train as a missionary. There she and her friends, including Pat Govan, whom I was afterwards to know as the wife of Professor Sir Norman Anderson, set to work to pray for brother John. I in the meantime had not been entirely static spiritually. I believed in God – I do not think it had ever seemed the least plausible to me that this amazing world just happened. But God also seemed to me remote as he had seemed to Eleanor. I had once boasted in Uncle John's hearing of the speed at which it was possible to get up at school in the morning – to leap out of bed at the breakfast bell and be down and dressed in time for breakfast. He had gently remarked, 'Wouldn't it be good to give yourself time to say your prayers?' So I had tried praying but my prayers never seemed to rise higher than the ceiling. I had tried reading the Bible; I had even tried learning the first chapter of Genesis by heart, but it had not gripped me. As to belief about Jesus, I think my scientific ideas had completely taken over. I didn't imagine that people in the twentieth century believed that the creator of this vast and wonderful universe had somehow taken a human body and had walked around in Palestine for thirty years. Jesus was certainly a wonderful man; my godfather Frank Sotham gave me a book *The Man Nobody Knows* which was one attempt to show him as such. Frank, I believe, had been at Trinity College, Cambridge in the days of E.W. Barnes, the modernist mathematician who was made Bishop of Birmingham by Ramsay MacDonald, our first Labour Prime Minister. His version of Christianity presented an entirely non-supernatural Jesus, and Frank, who attended church regularly, complained to the end of his days of the confusion into which the clergy threw the laity. To me the Incarnation seemed out of the question – Jesus was a great man. But God? Surely not.

A much more important influence on my life at Uppingham
was the Reverend R.F. McNeile, known to us as Fergie. He was
a brilliant mathematician, having been a so-called 'Student' at
Christ Church, Oxford – that is, he was a don there. He gave up
his work at Christ Church and went to Wycliffe Hall to train for
the ministry. He then went out to Egypt. The libellous story that
we were told was that he hated the Egyptians and soon came
home. (As a matter of fact he stayed there for seven years and
gained some reputation as an Arabic scholar.) When he did come
home he came to Uppingham as chaplain. At that time the school
had a young and able headmaster, R.H. Owen, who was a deeply
religious man, fairly low church, who conducted religious matters
at the school very well. The music was in the charge of Sterndale
Bennett who trained the choir; I was a treble in it until my voice
broke. It unfortunately began to break when we were singing the
Hallelujah Chorus. Owen left while still fairly young, through
illness. He became chaplain at Brasenose College, Oxford,
coached the college boat and finally landed up as Archbishop of
Wellington in New Zealand.

Fergie taught us maths and divinity for the higher school
certificate – divinity as a subsidiary subject. At the beginning of the
year he read out to us the various options we might choose from.
We had a good deal of Bible at the school; so the topic which really
interested us was Daniel and the Maccabees, as we knew nothing
about the Maccabees. So for the higher certificate we had to do
twelve chapters of Daniel and sixteen chapters of 1 Maccabees. (It
makes the average student at Oxford green with envy to hear that
we had two and a half terms to cover so small a syllabus.) Fergie
used for Daniel the Cambridge commentary by S.R. Driver,
Driver's books being the most highly respected Old Testament
higher critical works in the English-speaking world at that time
and for many years to come. We were given *The Century Bible* by
R.H. Charles, who was the greatest authority on apocrypha and
pseudepigrapha. I was totally convinced by these writers and by

Fergie's exposition of Daniel. They held that the miracles were
obviously legends and that what purported to be predictive prophecy was really history written after the event.

In the meantime the Ridgelands praying was having an effect.
It was suggested that I should go on a Varsity and Public Schools
house party at Leukerbad in the Rhône Valley. I duly went and
with me two others from my house. We had a fine time skiing,
skating and in the evenings swimming. There were delightful
natural hot baths there in which we could soak out our aches and
pains. After supper there would be a Christian meeting. It was all
very lively and earnest, and conveyed a great sense of reality.
Though musically rather thin, I was taken by the choruses which
we sang. They were short, simple and easily remembered and
carried a potent message, which was not buried in flowery language but spoke directly to both heart and mind. The party was
led by senior people including Bishop Taylor Smith, who had
been Chaplain General to the Forces for twenty-four years, and
by university students.

The student whom I had most to do with was Jack Collins, an
old Etonian, six foot seven tall, who rowed number six in the
Cambridge boat. The meetings told very simply the Christian
gospel, laying the foundation of the reality of sin, the provision
of atonement through the death of Christ, the need for new birth,
repentance and faith. One afternoon as I was going off skiing I
was joined by Jack. He chatted and then asked me directly
whether I was a Christian. In the sense in which he meant it, I
knew I was not. I began to feel a deep desire for this that the others
seemed to have. Although I believed that it was quite real for
them, I did not feel that it would work for me. Then he quoted to
me the man whose epileptic son the disciples could not cure, and
who, when Jesus asked him if he believed, said, 'Lord, I believe,
help my unbelief.' That seemed precisely to fit my case. I turned
round and tried to ski back to the hotel, but my knees were
shaking so much that I could barely stay on my feet. Eventually

I got back and went straight up to my room. I knelt down at the bedside and said, 'Lord Jesus, come into my heart.' I have no recollection of any immediate emotion but I knew what I had done.

When it came to the last evening of the house party we had a meeting during which we were invited to declare ourselves publicly if we had turned to Christ. With my two school acquaintances who had not become Christians sitting there in the audience it was quite a test. But I got to my feet and I said that I had done so.

Three

Bible, Prayer and World Vision

Lord Hailsham in his autobiography *A Sparrow's Flight* talks about life 'in a dormitory of thirteen or fourteen other boys where the smallest eccentricity or weakness was treated with derision.' When I read this, it rang a bell with me. In 1930 returning to the house a marked man was quite an awesome prospect. Someone gave me a pocket New Testament which I read in the train going home from Switzerland. Then I had my first experience of a Bible verse which really hit me; it said, 'Stand fast in the faith, quit you like men, be strong.' I read and re-read and read again those words which gave me great comfort and strength. For the first time the Bible had become the Word of God to me.

There were two memorable events towards the end of the holidays before going back to school. Prayer had now become instinctive and the desire to pass on one's knowledge of Christ was also something which came naturally. My sister and I used to kneel together and pray out loud. One object of prayer was my mother's mother. This granny was to some extent a religious woman, but how real her religion was I cannot say. Her marriage was an unhappy one, and there were evidently faults on both sides. Her husband was a man of means and a great fisherman, but, as far as I can make out, he appears to have had no job and to have been an atheist. When I first knew them, they lived at Addiscombe, not far away, but when he died Granny bought a small house right by us in Beech Avenue, Sanderstead. I liked her and she clearly enjoyed her grandchildren, but she embarrassed me by getting hold of some stitching which I had done, which she framed and hung up on her drawing room wall; needlework seemed to me to be an unsuitable thing for a boy to have advertised.

She was quite a difficult woman and my father said that on no account should she ever come to live with us, but the time came when we moved from Rednal to a new house a little further out called Portley Wood at Whyteleafe. It became unavoidable that she should come there too. She had her own room and a nurse attendant to look after her, who was a fine Christian woman. My sister and I, full of our new-found faith, would go to see her. She was unhappy in spirit and now rather deaf. One day she was sitting up in bed talking to me about her past and about the good deeds which she had done and the letters of thanks which she had received. She then raised her hands in anguish and said, 'But it wasn't pleasing in God's sight.' Her eyes filled with tears, her deafness became total and that was the end of the conversation for the young evangelist. As time went on she found peace and even my father had to admit that a great change had taken place in her.

The other event came from a visit to the Scripture Union book shop in London. I saw a book on the shelves with the intriguing title, *Daniel in the Critics' Den.* I took this down and found that it was a point by point answer to Driver's commentary on Daniel. I bought the book and read it in the train going home. I found myself chortling with delight because here was a totally unexpected answer to the book from which we had been taught for higher certificate. The author of the book was Sir Robert Anderson; he was not a professional theologian, but a distinguished lawyer. (I believe he was Attorney General in Ireland.) He probably got his material from the great Tractarian scholar E.B. Pusey. Pusey had been to Germany and had been shocked by the anti-Christian slant of the new biblical criticism. Back in Oxford he had given nine lectures on Daniel the Prophet which were published in a 688-page book. The skilful lawyer had, no doubt, reduced this to simple terms.

Reading his book taught me a lesson for life: it is unwise to accept any argument however apparently convincing until you have heard both sides of a question. Later on when I became an accountant's clerk I used to go into the law courts in the lunch hour and listen to the cases. When one heard an able advocate state a case one's natural reaction was, 'Yes, of course!' But then when an equally competent barrister conducted the cross-examination one's reaction might well be, 'No, of course not'. So this book resulted in my putting Daniel, which I had thought I must more or less disregard, back into my canon. It would not be true to say that I have never had any doubts about Daniel since, because the case against Daniel can be put with very great skill. All the same I have never gone back on what Robert Anderson taught me and what has been reinforced so well by people like Donald Wiseman, Ken Kitchen, Terence Mitchell and Joyce Baldwin.

Then came the return to school. I owe an enormous debt to the wisdom of Edward Thring, since he believed that every boy should have some privacy. The result was that at Uppingham nearly every boy had a tiny study with just room for a small table and chair, a tuck box and an easy chair. This meant that I always had somewhere where I could read my Bible and pray in private. I could also escape to the music school and strum away at the new-found choruses which I had enjoyed so much. I read the Bible from cover to cover. Opposition in the house was not too bad. John Lyon, a powerful personality who became head of the house in due course, delighted to say that all the world's ills derived from either science or religion – which he knew were my two passions. My sister kept some of the letters which I wrote to her at this time, and it is clear that I was by no means intimidated. I was praying hard that others in the house would respond to the

Good News and eventually three or four of us met for Bible reading and prayer. When news of my conversion reached my grandfather in Oban, the old man wept tears of thanksgiving and doubtless he prayed the more fervently for me. It is not surprising that with this great new interest occupying my mind, my interest in maths declined, though my interest in science was quite unabated.

During this time I was particularly indebted to certain books, of which I will mention three. First was *C.T. Studd: Cricketer and Pioneer* by Norman Grubb. One could hardly imagine anyone more unlike me than C.T. Studd. Here was a man who was a wonderful cricketer, captain of England, physically without a fear. He was one of the Cambridge Seven who went off to inland China under the influence of D.L. Moody. He had been invalided home, and it looked as though his career as a missionary was at an end; but one day he saw an advertisement for a missionary meeting which said, 'Cannibals want missionaries.' It took his fancy and he heard the speaker telling about the vast areas of central Africa where the name of Jesus was not known. As a man far from fit, at fifty years of age, he went out to the Belgian Congo and stayed there for the remaining twenty years of his life. He was the man who said, 'If Jesus Christ be God and died for me, then no sacrifice can be too great for me to make for him.' Missionary biographies in those days tended to glorify God by telling you all the good things about the missionaries, but seldom revealing their weaknesses. Studd with his health problems became a drug addict, saying that heroin was one of God's greatest gifts to mankind. This seems to have caused him to become somewhat unbalanced, calling on his fellow-workers to ever greater dedication. He asked what a tommy in the trenches would say when ordered to go over the top. He would say, 'I don't care a damn,' and obey. DCD was to be their response whenever they were frightened or discouraged by the devil. Sadly his society, the Worldwide Evangelization Crusade, had several splits and a number of excellent missionaries hived off in various directions, but after Studd's death WEC leapt forward and became a tremendous missionary society. I owe to C.T. Studd perhaps more than anyone else the deep conviction that the purpose of the church is that people of every tribe and nation and tongue should hear about Jesus and that from all parts of the world the saved should come and worship the Lamb of God.

Another book which particularly impressed me with my interest in science was A.T. Pierson's *George Müller of Bristol*. Müller, brought up as a boy in Germany, had been a ne'er-do-well who had actually landed up in prison. He had been given to a great deal of lying and cheating and seemed beyond reformation. But one day an acquaintance of his persuaded him to go to a meeting of unlearned Christians who had come together for prayer and Bible study; he was deeply moved and before long was rejoicing in new birth. He came to England in 1830, an England of course without any National Health Service, and was shocked at the state of the poor, particularly of orphaned children. He had read the life of Franke who had started a home for orphans in Germany. Franke ran this home in complete dependence on God, making no appeals for money, all the asking being directed to God alone. Müller was led into the same sort of work and he kept a scrupulous, matter-of-fact account of '*The Lord's Dealing with his Servant George Müller*'. It became his lifelong work and he exercised an extraordinary influence. Eventually he built five vast homes on Ashley Down in Bristol and was caring for something like two thousand orphan children year in, year out. He was a great man of prayer and during his lifetime a million and a half pounds was given towards the work he was doing. In those days a million pounds was a great deal of money. He was frequently in the position of having the responsibility for all these children and being left without food or money, and only at the very last moment did the answer to prayer come. When I saw the scrupulous way in which George Müller kept an account of God's working it seemed to me almost a scientific proof of the existence of the living God. He gives an account of his devotional practice which I think is worth repeating as it had quite an influence on my own practice.

It has pleased the Lord to teach me the truth, the benefit of which I have not lost for more than fourteen years. I saw that the primary business to which I ought to attend every day was to have my soul happy in the Lord. The first thing to be concerned about was not how much I might serve the Lord, or how I might glorify the Lord; but how I might get my soul into a happy state, and how my inner man might be nourished. For I might seek to set the truth before the unconverted, I might seek to benefit believers, I might seek to relieve the distressed, I might in other ways seek to behave myself as it becomes a child of God in this world; and yet, not being happy in the Lord, and not being nourished and strengthened in my inner man day by day, all this might not be attended to in a right spirit. Before this time my practice had been, at least for ten years previously, to give myself to prayer after having dressed myself in the morning. Now I saw that the most important thing I had to do was to give myself to the reading of the Word of God, and to meditation on it, that thus my heart might be comforted, encouraged, warned, reproved, instructed; and that thus, by means of the Word of God, my heart might be brought into experimental communion with the Lord.

I began, therefore, to meditate on the New Testament from the beginning, early in the morning. The first thing I did, after having asked in a few words the Lord's blessing upon His precious Word, was to begin to meditate on the Word of God, searching as it were into every verse to get blessing out of it; not for the sake of preaching on what I had meditated upon, but for the sake of obtaining food for my own soul. The result I have found to be almost invariably this, that after a very few minutes my soul has been led to confession, or to thanksgiving, or to intercession, or to supplication; so that, though I did not, as it were, give myself to prayer but to meditation, yet it turned almost immediately more or less into prayer. When thus I have been for a while making confession or intercession or supplication, or have given thanks, I go on to the next words, turning all, as I go, into prayer for myself or others, as the Word may lead to it, but still continually keeping before me that food for my own soul is the object of my meditation. The result of this is that by breakfast time, with rare exceptions, I am in a peaceful if not happy state of heart.

I was probably influenced most of all by Marshall Broomhall, *Hudson Taylor: The Man Who Believed God.* I felt a closer sympathy with Hudson Taylor than with C.T. Studd. He does not seem to have been an outstanding personality. In a worldly sense he had few advantages in life. He worked away at his medicine under considerable difficulties, passed his exams and then learned the way of faith by hard experience. Following the same principles as George Müller, he went off to evangelize the great inland areas of China. At one time the China Inland Mission came to have well over a thousand workers in the field and this work was all based on the simplest possible creed. Hudson Taylor said, 'I believe that God has spoken, I believe that his Word is recorded in the Bible, I believe that he means what he says and will do all that he has promised.' To me, being taught how to disbelieve the Bible, the witness of these great warriors was a tremendous inspiration, and I said to myself, 'No liberal theologian could achieve such things.'

Hudson Taylor was profoundly concerned about the hundreds of millions of 'immortal souls' who were dying in China with no

knowledge of the Saviour. The question came home acutely to
me, what were we to make of other religions? There were a
number of good books in the school library on other faiths and
I read about each in turn. I don't think I came to any conclusion
as to what the state of people was who had no chance of hearing
the gospel, but it was quite clear to me that everyone on earth
ought to hear about the wonderful Saviour who had come into
the world for their sake. Reading about these spiritual giants
brought home to me the shocking state of a church which disbe-
lieved its textbook. It seemed to me that Protestantism without a
truly inspired Bible was heading for disaster. The testimony of
these men of faith did three things for me. They mightily reinforced my experience of the inspiration of scripture and the
academic arguments of such as Robert Anderson; they confirmed
my conviction that all good spiritual work must be steeped in
prayer; and they gave me a passion for the evangelization of the
world, which made me wish to become a missionary.

Two items of theological progress merit mention. I had little
difficulty with the great Christian doctrines at the beginning of
my spiritual career. I remember thinking that the really crucial
question is, 'Was Jesus God?' I think it was a little book by W.H.
Griffith Thomas, *Christianity is Christ* which helped me to articu-
late the reasons for this belief. He brought out the significance of
Christ's character, his words, his works, his resurrection and
finally his influence. I had sufficient knowledge of the Jesus of the
gospels to be entirely convinced as he developed those five
themes.

There was progress too with biblical criticism. When the sixth
form had finished with Daniel and the Maccabees, we went on
the next year to the book of Genesis. This was a marvellously
providential choice because the way one treats the Pentateuch is
the most crucial of all higher critical questions. I went through a
similar experience to that with Daniel. I found the presentation
of the theory of the four late documents J, E, D and P, which are

supposed to have made up the Pentateuch, very convincing, and I almost came to believe it. Mercifully when I wrote to my sister about this, she got from the Ridgelands library what was one of the very best books on the subject: James Orr, *The Problem of the Old Testament*. Orr pointed out the enormous difficulties of the JEDP theory, of which I had been unaware when I had only heard one side of the question. I devoured this book and found it completely convincing. I can say quite truthfully that, having abandoned this documentary theory and having read many books on the subject, I have never felt the slightest inclination to go back to it; it is simply riddled with implausibilities. I think that the Graf-Wellhausen hypothesis as it is called has been the most powerful single factor undermining the credibility of the Christian faith. It is very difficult to square this view of the Old Testament Torah with the teaching of our Lord Jesus Christ. Once you undermine his authority as a teacher you undermine his deity; when you undermine his deity you undermine his saviourhood and you undermine belief in a God who reveals himself. (I also read before I left Uppingham a book which sowed seeds of doubt about Darwin. It was H.C. Morton, *The Bankruptcy of Evolution*, which showed me that there were two sides even to that highly complex question.)

Developing sexuality presented no very difficult problems at this time, though we were lamentably ill-prepared to cope with it. I had absolutely no instruction in sex at home and I was long puzzled as to how the baby got out of its mother's tummy! Boys got most of their sex instruction from 'dirty' stories and 'dirty' jokes. Of course I thought these wrong and all I could do was to pray that I might learn what I needed to know as I needed it. The mind boggles at the thought that for a thousand years all the sexual instruction of Christendom came from men with no experience of a pure married union. The VPS camps tried to give some help but as they could not claim to be *in loco parentis* this was necessarily very restrained. I think it may have been Bishop

Taylor Smith who taught me to pray daily for Miss Right, that
she might be prepared for me and I for her – an excellent practice.
I remember a stage when I was distinctly attracted to a good-look-
ing senior boy. I can understand the danger of a boy's sexual
orientation becoming distorted if he is encouraged to think of
himself as homosexual at this stage and is not allowed to grow
through it naturally. Fortunately for me this problem did not
arise and my prayer for needed knowledge was answered.

An interesting new opportunity for passing on the faith came
during the first summer holiday after the trip to Leukerbad. I was
asked to help with a children's beach mission at Elie in Fife on
the east coast of Scotland. The sheer happiness of working with
a group of like-minded Christians was remarkable – I remember
how forcibly Psalm 133 struck me: 'How good and pleasant it is
when brothers dwell in unity.' I had my first experience of giving
a talk in public. I worked hard to make it direct and simple and
was quite nervous. Our housefather told a story of a nervous
young man who had carefully memorized his sermon. When he
got to the sand pulpit, he blurted out his text loud and clear, but
then entirely forgot what he had intended to say. Silence. He said
his text again. Further silence. He said it a third time; and then
fled from the scene. 'I have never forgotten that text,' said the
housefather, 'it was the most memorable sermon I have ever
listened to.' Certainly it achieved the first aim of a sermon – to
say a bit of God's Word memorably. Some nervousness is the
preacher's friend; it encourages prayer without which the word
will have no power. My little talk seemed to go all right.

Another, very unexpected, opportunity came. In my last year,
Fergie sprang a surprise on us. He offered to preach a sermon by
a member of the sixth form, if anyone would undertake to write
one for him. At this time I was meeting with two or three others
and we betook ourselves to prayer about this matter and I duly
wrote my first sermon. The text was, 'I have come that they might
have life and might have it more abundantly.' As it happened

another member of the form, named Smart, who was a very clever boy, also wrote a sermon, and when it came to the end of term and the sermon was due to be delivered, Fergie took extracts from the two sermons and put them into his own. Of course I felt that he had left out the best bits!

On the Monday after morning school I went to collect this sermon from Fergie. He said he was very impressed with the sermon, but warned me against minimizing the reality of moral endeavour by talking too glibly about letting the Holy Spirit take over; and against a divorce of the intellectual and the spiritual. Little did he know how busy my intellect had been, trying to confute his unbeliefs! As I returned to my boarding house I fell in with another member of the house, Gordon Sinclair. We walked back together; when we got there he said, 'Let's have a look at this,' and he snatched the sermon from me and took it away to read. The praying group of course was quite excited by this and we prayed that he would read to his own profit. It was his very last term and in a few days he was gone for good, but he seemed to have come to a personal faith. Later on he told me how he had gone home and found that his father was contemplating suicide. He felt that through his faith he had been able to talk his father out of killing himself. He went out to Ceylon (I think it was) as a tea planter and became a wealthy man; but one day in Durham, having seen a letter of mine in *The Times*, he came and looked me up. He still seemed to be a believing Christian and he told me how out in Ceylon he would support the parson when he came to take a service. So that was very thrilling.

Our spiritual convictions created certain difficulties at home. The one which I remember most clearly was the question of Sunday games. We thought that the Fourth Commandment was binding on us and that refraining from sport was involved in keeping the day holy, though my views on this were to be modified later on. This point of conscience made it particularly difficult if a tennis party had been arranged at home. The difficulty was largely evaded by the fact that a Crusader Bible class had just been started up locally, which made it possible for me to slip off to Crusaders on a Sunday afternoon. The leader of this newly founded class was David Stokes, who was later to go out with the Bible Churchman's Missionary Society to Ethiopia, there to try to help the Ethiopian Church to reform itself through a knowledge of the Bible in the vernacular. It was interesting that a strongly evangelical society like BCMS should not try to get members to leave their unreformed church, but should try to promote reformation from within.

In connection with Crusaders I met a fine missionary from Egypt called Sandy Bradley. A saying of his has stuck with me all my life. He said, 'If the devil cannot pull you back and make you unkeen, he will try to push you forward to unhealthy extremes.' How often did I observe this in the years that followed.

Four

A Significant Interlude — 1932

As my final year at school drew on I found that I had little interest in maths and that a consuming interest in the Christian faith possessed me. It somehow came to my ears that there was a place of Christian training near at hand where young men did some preliminary training for the ministry or for missionary work. I persuaded my father to let me leave school a term early and spend the time at Woodridge, Woldingham, under the care of the Revd H.D. Salmon. 'Pa' Salmon, as he was always called, was a doughty evangelical who had made a name for himself as head of the Cambridge University Mission at Bermondsey in inner London for fifteen years. To quote John Pollock:

> In the late nineties a young business man in South London had been invited one Sunday by the Rector of Bermondsey to come over and speak at an evening meeting. As Harold Salmon walked through the neighbourhood, squalid, tumbledown and wretched, he was so horrified that he resolved to do what he could for it in the future. At first he gave his spare time; then he threw up his business and went to Cambridge in order to take a degree, be ordained and start a university settlement.
>
> As an undergraduate he had tried to procure someone to launch his settlement, but it was not until 1906 that a

committee of Cambridge men headed by the Bishop of Durham formed a trust, raised funds and appointed Salmon as Honorary Head of the new venture.

The neighbourhood was debased and drunken, a vast unrelieved expanse of mean dwellings, yet containing numbers of respectable though struggling families whose attempt to keep above the prevalent level seemed to Salmon one of the strongest pleas of the place. The mission aimed to reach the boys of the area, catering for mind, body and spirit, and working in partnership with St James's Parish Church. A boys' club and a public dispensary were provided and the doors opened in October 1906. The club was soon full and the dispensary never lacked cases, but the gambling in the streets, the usual obscenity, free fights and prostitution went on as before. 'When we came to the district,' wrote Salmon a few years later, 'we were convinced very strongly that the only remedy for this evil was the power of Jesus Christ . . . We determined that we would put our belief into practice and start from the very beginning with knowing nothing among them but Jesus Christ and Him crucified.' But for eighteen months they lacked result. 'At last a lad of seventeen made a stand for Jesus Christ before his fellows, and his stand brought upon him a terrible persecution.' This was the beginning. In course of time, despite frequent disappointment, Salmon saw several of his boys active Christians. He even educated some at his own expense, sending them to public school and university in order that they might enter the ministry.

(*A Cambridge Movement*, pp. 153 ff.)

He saw the need that young men should not only be soundly converted and deeply dedicated, but also well taught. He dedicated his money to the establishment of the Ordination Candidates Training Fund and bought a sizeable property on the North

Downs with a glorious view of the Kent and Surrey countryside where such men could come and study. So to Woldingham I went.

This was quite a significant interlude, because thus far my experiences had given me very little interest in the church. My admiration for C.T. Studd had tended to make me somewhat anti-church. In his call for pioneer missionaries to enter the great unevangelized areas of the world, he said:

> This can only be accomplished by a red-hot, unconventional, unfettered Holy Ghost religion, where neither Church nor State, neither man nor traditions are worshipped or preached, but only Christ and Him crucified. Not to confess Christ by fancy collars, clothes, silver croziers, church steeples or richly embroidered altar-cloths, but by reckless sacrifice and heroism in the foremost trenches.

I had to learn that the work of Christ covered a wider field than pioneer evangelism, crucial though that was.

The influence that George Müller and Hudson Taylor had had upon me was also typical of a major strand of twentieth-century evangelicalism. These two men were heroes of the (Plymouth) Brethren movement who demonstrated in a practical way their belief in the priesthood of all believers. All Christians, they held, should be witnesses to Christ and all gifts should be exercised in the church. In the dark days of the liberal inroads into the life of the churches, evangelicals recognized their oneness in the fundamentals and drew together, whether Anglican, Methodist, Brethren, Salvation Army or anything else. Hudson Taylor recognized that denominational differences, though secondary matters, were important, and his mission was interdenominational, not undenominational. That is to say he allocated each area of the field to missionaries of one denomination only and so largely avoided the tensions which would have arisen, if, say, Baptists and paedobaptists had worked side by side.

I did in fact appreciate certain aspects of the Church of England, most notably Morning and Evening Prayer and the Holy Communion service, in which I had taken part so often. I appreciated the way in which they were steeped in scripture and I appreciated the deeply devotional language of Thomas Cranmer. I was glad too to have been able to confess my faith in Confirmation shortly after my conversion. But the church as such did not greatly interest me and certainly did not excite me. My time at Pa Salmon's began in a tentative way to widen my horizons, since the specific aim of Woodridge was preparation of men for service in the Church of England. Pa's 'boys' normally came for about a year to get some instruction in the Bible and to read some good books. The fellowship was great and it was a pleasant way to spend the summer, but I was a bit shocked at the standard of work expected. Pa seemed a little passé; having married late in life he was too preoccupied with raising a large family and administering the establishment single-handed to be able to give much time to seeing that his students worked hard. He would give a Bible exposition each day and then leave his students to get on with their reading, which most of them did in a leisurely way.

I can only remember two of the set books: James Denney, *The Death of Christ*, an excellent work on the atonement, and A.T. Robertson, *The Minister and his Greek New Testament*, a book well worth reading. Robertson was a Southern Baptist from the USA, a scholar for whom I have the greatest respect. He is best known for his *A Grammar of the Greek New Testament in the Light of Historical Research*. My copy has 1,454 pages. It was a revision and up-dating of G.B. Winer's standard work of 1867. The marvellous thing is that, for all its detail and condensation, it is remarkably lively. The author is a scholar who wished to put his scholarship to the service of the gospel. It seems sound sense to me to revise good books which have serious defects; all that is good can be kept without the charge of plagiarism and all that is defective can be improved. Knowing A.T. Robertson, I cannot join in the view that all Southern Baptists are Bible-thumping ignoramuses. Billy Graham has a tradition of sound learning behind him.

Pa was no theologian and I can only recall one of his expositions. It was on a favourite theme of evangelicals at that time, the need for Christians to be separate from the world. It began with the text, 'Solomon made affinity with Pharaoh King of Egypt'. It was a searching and relevant subject, but how to apply it to the twentieth century is not easy and it became a topic for earnest debate for years to come. Amongst other books read at this time was J.C. Ryle, *Knots Untied*, which was not one of the prescribed texts, but it dealt lucidly with the points which divided evangelicals, such as baptism, episcopacy and liturgy. Ryle had learnt the art of expounding Christian doctrine with great clarity as a result of many years work in a country parish, and this resulted in robust Reformation teaching. His work brought the mind into more serious touch with church thinking, as did also a little later the recommended books of the Protestant Reformation Society. I was very thrilled with G.R. Balleine's *A History of the Evangelical Party in the Church of England*, particularly of course with the eighteenth-century revival under Whitefield, the Wesleys and their friends. W.P. Upton, *The Churchman's History of the Oxford Movement*, gave me some knowledge of the High-Church party as viewed by an evangelical, but naturally it did not convey to me the power and attractiveness felt by its many adherents. It seemed to me an illogical and unstable attempt to reconcile the irreconcilable – Rome and the Reformation. Though Rome seemed to me far removed from New Testament Christianity, it had a logical coherence which Anglo-Catholicism lacked, and I was attracted neither to the one nor to the other.

Of the subjects with which Ryle dealt, the most divisive was the question of baptism. To a person who has come to a living faith after the years of childhood the Baptist case looks extremely plausible. Baptism in the New Testament was administered to adults on profession of repentance and faith, and public baptism by immersion is a powerful, and often costly way of confessing one's faith. All this seems so self-evident to a new convert that it is often difficult to get a young believer to look at the case for infant baptism seriously. Ryle convinced me that under both the old covenant and the new, children of believers should be regarded as children of God (at least until such time as they repudiated the faith). I was to discover later when I came to have children of my own how important this was as a principle of child nurture. Does one bring one's children up to call God 'Father', or is that something to be left till they have reached the age of discretion? We brought up our children as children of God and warned them against thinking that they needed to have a particular type of conversion experience. From the very beginning they were very secure in their parents' love and in God's love. Colin Buchanan's Grove booklet *A Case for Infant Baptism* was later to up-date the argument convincingly.

Quite the most important contact of those days was Eric Nash, known to all his friends as 'Bash'. It is no exaggeration to say that, although he was known to a comparatively small circle, Bash has probably had a greater influence on the Church of England in the twentieth century than any of his better known contemporaries. For some fifty years he dedicated his life to the winning of public-schoolboys to Christ and to building them up in the Christian faith – and with astonishing success. His success at first sight is most surprising, since he had none of the gifts usually associated with the typical youth worker. He was (one would think) neither a boy's man nor a man's man. He was not athletic or adventurous; he was in fact a bit of a softie. There was nothing of the ascetic about him. He much preferred sleeping in a proper bed to sleeping in a tent, and he was a bit of a hypochondriac, often fussing about his health. He was not particularly bright intellectually, nor of wide interests – he scarcely ever travelled abroad or took a proper holiday – nor a very impressive personality; yet he brought hundreds of gifted boys to faith in Christ.

Born in 1898, the son of an evangelical clergyman, he came to personal faith at the age of 19. After working in the city for a few years he went to Trinity College, Cambridge and thence to Ridley Hall to prepare for ordination in the ministry of the Church of England. He was in Cambridge at the time of the famous William Nicholson mission, of which we shall hear more in the next chapter. The Christian Union which he joined was utterly given over to evangelism, and he emerged from Ridley Hall with his fervour undimmed. After two curacies he became chaplain of a public school (Wrekin College, Shropshire), where his evangelistic zeal was not altogether appreciated by the school authorities. (Though it was mightily appreciated by some of the boys who found Christ through him, including David Milnes who became a missionary in Peru and a close friend of mine.) He was then appointed to the staff of the Scripture Union to work amongst public schoolboys. It was at this juncture that I met him.

He had already been gaining experience of running camps and house parties for boys. He and Wilfred Burton and Graham Leask had formed themselves into a team and he came to Pa Salmon's on the look-out for officers to help run the next camp, which was to be at Whitecliffe Bay, Isle of Wight. Young though I was, he took me on as an officer and put me in charge of a tentful of boys. Though I had already had experience of working in a mission team, this was something more; it was part of an ongoing work in which preparation, execution and follow-up were carefully integrated. The camp was prepared for by much prayer, it was meticulously carried through and contact was maintained with each boy as far as possible afterwards.

Officers would meet for prayer and planning each day. The boys were kept busy working off their energy with games-playing and other fun until the camp's main activity – the meeting. This was led by one of the officers and was lively and informal without ever becoming cheap or irreverent. 'Monty' Burton, the quarter-master, was a great wag, who, he claimed, had escaped from Churchianity into Christianity. He would have us rocking with laughter one moment and deadly serious the next. The simple choruses would be explained and then sung with deep feeling. The talk, following the pattern pioneered by Bash himself, would be straightforward and challenging. One of Bash's heroes was the American evangelist, R.A. Torrey, who was successor to D.L. Moody. Torrey as a student had tested his Christ-centred and Bible-centred faith in Germany when that country was being swept by a higher criticism which threatened completely to undermine all true Christian faith. He came out with his belief in the Bible as the Word of God strengthened, and he added to the down-to-earth type of preaching which he had learnt from Moody an intellectual element to which Moody could not aspire. One of his favourite addresses was 'Ten Reasons Why I Believe the Bible to be The Word of God', and all his preaching was direct, reasoned and Bible-based.

Bash followed this example. There was nothing clever or emotional in what he said, but it was relevant, logical and scrip-tural, and the boys listened. One famous outline of his many of us have used: the ABC of Salvation. How can one come to experience Christ's salvation? Three steps are necessary: I must Admit that I am a sinner; I must Believe that Jesus bore my sins on the cross; I must Come to him. It has been said rightly that what a man is going to explain simply he must understand deeply. Bash had no great breadth of understanding, but he certainly had depth; he understood the heart of the gospel, knew it was the Word of God, and trusted it to do its work when spoken in the power of the Spirit of God. He was totally against hot-gospelling – he did not mind in the least if a powerful evening meeting was followed by a pillow-fight in the dormitory. There need be no attempt to sustain an atmosphere, simply trust the Word, the

Spirit and the promises of answered prayer. And, sure enough, boy after boy experienced the deep desire to get right; they came to Jesus and experienced the new life in which the Spirit set them praying and loving the Word. It is this which explains the influence of this extraordinary man. The symposium concerning him to which John Eddison, Dick Lucas, David Fletcher, Dick Knight, John Stott, Michael Green, John Pollock and others contributed is entitled *A Study in Spiritual Power*. That spiritual power was awesome.

In addition to the main camp meeting, the day would end with a short 'quiet time' led by the officer in his tent or dormitory, and the officer would feel a special responsibility to pray for those boys and to follow them up. He would write letters after camp was over – Bash said that we needed not only apostleship, but epistleship. He himself wrote a letter every week for five years to one of his 'key boys' – John Stott. John read them almost as encyclicals, so great was his respect for his mentor. We were encouraged also to visit boys, either to speak at a school Christian union or just to take them out for tea. I remember taking out a studious boy from Bedford School, who became a great authority on evangelicalism: John Reynolds, the author of *The Evangelicals at Oxford* and *Canon Christopher of St Aldate's, Oxford*. One of the jobs which I got at camp before long was the running of the bookstall. I was interested in the books and booklets which helped new converts to understand their Bibles, and I was thrilled with books which told of the exploits of those who took the gospel to the hard places of the earth. I sold the two volumes of Hudson Taylor's life to David Bentley-Taylor, who was to land up in mainland China. In later years Bash became very cautious what books he allowed to be taken home from camp. Understandably parents who had paid vast sums to get their sons equipped for some respectable job did not always take kindly to the idea of their blue-eyed boy becoming a missionary. To some of us the Second Coming was a thrilling new truth, but Bash likewise

wished this truth soft-pedalled; 'those who become too keen on
the Second Advent tend to forget the First', he said.

I remained with Bash throughout my first three years at
Cambridge, a privilege never to be forgotten.

Five

CICCU — 1932/3

Encouraged by these new-found friends, my natural spiritual home in Cambridge was the Cambridge Inter-Collegiate Christian Union. The CICCU effectively dated from the middle of the nineteenth century and was the outcome of the earlier work of Charles Simeon. Simeon, with very little religious background, went up to a Cambridge with very little serious religion and was told he must attend Holy Communion. At this he was horrified saying: 'Conscience told me that Satan was as fit to go there as I.' As he tried to prepare himself, he read about the Old Testament sacrifices and saw how God had 'provided an offering for me, that I may lay my sins on another.' This he tried to do and he woke up on Easter Day 1779 with peace of mind and an overwhelming sense that Christ was risen. He went on to have an extraordinary ministry in Cambridge for fifty-four years, training generation after generation of undergraduates to understand the scriptures in their natural sense and to proclaim the whole counsel of God in a direct and positive way.

The Christian Union with its daily prayer meeting had been a great focus for evangelism at home and overseas. Through the influence of D.L. Moody had arisen in the 1880s the Cambridge Seven, who stirred the country to its depths with their missionary call. Early in the next century the CICCU was part of a wider Student Christian Movement, which began to be infiltrated by ideas which threatened to undermine all that the CICCU stood for, questioning the very need of salvation and denying the truth of the Bible. A long period of stress followed during which some of its members advocated staying in the old paths, while others advocated a broadening out into more liberal ways. In 1910 Torrey conducted a highly successful mission which greatly heartened the members, but then World War I came and nearly extinguished the union. When the war was over SCM grew rapidly, while CICCU remained small. Repeated efforts were made to bring CICCU into the broader body and in 1925 they succeeded in getting its leaders to consent to a united mission the following year. There was to be a joint meeting on the opening night, after which the three missioners, Anglican, Nonconformist and CICCU, would conduct their separate campaigns. William Temple and Cyril Norwood had already been selected; the CICCU decided to invite John Stuart Holden, vicar of St Paul's, Portman Square, to represent them. He was a widely read, eloquent man who had frequently preached for them. He had suggested that William Nicholson, an Ulster evangelist, a minister of the Presbyterian Church of Ireland, should be invited to Cambridge for three days before the mission to stir up the CICCU. Then something very strange happened.

Dr B.F.C. Atkinson of Magdalene, a double-first in classics, who had recently gained his PhD in linguistics and was now Under-Librarian at the University Library, had been disturbed by a message which had been sent out by the missioners and signed by Holden, which he thought would compromise the gospel. He prayed 'definitely and urgently' throughout the winter that Holden would not come. Less than a week before the mission was due, a telegram arrived saying that Holden was ill. All attempts to get a substitute at such short notice failed. When Nicholson got off the train at Euston station they asked him to take his place. 'In great fear and trembling' he accepted. On the face of it it seemed a totally unsuitable appointment – the man was a converted seaman with a wild past and practically no formal education, experienced only in speaking to the Irish working classes. What followed put off some people for life but it put the CICCU on for the rest of the century.

The opening meeting took place in the Guildhall on the Saturday. In the chair was Michael Ramsey, President of the Union Society, later to be Regius Professor of Divinity in Cambridge and Archbishop of Canterbury. Temple spoke first giving a scholarly and impressive address arguing the reasonableness of Christianity. Then, to quote from John Pollock's moving account in *A Cambridge Movement* (London, 1953) p. 222:

Norwood spoke next, somewhat lamely. Then the Chairman formally announced Stuart Holden's withdrawal and asked Nicholson to speak. 'I understand', began Nicholson, 'that the purpose of this gathering is to introduce the missioners to you. My lord bishop is well known, and so is Dr Norwood. But I am an unknown quantity. Who am I?' And then, with a voice like a bull, he announced: 'My name is William P. Nicholson of Bangor, County Down, Northern Ireland. I was born on 15 April 1880, I was born again on 22 May 1898, and I was filled with the Spirit in November 1898 through the ministry of Dr J. Stuart Holden of London. And what do I believe? I believe in God the Father Almighty, Maker of heaven and earth, and in Jesus Christ His only Son our Lord. I believe He was conceived by the Holy Ghost. I believe He was born of the Virgin Mary, yes, born of the Virgin Mary.' And so he continued, enunciating each clause of the the Apostles' Creed, with briefest comment but without reservation – and when he came to the phrase, 'From whence also He shall come again to judge both the quick and the dead' and spoke of the Second Coming of Christ, a ripple of laughter ran round the room. He reached the last clause: 'I believe in the Life everlasting

– yes, the eternity of Hell and the eternity of Heaven. That's me and that's my message.' He then sat down.

On the Sunday night the missioners were on their own. A crowd flocked to hear Temple and a modest congregation assembled to hear an hour's sermon from Nicholson on the text, 'Ye must be born again.' He was 'in full tilt against the ideas of the age.' To quote Pollock again:

> It was not what he said which astonished so much as his manner, and the man himself. 'It was extraordinary,' said one freshman whom a friend had taken along, 'very vulgar and yet – very attractive at the same time.' Stories and anecdotes flowed from the pulpit. Humour and pathos were unbounded, and a dogmatism which was almost alarming. Many senior members were horrified. 'Alack, a ranting Protestant,' wrote one, 'and this in Cambridge of all places.'

Numbers began to build up. Nicholson with his puckish sense of humour and his transparent sincerity riveted his audience.

Nicholson's statements were sweeping, yet he knew what he was doing. 'We have come to a place where the Christ of denunciation needs to be preached,' he once wrote. 'Amid the hypocrisies and insincerities which permeate our modern life we too seldom hear in the pulpit the burning indignation, the splendid scorn, and the fiery arraignment which distinguished the old prophets of God when they looked upon social sin and corruption.' He had no fear of preaching on Hell.

> If this Bible is the Word of God – and it is – and if Jesus Christ is the Son of God – and He is – then there is a hell. You may deny the fact, but that will not destroy it. How are we to escape hell? This is the part of my message that I like. The other part has been very hard to declare to you, but to be true to your soul I had to do it . . . there is mercy with

the Lord here and now. Jesus Christ has died, the just, for you the unjust. Surely you will not go to hell with your eyes open and your feet stained with the blood of Christ?

There was much in the Nicholson mission that bore the stamp of human frailty and roused understandable antagonism. Michael Ramsey, with whom I was to have many contacts later on, seems to have got his image of evangelicals from this event and never to have felt able really to tolerate them; for all his charity he never in his heart accepted Billy Graham. But the mission proved a turning point for CICCU. In spite of poor follow-up and a good many unsatisfactory converts, there were deep conversions and, most important, CICCU had lost its reputation for respectability. A Christianity which said, and meant, 'you must be born again', could never be popular. From that day to this the churches in which this message is fearlessly and warmly proclaimed are a small minority, but they are often richly blessed, probably owing more than they realize to the stream of witness that flowed from the Ulsterman's ministry.

It was into this CICCU that I came in 1932. Whole-hearted membership was very time-consuming. We would normally start the day with an hour or so of private Bible reading and prayer; at midday was the daily prayer meeting, if one could find time to attend it; at the week-end was a Bible exposition and an evangelistic sermon (to which we tried to bring our friends) and in the summer an open-air meeting in the market-place. I remember Donald Coggan (the first historian of the new evangelical student movement) speaking at one of these, and I have memories of speaking once myself – on the Second Coming. In addition to this were the demands of the college group in Pembroke. We were four in number: Donald Lynch (third year) who had a first in classics and went on to be Chief Secretary of the Church Army; Kenneth Kitley (second year) who was a modern linguist with a first and gained a half-blue at athletics, becoming in due course

a missionary in Africa; Trounson Capon and I represented the
first year, but Trounson sadly died after only one term at college.
The evening meal at Pembroke was in two sittings and during the
previous year Donald went to the first, while Kenneth went to the
second. They had made a habit of meeting in Donald's room in
Old Court between the halls. They often felt like letting off some
steam as well as praying; so they had a bit of a rough house and
threw each other about the furniture. The diminutive bed-maker,
Mrs Barker, didn't intrude on these occasions, but she was
curious and said one day, 'Mr Lynch, do you always fight when
you pray?' Trounson and I joined them, and we were much
concerned about the evangelization of our own college.

In the early days I also attended college SCM meetings, but
pressure of time squeezed these out. I also took on some Sunday
school teaching at the Castle End Mission, a Free Church centre
for townspeople. One Saturday, not being very pleased with my
performance with my class, I thought I ought to follow the Lord's
example and attempt a night of prayer beforehand. I arrived at
the class on Sunday feeling rather jaded and felt that I performed
if anything worse than before. I did not do it again! I got friendly
with a tramp on one occasion and took him to my rooms and
then to the mission. He was very frank and said that it was useless
to give money to his kind as it would only be spent on drink. There
was also a regular prayer meeting for Bash's camps; I remember
J.V. Taylor attending these and unfailingly livening the proceedings with two or three new jokes. In addition, in a place like
Cambridge, there were miscellaneous activities galore.

Then there was rowing in the winter and tennis in the summer.
Rowing meant an outing every weekday afternoon, another time
consuming activity but one which kept us very fit. My second year
I stroked the college fourth boat in the Lents with disastrous
results – we were bumped four days running. Tennis was a little
more successful, I usually played in the college second six. Finally,
of course, there was academic work to be done! We were not lazy,

but our idea of putting the kingdom of God first was to do academic work when there was nothing of greater importance to do. This was not an ideal way of mapping out one's time and many (particularly later generations) managed things more sensibly. It will be noticed that church and college chapel played a small part in my spiritual life at this time. Indeed Anglicanism as such did not particularly interest me. There was a small Anglo-Catholic group in the college centred on Edward Wynn, the Dean, who was later Bishop of Ely. He was a charming man but the two groups were on quite different wavelengths and there was little communication between them. All in all we were as busy as bees from morning to night and one CICCU speaker warned us, 'Beware of the barrenness of a busy life.'

The CICCU in all its history was never without problems. In 1932 it was perturbed by the presence of Frank Buchman's Oxford Group Movement, which seemed to offer a fresh and promising approach to the spiritual life and to the winning of the outsider to Christ. The undergraduate question was: Is it of God or of the Devil? Jack Cobb, who was CICCU president at the time, was slightly older than the average undergraduate, and he realised that the movement was based on subjective experience with only the slimmest basis in Christian doctrine. In the May term he got T.C. Hammond, who was a competent theologian and later to become Principal of Moore Theological College, Sydney, to come and give a course on Christian doctrine. The influence of the Oxford Group waned and CICCU continued to try to maintain its dual emphasis on Word and Spirit, grounding its members in the Bible and encouraging them in prayer and Christian witness. I came to see as time went on that it is usually wrong to see any Christian movement in terms of black or white. The good is always mixed with the bad and we are all different shades of grey. Some of the Oxford Group members were deeply rooted in the New Testament and did solid work, one of whom was Garth Lean whom I came to know and appreciate after retirement.

Six
Sanctification, Sex and Separation

The evangelicalism which owed much to Moody was vexed by another problem. Mission preaching which preached for a decision and which was not firmly church-based was peculiarly prone to the spectacle of 'converts' who seemed only half converted. This led to the need for a 'second blessing' and to a proliferation of movements and conventions in which was sought Holiness, or the Fullness of the Holy Spirit, or the Victorious Life, or Entire Sanctification or Christian Perfection. What was required from the seeker was total renunciation of sin and total trust in the power of the Holy Spirit. To many who attempted this second step (including Nicholson) the second blessing was more wonderful than the first. Indeed in many cases the second blessing may have been the first actual experience of true repentance and new birth. Throughout its history, zealous CICCU men had indulged in much introspection in quest of this blessing in the fullest degree, and in our day the speakers who took our Bible expositions usually took some aspect of sanctification.

To many of us – it was certainly so to me – this talk of victory over sin came to mean particularly and concretely victory over masturbation. I heard an Oxford theological college principal recently quoted as saying: 'If Jesus had known the agony which his statement, "Whoever looks on a woman to lust after her has committed adultery with her already in his heart" would cause millions of young men, he would have torn his tongue out.' It would be an overstatement to say in my case that it caused me agony, though one of my contemporaries was suicidal at one stage, as was a theological student whom I knew later on, but it was very troublesome and it was a long time before I came to a satisfactory understanding of the problem.

A number of considerations helped to save me in the matter of masturbation. For one thing my whole spiritual experience was built on the assumption that the Bible was God's Word and that it was to this primary source that we should go for guidance. I found the Bible condemning all manner of sexual sins but this activity (said to be practised by the great majority of men) is nowhere mentioned. I noticed too that it was most likely to take place when I had had a blissful time of bedtime prayer with a great sense of love for God, when presumably erotic pressures were strong. In any case it was very near to nature, not far removed from a wet-dream, therefore surely not a very heinous sin. Finally, I felt sure that such an occurrence must not be allowed to drive me away from God but to him – to ask forgiveness for all that needs forgiving and cleansing for all that needs cleansing and for the power of the Holy Spirit to flow through me during the coming day.

It was sometime later that I came to see the importance of the word *eis* in Jesus' sentence. He is speaking of the man who looks on a woman with the intention of lusting after her. To be aroused by a woman's attractions is part of the temptation; it is only when the will consents that the attraction becomes sin. Admittedly it is a small step from admiring a woman's beauty to desiring her but it is this step which is crucial. It is a shame that for a millennium Christendom had all its sexual instruction from men who had had no experience of pure and happy sexual intercourse. It makes it difficult now to steer a course between a guilt-ridden anxiety on the one hand and a sinful laxity on the other. It is clear that God has put us in a world with a sexual nature which somehow has to be coped with. Retreat to a monastery or strict veiling provide no escape. Jesus mixed freely with womenfolk, he talked alone to the Samaritan woman at the well about her sex life, he even allowed a prostitute to wipe her tears from his feet with her hair. We have to learn to manage our sexual natures, not to suppress them. It is good to recognize the animal-like nature of our instincts and laugh at ourselves. But it is still necessary to avoid needless temptation. For instance, it is probably unwise to counsel members of the other sex at any depth. Is not the confessional box with its physical separation of priest and penitent a permanent witness to this truth? On the other hand, does not the ban on contraception by three successive Popes lead to unnecessary temptation? Does it not indeed put an intolerable strain on the millions of devout couples who feel unable to obey their direction?

All of us in the CICCU, I think, accepted the fact that a Christian should not have sex before marriage. With all the colleges being single-sex and only two of them being for women, there was not the pressure of continual contact experienced in modern universities. Most of us hoped to be happily married and were content to wait till marriage had come into sight as a practical possibility before forming alliances with girl friends. The women of the two colleges had recently formed their own Christian union and they brought their friends to the CICCU evangelistic sermon where they sat in rows reserved for them, but there was virtually no mixing up of men and women. Incredible though it may sound today, this was to us one way of 'seeking first the kingdom of God'. And God wonderfully added the blessing of happy marriages to nearly all of us. Some sixty of us went down from Cambridge in 1934 and we kept in touch with each other by six-monthly duplicated letters thereafter and, in spite of prudish upbringings and lack of sexual knowledge, not a single one of our first marriages went wrong.

The sanctification teaching so much in vogue in the thirties owed a great deal to a visit to England in 1873 by Pearsall and Hannah Smith. They argued that Christianity was not meant to be a gloomy struggle but a steady experience of joy in the Holy Spirit. The cry was total renunciation of sin and self and total surrender to the Spirit: 'Let go and let God'. This teaching found expression in institutional form in the Keswick Convention to which CICCU took a party every year. I found that this teaching tended to make the extroverts who had 'got the blessing' self-satisfied and the introverts who could never quite get it more and more depressed. I came to the conclusion that eternal life meant having Christ, the greatest gift imaginable, and that all growth in grace was simply appropriating more of him. This might come with the help of one or more noteworthy experiences but, since experiences differed tremendously, no one's experience should be the basis for doctrine. I visited Keswick three times and my disillusion grew – I felt that many in the great concourse would be better employed getting themselves trained for some Christian work than in listening to convention orators. I was therefore more than ready to side with James Packer twenty years later when he wrote an article for the *Evangelical Quarterly* (July 1955), 'Keswick and the Reformed Doctrine of Sanctification' which repudiated the Pearsall Smith doctrine. Packer's article was very unpopular in some quarters since it attacked a much treasured sacred cow, but it was a step in the direction of sanity.

Incidentally Bash had no use for second blessing teaching, even declaring that his favourite theologian, Torrey, 'went loopy' when in later life he had an experience which made him advocate 'baptism with the Spirit'. C.T. Studd was likewise impatient with this sort of 'deep teaching', declaring that obedience to the plain teaching of the Bible was enough to keep anyone fully occupied. On the other hand the CICCU had its own missionary, Dr Joe Church, who worked in the Ruanda Mission (of the Church Missionary Society) which embraced Keswick principles in its basis of faith. He was a major instrument in the East African Revival which began in the mid-thirties, which shows that doctrinal semantics are not always important.

In common with other evangelicals we had a strong doctrine of separation from the world. This consisted of a taboo on smoking, dancing, theatre, cinema, gambling and alcohol, and is often thought of as something negative, when Christianity with its belief in a Sovereign Creator ought to be supremely world-affirming. Whether all these taboos were wise and necessary is open to question but they certainly were not thought of as negative. They were an attempt to set the very highest ethical standards to be lived out by the Christian in nearly every walk of life and every stratum of society, whether in the professions, in business, in politics, in manual labour, in the arts, or in the armed forces. (Pacifism was much debated among us – some went the Quaker way, but more believed it sometimes right to fight.) The Christian was called to live a holy life right in the world. The case was put in a widely read booklet *Questionable Amusements* by Frederick Wood, one of the Brethren and a founder of the Young Life Campaign, and argued as part of the cost of honouring God and loving your neighbour. As Elizabeth Goudge puts it in her account of the thirteenth-century Cardinal John of Saint Paul who helped Francis of Assisi in his approach to the Pope: 'He would have stripped himself as gladly as Francis had done. That would have been the easier way for him, but God had called him to the infinitely harder task of living the dedicated life within the world' (*Saint Francis of Assisi*, p. 82).

Seven

Communism and Christianity — 1933/4

A breath of fresh air came to the Pembroke CU in my second year in the person of Tony Biddulph. He came of a well known Christian military family and had been sent to Cambridge by the Sappers to get a degree in engineering. He was a fire-eating daredevil, whose driving terrified me and who seemed to long for nothing better than to die a hero's death in battle, which, alas, he did in the war which was so soon to come. He defined Christianity as 'betting your life there's God'. He must have found it a culture shock to come from the Sappers' mess to our pious hothouse but fellowship in Christ bound us together. One of my most enduring memories of him was an entirely trivial one. We were walking together towards the great university library and he said: 'When I was a little boy I thought that if I worked really hard I could learn everything. Now I know better.' It illustrated in a vivid way the dilemma of academia. We have access to an infinity of facts which we cannot hope to make sense of unless we have revelation to tell us which are the significant ones. It reminds me also of another piece of sound advice given at that time: It is true that what we don't know is infinitely more than what we do know, but never let what you don't know – be it psychology, sociology, geology or any of the other bogies which may frighten a Bible-based Christian – overturn what you do know.

I had ended the first year with an inglorious third in mathematics and had had to decide what to read next. The advice was all against reading theology and Bash's right-hand man, Graham Leask, got me interested in Geography Part One which he had just read. Geography was the meeting-ground of the arts and the sciences and I thoroughly enjoyed it. It was really a two-year course, but I came up for a preparatory Long Vac Term in order to read it in one year. I remember very pleasant times surveying Coe Fen during that term. The range covered by the course was tremendous, including geology, land forms, meteorology, anthropology, historical geography, economic geography and political geography, and it is not surprising that I finished up with another third.

Political geography had special interest since Cambridge was at this time a hotbed of Communism with Burgess and Maclean being recruited for the cause. One of our lecturers recommended John Strachey's *The Coming Struggle for Power* which greatly impressed me, except for its chapter on religion, which struck me as feeble. I gather that the economists also gave him a rough ride, but I could well understand people who were not well informed about either religion or economics finding his book compelling; it read almost like a prophecy. Another impressive book which had many reprints was *The Socialist Sixth of the World* by Hewlett Johnson, the Dean of Canterbury – another of Ramsay MacDonald's appointments.

My supervisor, a brilliant young man called Dr O.H.K. Spate, was an ardent Communist of (I believe) German extraction. At one supervision he produced what looked like a booklet advertising Electrolux, inside which was a Communist tract. He told me with bated breath of the thousands of these which they had distributed in Berlin, in telephone kiosks and other such places, before the Nazis got on to them. He and I got on very well because at least we both believed something. Politics and world affairs provide a very good starting point for evangelism. I had a long talk during the war on board ship with an army officer who was heading for India intending in his spare time to spread Communism there. He already gave half his pay to the party. Starting from the state of the world, it is an easy step to the fact of human sin, and it is an easy step from there to the need of a new birth. And it is easy to show that the stirring up of hatred can do no lasting good, whereas the love which springs from new birth offers the only realistic hope for human beings.

It is often impossible to recall precisely when one read particular books but I was ravenously reading Christian literature all the time, especially the Bible. It was during my second year that I read through the prophets in the Revised Version writing in the margin my own summary of each paragraph. It was also while at Pembroke that I read that classic of the Roman controversy, George Salmon's *The Infallibility of the Church*. I was so impressed that I wrote a digest of these twenty-three lectures in a large exercise book, running to forty-eight pages. Salmon was the Provost of Trinity College, Dublin, a mathematician turned theologian, with a clear head and great command of his material. I was told that the book was used at one time in training men for the bar, showing them how to present a case. Not surprisingly the Roman Catholic lobby resented this and managed to secure its removal. The Roman Church was not a great force in Cambridge in my day but I obviously realized that it is a world phenomenon which every Protestant needs to take seriously. Salmon was reprinted in abridged form in 1952, which evoked a reply (*The Church and Infallibility*) from B.C. Butler, at that time Abbot of Downside. I went over to Downside and had a long and useful talk with him. But although Butler makes some effective debating points, he does not seem to me to answer Salmon.

I was also concerned at this time with one of the doctrinal debates which perennially agitates evangelicals: Should we be Arminians or Calvinists? In the thrilling story of the evangelical revival, John Wesley and George Whitefield took opposite sides, while Charles Simeon refused to take sides, affirming that the truth lay not in one extreme or the other but in both together. During my time in Cambridge I was gaining much help on the question of biblical inspiration and in the fight against liberalism from American Calvinists like J.G. Machen and B.B. Warfield, who were fine scholars. They all followed the so-called Five Point Calvinism which had been developed in the seventeenth century in answer to Arminius who thought that Reformation doctrine was being expounded in a way that undermined human responsibility. The five points (remembered by the acrostic TULIP) were Total inability, Unconditional election, Limited atonement, Irresistible grace and Perseverance of the Saints, which were given their classical expression in the Westminster Confession of Faith. I read L. Boettner, *The Reformed Doctrine of Predestination* (1932), a volume dedicated to the faculty of Westminster Theological Seminary, Philadelphia, the college founded by those (like Machen) who had broken away from Princeton. I was very sympathetic towards his exposition, knowing full well that election is a central doctrine of the Bible and that predestination has an important place. These men were thinkers who knew the Bible and were trying to plumb it to its depths. But while Boettner gave full scripture proofs for points 1, 2 and 5, he did not do so for points 3 and 4. I could not accept point 3, since if Christ died only for the elect and we do not know who is elect, it would be impossible to say to my unbelieving friends: Christ died for you. All Christians recognize that there are deep mysteries here and I was not persuaded that the Five Point Calvinism left the mysteries in the proper place. I felt myself a true Simeonite, and incidentally a true Anglican, since Article 17 of the Thirty-Nine Articles affirms only predestination to life and does not go on to espouse double predestination, however logically predestination to damnation might seem to follow.

I was more impressed by a Dutch Calvinist who deserves a note to himself. Abraham Kuyper (1837–1920) was in his time one of the leading statesmen of Europe and as Prime Minister he became the

Grand Old Man of the Netherlands. He was founder and first theological professor of the Free University of Amsterdam; he created a national system of Calvinistic schools; he founded the Gereformeerde church; he founded a political party and a system of trade unions; he wrote books on Dutch art, and (as if that were not enough) for fifty years he edited a daily newspaper. I once received an ordinary second-hand theological book catalogue from Holland; it had nearly six hundred books either by or about Kuyper. Though brought up in a Christian home he lost his faith during his studies in the University of Leyden; nevertheless he got ordained and accepted a small country parish. What happened there is worth quoting:

> Here he found a dedicated group of Christians who in many ways seemed far beneath their brilliant pastor, an 'intellectual superman'. Yet, he quickly recognized that they were in many ways his superior. 'I could not measure my impoverished Bible knowledge, the fruit of university study,' he wrote, 'with that of these plain people . . . What drew me most to them was that here the heart spoke – there was inner experience. I found myself ever at the fork of the way. Either must I take sharp position against them or go with them without conditions, putting myself under sovereign grace.' His conversion came through the counsel of a young girl named Pietje Baltus. She had none of this world's luxuries, but she had a deep faith that amazed Abraham. In his first visit to her parents' home the new dominie sat for two hours listening to the statement of the hope that was in her. She warned him that he, too, must have this hope if he would not perish eternally. She confessed how she had prayed almost constantly for him. 'I could not relax until the Lord Himself came and took him from my soul.'
>
> What a contrast! This gifted, cultured son of the university, versed in all the philosophies, chatting in five languages

with ease at his dinner-table . . . and the unschooled but Spirit-taught peasant girl. Kuyper throughout life retained a profound gratitude to this intercessor and her photograph stood in his study till the end.

(R.A. Tucker, *Sacred Stories* p. 140)

In 1898 he delivered the Stone Lectures which were published under the title *Calvinism*. This book thrilled me – it showed me reformed Christianity as a life system which had something to say about every area of life: religion, politics, science and art. It was set over against other systems – Roman Catholicism, Islam, liberalism – the comprehensive vision of a big mind. I was to hear many years later from Alvin Plantinga (our greatest living philosopher of religion) that the Stone Lectures were still being studied as a textbook when he taught at Calvin College, Grand Rapids. This book broadened and deepened for life my understanding of evangelical faith. Sad to say, Kuyper's experiments were not an entire success in the long term. The Free University greatly prospered, but it was unable to maintain its strictly Reformed basis, and the Gereformeerde church was plagued by schisms. My two passions for a long time were C.T. Studd and world evangelism and Abraham Kuyper and an academic world view. I fear that Kuyper's theology could not bear so vast a weight. A Dutchman made a remark which appealed to my pragmatic mind: 'It is not we Dutch Calvinists who have evangelized the world, it is you evangelical Anglo-Saxons.'

At this time my views on hell were particularly influenced by R.A. Torrey, *What the Bible Teaches*. This book is an inductive study of the Bible; it sets out the main passages on a given topic and then summarizes what they say as far as possible in the words of Scripture. Of course there has to be interpretation at various places and at places questions are raised and answered. The conclusion to which Torrey comes is:

When we see sin in all its hideousness and enormity, the Holiness of God in all its perfection, and the glory of Jesus Christ in all its infinity, nothing but a doctrine that those who persist in the choice of sin, who love darkness rather than light, and persist in the rejection of the Son of God, shall endure everlasting anguish, will satisfy the demands of our own moral intuitions.

He maintains that weak doctrines of sin and worldliness of life lead Christians to abandon the plain teaching of Scripture and so lose spiritual power. I had prayed that I might be used by God and I dreaded that this might happen to me and I was eager at all costs to rescue all around me from this terrible fate.

Eight

Cambridge Theology — 1934/5

In my third year I launched into the Theological Tripos Part One with my eyes wide open. I knew that my beliefs about the Bible would not be shared by any of my teachers and would be assailed with much learning and with a cool urbanity. I knew that it was customary to ignore the conservative case with which I had become acquainted, so that a difficult battle lay ahead. I had the great good fortune to be put under the supervision of Sir Edwyn Hoskyns, Bt, the Dean of Corpus Christi College which was next door to Pembroke. Hoskyns was a somewhat lonely figure in liberal Cambridge, being a High-Churchman strongly influenced by Karl Barth. He made a name for himself by translating Barth's *Epistle to the Romans*, which I remember taking with me on a punting expedition up the Cam. The supervision system was extraordinarily inadequate. I would write a New Testament essay for Hoskyns each week which was very worth while, but as far as other subjects went, I had to be content with a query at the beginning and end of term as to whether they were all right, to which the invariable answer was 'Yes'.

The first necessity was to get some Greek, as recollections from my preparatory school days amounted to little more than an ability to recite the definite article. I was dispatched to Dr Lukyn Williams, who had been associated with Handley Moule, Bishop of Durham, who had been a staunch supporter of the CICCU.

Lukyn Williams no longer held these views but was not unsympathetic to them. His positive work had led him to become an expert in Christian apologetics to the Jews, which meant that he had much of interest to say. I remember the warning he gave against accepting the idea that Jewish authors of books of the New Testament made mistakes when quoting the Old Testament – they knew their Old Testament better than even Bible-loving Christians know the New. We worked away at Nunn's *Elements of New Testament Greek* for a term and I was then left to mug up what I could for purposes of the exams.

Lectures which I remember included those of 'Froggie' Marsh at Selwyn on Old Testament. (Canon F.S. Marsh, Lady Margaret Professor of Divinity, lectured sitting on a stool looking for all the world like a giant frog!) It was useful of course to get the current teaching on Old Testament criticism, though in fact it differed very little from the position of S.R. Driver which I had learnt at school. It encouraged me to read A.H. Finn, *The Unity of the Pentateuch* (3rd edition, 1928) which was a thorough examination of the main works in English which advocated the JEDP analysis. This was valuable in its own right but I thought I ought to be able to say that I had read it, if ever I found myself in debate on the subject. It is remarkable how good the answers are and how persistently they are ignored. The one topic which Finn failed to tackle satisfactorily was the very large numbers in the Pentateuch – a subject to which I came back later.

For New Testament, Hoskyns' own lectures thrilled CICCU men. He got down to the text itself and tried to bring out the spiritual realities of which it spoke. On one occasion the packed lecture room looked puzzled; Hoskyns said: 'Paul expected the servant girl in Rome to understand this. The trouble is we are *sarkinoi* (carnal).' He spoke with great intensity and I believe always rewrote old lectures before delivering them again. Charles Raven also lectured on the New Testament with much eloquence to large audiences but I felt with him that we were getting Raven's

ideas more than those of the apostolic writers. But what he was
trying to say proceeded from the positive vision of a man trying
to wed the best of Christianity to the best of science. This, alas,
could not be said of B.T.D. Smith, who was the spokesman for
Rudolph Bultmann in Cambridge. He was an Anglican clergyman who had resigned his orders and presented the sad spectacle
of a sceptic. He was always immaculately dressed and spoke with
a slight lisp. One student used to sit in the front row and prefaced
his note-taking with an account of the lecturer's attire for the day:
tie, shirt, shoes, suit. He tried to get a glimpse of his socks as he
mounted the rostrum but always in vain!

As there were no conservative New Testament scholars writing, I used to look at the old ones. I often found Henry Alford's
commentary on the Greek Testament helpful. He taught me that
the synoptics were written before the fall of Jerusalem in AD 70
and that Acts was completed at the point where it ends – in AD 62.
E.F. Scott was the recommended book on The Fourth Gospel
but I found B.F. Westcott in the Speaker's Commentary much
more convincing. The Cambridge trio, Lightfoot, Westcott and
Hort, were superb scholars, and I have never doubted that the
fourth gospel came from the apostle John since reading Westcott.
I would only take issue with him in dating it so very late in the
first century; I believe that John Robinson is nearer the mark in
placing it before AD 70.

Early Church History was another exciting subject. I much
enjoyed H.M. Gwatkin's *Early Church History to AD 313*, and
also the lectures of Percy Gardner-Smith in Jesus College. I found
the doctrinal debates concerning the Trinity and the Person of
Christ interesting and important in establishing the fundamental
antinomies of Christian doctrine. Just as I had learnt about
complementarity in physics, here was the same thing in revelation: two propositions (Oneness and Threeness; Godhood and
Manhood) both inescapably true, but irreconcilable by the human mind. I was to discover the same thing in philosophy. Some

of the debating seemed to me more a matter of words than of substance but the conclusions of Nicea and Chalcedon undoubtedly point to something objectively real in the New Testament.

Theological light also came to me from quite another quarter, none other than the redoubtable Basil Atkinson who had prayed all winter that Stuart Holden might not take part in the united Cambridge mission. Basil was a remarkable man, a brilliant linguist who would reckon to learn the language before visiting a new country. He was chosen to write the book on the Greek language in a prestigious Cambridge series. As under-librarian he had responsibility for the university's ancient manuscripts. There was a problem about insuring Codex Bezae when the library moved into its new premises. 'What did you do?' 'I popped it into the back of my Baby Austin and drove it round.' He had beautiful, legible, flowing handwriting. At that time he was virtually the only senior member of the university in sympathy with the CICCU, and he was not a fellow of his college. He was the unofficial, but very powerful, guardian of the CICCU's theological soundness for some forty-five years. Long after his retirement officials of the CICCU committee visited him regularly for prayer and counsel.

Theologically he was an amateur but very well informed in many directions. He went for the primary sources, studying his Bible in the Hebrew and Greek. He knew the debates of critical scholarship with all its supposed biblical contradictions and inconsistencies. He gave the sensible advice: 'Face them boldly; with the application of accuracy and common sense most of them will melt away.' He was unquestionably what Barr would call a fundamentalist, believing the very text of scripture to be inspired and infallibly true. He wrote a lively little book *Is the Bible True?* advocating this view. He was also a fairly extreme Protestant. This comes out in a book on church history *Valiant in Fight* and in his exposition of the Book of Revelation called *The War with Satan*. The latter takes a traditional 'historicist' line of interpretation, which sees the whole history of the Christian church hidden in the symbols of the book with the beast of 13:1–10 representing the Bishop of Rome. R.E.D. Clark mentions Isaac Newton's interest in this prophecy and adds that 'over a long period every (other) Lucasian Professor of Mathematics in the University of Cambridge wrote a commentary on the Revelation' (*Tomorrow's Word*, p. 1). I was myself impressed by 'historicist' reasoning which at least takes the book as a whole and tries to make sense of it as a whole, but like both Luther and Calvin I never felt able to commit myself to this view. I did, however, feel horrified at the way paganism flooded the church after Constantine and how the Papacy tried to crush the great spiritual revival of the glorious Reformation. I think my Protestantism must have reached its lowest point at this time; I hated the very smell of stale incense in a church.

Stories and good-natured undergraduate jokes abounded about 'Basil At'. He was said to read the Bible as though he had written it; when he read the lesson in St Paul's church he emphasized every other word! But we respected him as a great man of the Word and of prayer and of witness. I was very touched when I heard one day that he, a man whose head was stuffed with academic thoughts, had been chatting to some lads who were loafing in the market-place and had told them that Jesus loved them. He was always ready to put in a word for Jesus. He and his sister used to keep open house on Sunday afternoons at their home in Grange Road and students flocked to enjoy the excellent tea which they laid on. Sometimes when tea was over Basil would expound in an informal way some topic of interest. It was on one such occasion that I heard him talk about conditional immortality and the ultimate destruction of all evil.

I do not remember precisely what he said on that occasion and we shall come back to this subject later, when I can give my views as digested in the subsequent sixty years. His main ideas included the following points:

1. The Bible nowhere teaches that man is immortal. This is a Greek idea.
2. God alone has immortality.
3. Immortality has been brought to light by the gospel.
4. Immortality is received when someone is born again to eternal life and becomes a partaker of the divine nature.
5. Death means the cessation of life, followed by deep unconscious sleep, until the resurrection to judgment of the just and the unjust.
6. The second death in the lake of fire means the cessation of life for ever.
7. The fires of hell burn up what is evil, they do not torment for ever.
8. *Aionios*, the word often translated 'everlasting', means 'of the age to come'.
9. The doctrine of everlasting punishment is a doctrine of everlasting pain and of everlasting sin, since punishment would not continue for anyone who was reconciled to God.
10. In the end God will be all in all, all evil destroyed with no one living in opposition to him.

I saw at once that this teaching was quite contrary to what I had learnt from Torrey and it seemed most plausible. I felt deflated; it removed some of my motivation for evangelism and some of my motive for prayer. But when I came to pray it over I realized that rescue from torment was not a primary motive for evangelism, rather one wished to see God glorified through the loving response of a sinner to the one who loved him. The conviction that Basil was basically right deepened as the years went by. From this point onwards I found I had a new freedom to teach the awesome judgments of God and the perfection of his love without having to represent him as the everlasting torturer.

One other matter in my third year merits a mention. The CICCU (I suppose in common with all institutions that have a zeal for orthodoxy) had a very unpleasant trait. If any member dared to voice doubts about the received orthodoxy, the word quickly went round that 'so-and-so was going off the rails'. This was potentially most damaging to the suspect and also to the cause. This happened to David Milnes, who was a very fair-minded and independent-minded man. He was troubled about evolution and found that I was very ready to listen without condemning him. We became lifelong friends. He in turn challenged me (not by words but by his actions). He felt from reading the Bible that a Christian should fast, so on Fridays he took no food until the evening meal. This is something on which I think I have failed, since undoubtedly men of God in both Old and New Testament times fasted at points of need. My attempts have been without clear aims or convictions and have usually been discouraged by the womenfolk: 'You're far too skinny as it is!' I was impressed by my wife's uncle, Gordon Bulstrode, better known as Brother Edward, co-founder with Bishop Walter Carey of Village Evangelism, who was a powerful and scriptural preacher. He fasted. He told the story of a monk who was on his third day of a fast and feeling rather cheap. He was out in the country and met a tramp who asked him for something to eat. He said that he himself had had nothing to eat for two days. The tramp replied: 'You does it 'obby-like, I does it real!' I do not doubt that members of a fully committed church will be the better for adopting this practice.

Nine

Working with Douglas Johnson — 1935/6

My third year in Cambridge ended my days at Pembroke, but the work on the theological tripos was only half done. This was to be completed at Ridley Hall. Ridley Hall was a college (less than half a mile from Pembroke) founded by evangelicals in the nineteenth century to train men for the Anglican ministry. Unfortunately with my departure from Pembroke, the CICCU group in the college died out, but I undertook to organize a meeting for freshers from my new base at Ridley. Amongst those who came to the meeting was the Honourable Malcolm Kenworthy. He was the second son of Lord Strobolgi, who had successfully laid claim to a very ancient peerage and had secured a seat in the House of Lords as a Labour Peer. Malcolm showed some interest so I introduced him to Bash, under whose influence he was roundly and soundly converted. He was a delightful man, with absolutely no side; he gave himself at once to evangelism and the CICCU was soon a force in the college again. He had a serious head injury during his war service as army chaplain which was a severe handicap, but he continued a faithful ministry to the end.

Ridley, with its location in Cambridge and its supposedly evangelical tradition, was still attractive to CICCU men, and a good bunch of us went there. But it was soon obvious that the theology of the staff was not ours, and we found it necessary to organize ourselves into a theological opposition in order to

defend our cherished convictions. The liberal evangelicalism of
those days had not for the most part given up belief in the bodily
resurrection of Jesus but it denied both the substitutionary atonement of our Lord and the infallibility of the Bible. The emphasis
of the training was not on the ministry of the Word but on coming
to terms with the contemporary world and the contemporary
church. This had its value but it left out the heart of Christianity.

The principal was Paul (alias 'Hoot') Gibson. (Hoot Gibson
was the name of a contemporary film star.) Gibson's favourite
theologian was John Oman, who broadly followed in the footsteps of Friedrich Schleiermacher, perhaps the greatest of the
German liberal theologians. The vice-principal for some years
was Charlie Moule, who was to remain in Cambridge for most
of his life, eventually becoming Lady Margaret Professor of
Divinity, and regarded as quite a conservative scholar. But he was
not conservative enough for us, and we used to try to ask searching questions during lectures and we would put our heads together out of class attempting to sort out the unsolved problems.
This was all done in a friendly way but with deadly serious intent.
We dreaded the idea of becoming woolly liberals and losing the
cutting edge of the revealed Word. Geoffrey Bromiley, whom
Moule regarded as one of the brightest of his students, could not
stand Ridley and went off to the Bible Churchmen's College in
Bristol to complete his training. He eventually got to America
and gained an international reputation as a theological transla-
tor, making Karl Barth's *Church Dogmatics* available to the
English speaking world. Other contemporaries were Eric Pitt who
became Dean of Sydney, Leo Stephens-Hodge who became a
competent liturgiologist, and Joe Parker, a humorous north
countryman, who kept us plied with Calvinistic literature.

We were concerned not only to resist the liberalism of the
staff but to encourage other students to come the evangelical
way. We had an unexpected opportunity when the college organized a mission to St Leonards-on-Sea. The rector of St

Leonards, Cuthbert Griffiths, turned out to be a man after our own hearts. The team allocated to his parish was a very mixed lot, some of whom he believed to be unconverted. When he came to tell us about the needs of his church, he felt that the first requirement was that the members of the mission team should be converted. He told us how he had been an army chaplain during the war with men dying in his arms and how he had not known how to point them to Christ. He showed how it was possible to get even as far as ordination and still have no personal knowledge of Christ. He made the mission initially a mission to Ridley and we rejoiced. He memorably illustrated the need for personal conversion and personal evangelism by taking a crateful of milk bottles and first sprinkling water over them to little effect (as one does in preaching a sermon) and then pouring water into them one by one.

But the biggest influence on my life during the three years from 1935 to 1939 came from outside Cambridge in the person of Douglas Johnson. Like Bash, Douglas Johnson though almost unknown to the world at large was one of the great influences on the church of the twentieth century – perhaps the greatest. He was the key figure in the rapidly burgeoning Inter-Varsity Fellowship of Evangelical Unions, the story of which is told in his *Contending for the Faith* (IVP, 1979). At the end of the War strong groups of dedicated Christians (many of them matured by their wartime experiences) sprang up in the universities, particularly in the London medical schools and in Cambridge. These had begun to come together in an annual conference for mutual support to encourage the foundation of groups in every university and for the development of missionary interest. It involved a prodigious amount of work, all of which was being done by volunteers in their spare time, mostly by students. This reached a peak in 1924/5 which proved to be a decisive year in Douglas Johnson's life.

The inside story is not written up in the official records but he wrote a private letter to me on the sixtieth anniversary of the day that ruined his medical career! He was a man of outstanding intellect who had read history and English before turning to medicine to prepare himself for missionary service. He became secretary of LIFCU (the London Inter-Faculty Christian Union), which had a membership of over one thousand scattered around the many colleges and hospitals of London. The secretary of the 1923/4 Inter-Varsity conference had been Julian Thornton-Duesbery, a Triple First, who did not take kindly to the use of so much time on this task. He urged the appointment of a full-time secretary, and had in mind a friend of Frank Buchman (the founder of Moral Rearmament), from whom also financial support might be expected. The LIFCU (I suspect strongly influenced by Douglas himself) was intractably against this appointment and complete deadlock was reached. So the committee said that LIFCU had better organize the next conference and they would soon see the need for paid help!

So the task was landed on Douglas, who had just completed his first term of medicine. He thus had three major jobs: work as a medical student, secretary of LIFCU and secretary of IVF. He carried through his three tasks, and eventually not only qualified as a doctor, but also acquired a qualification in theology, gaining the AKC (Associate of King's College). He could no doubt have become a high-flying medic (his two sons both became professors, one in ophthalmology and the other in surgery), but he had proved that his supreme gift was that of Christian secretary. He was prevented from becoming a missionary doctor and instead gave the rest of his life to the task of building up dynamic Christianity in the student world. Some measure of his success can be seen by the sheer size of the Universities and Colleges Christian Fellowship and the International Fellowship of Evangelical Students which grew directly out of his work. The former has a paid staff of more than a hundred workers and the latter of some one thousand five hundred in different parts of the world.

A very weak link in the early days of the IVF was the work amongst theological students. It was a depressingly common experience in all denominations to find that students with a vigorous, but somewhat naive, faith would hear a call to the ordained ministry and find that their theological training left them mentally confused and spiritually ineffective. In 1934/5 a Theological Colleges Prayer Fellowship was formed to unite evangelical theologs in prayer for one another with F.H. Wynne of Assembly's College, Belfast, as secretary. He was succeeded by T.F. Torrance, who was already well read in the new continental theologians, like Barth, Brunner and Heim. When the post fell vacant Douglas pounced on me and I was made Theological Students' Representative on the IVF Executive Committee and then began an important new phase in my education.

Like Bash, Douglas had the same singleness of purpose, the same simplicity in prayer, the same commitment to soul-winning and to the nurture of the new-born, the same shrewd common sense. But in a number of ways he was unlike Bash. He had almost boundless energy, working from morn to night six days a week and filling his home with visitors (often from abroad) on Sundays. He had a wonderful brain – reading to him whether in theology, philosophy, science, history or biography was a means of relaxation. He mercilessly scored his books and he retained most of what he read. He had a world vision; though his calling was to work amongst students and in the universities, it was all in the interest of church renewal and world evangelization. He had a remarkable sense of humour – at leisure times in conferences, wherever Douglas was there would be peals of laughter. He had a wonderful wife. In the midst of all this tornado of energy, Dorothy provided that unfailing centre of peace and support which kept him sane and enabled him to maintain the pace. She is undoubtedly one of the heroines of the Christian church.

His work showed a remarkable combination of the theoretical and the practical. His life was a contending for The Faith. He was

totally incapable of divorcing the intellectual and the spiritual
and to him preaching the gospel was telling the revealed truth
about God and man and the facts of the gospel story. He was
fully aware that different branches of the church in the quest for
accuracy had elaborated a number of somewhat different theolo-
gies. But these differences were largely irrelevant in a church that
was swamped by liberalism and ignored by the world. What was
needed was a return to the fundamentals – believed so fervently
that they would be the natural topic of conversation of Christians
in a non-Christian society. Such Christians, steeped in the Bible
and attempting to live 'by every word that proceeds from the
mouth of God', were to be found in all the Protestant denominations, and it was essential that they should band together to tell
the gospel to the world. Douglas called himself a Calvinist and
was a great admirer of B.B. Warfield whose books he read avidly,
but he never allowed himself to develop 'scholastic' leanings. His
aim was always to teach students to immerse themselves in the
actual Scriptures. In my first term on the IVF committee we
collectively resolved to make 'Loyalty to the Christ of the Scriptures' our aim for that year. A simple doctrinal Basis of Faith
underlay all the work of IVF and all its speakers were expected
to conform to that basis. It was that Faith for which we contended
and which we propagated whether by word of mouth or by
literature.

But Douglas was not only a discerning theologian, he was also
a brilliant secretary. He was bursting with ideas, which made all
the drudgery of committee work worthwhile, but he had great
practical common sense. He encouraged student initiative,
thereby making a virtue of necessity. The Bible lays much stress
on the wisdom of age, but senior advisers were few and we had
to make do with what we had and take courage from St Paul's
injunction, 'Let no man despise thy youth.' In committee he
would regale us with practical illustrations from the medical
chiefs under whom he sat, or bits of experience gained when he

worked in the Bermondsey Medical Mission. He would sometimes bring us down to earth by passing a note to the chairman:
'We have not DONE anything yet!!!'

He seemed to have a genius for making bricks without straw;
he could conjure something out of nothing. A classical example
was his production of *In Understanding be Men*. He saw the need
for a book on doctrine, fully Bible based. Who could do it? There
was an Irishman, not a writer but one renowned as a debater and
public speaker, who seemed to have Protestant doctrine at his
fingertips – T.C. Hammond, leader of Irish Church Missions,
who had just accepted an invitation to become Principal of
Moore Theological College in Sydney. Douglas offered to draw
up the outline of a book on Christian doctrine and come to
Dublin with a shorthand typist, if Hammond would consent to
fill in the text. They worked solidly for three days and (with a
good deal of editing and the supply of copious biblical references)
the manuscript became in 1936 IVF's first major publication,
which was still in print in 1993.

His practical genius was also shown in his ability to enthuse
and to enrol the support of trusted leaders. A notable instance
was G.T. Manley. Manley had been Senior Wrangler, that is the
top mathematician, in Cambridge in 1893, the same year as
Bertrand Russell graduated (Russell having been listed as sixth
equal). After a time as Fellow of Christ's College, Cambridge,
Manley decided to forgo an academic career and give himself to
the missionary work of the church, first among students in India
and then on the home front. He was fully aware of the great
debates that were going on with regard to the Bible and was well
informed on pentateuchal criticism. He had made a careful study
of Christ's view of Scripture and of its implications for Christian
belief which had been published by the Religious Tract Society
under the title *It Is Written*. Douglas roped him in as chairman
of the Publications Committee and later of the Biblical Research
Committee. After he took this task on Manley himself wrote an

original and useful work on Deuteronomy entitled *The Book of the Law*. Douglas also secured the services of another gifted missionary, H.E. Guillebaud, who wrote *Why the Cross?*, another of IVF's famous early books, this time on the atonement.

He also secured the advice and help of men in the business world. A student work which had to finance an office staff and travelling secretaries, develop publishing and own property, had to look beyond students for the necessary experience. Douglas set up a Business Advisory Committee of men trusted in the Christian world, whom he always consulted and whom he always kept informed. They kept a tight hold on the purse-strings but would always come up with the money when convinced that a scheme was right and that other supporters were doing their bit. John Laing, one of the Brethren, the founder of a most successful construction business, was a particularly noteworthy example of a wise and generous counsellor who stood behind the work. Meanwhile Douglas built up a great network of committees and kept them all running reasonably smoothly.

I busied myself writing to contacts in the various theological colleges and occasionally visiting them. These visits introduced me to certain aspects of the Anglican church of which I was barely aware. I remember visiting the Bible Churchmen's College in Bristol where the principal, the Revd W. Dodgson Sykes, received me very kindly. He had a first-class brain having run off with a number of theological prizes in Cambridge but, alas, his college was most inefficiently run and his lectures were sometimes incoherent. There were three other more or less definitely conservative Anglican evangelical colleges at the time: Clifton, Oak Hill and St John's, Highbury, all led by men who had played a notable part in the Prayer Book debates of 1927, but all of them men who seemed to have defects of character which prevented them from commanding the universal respect of their fellow evangelicals. Douglas Johnson had a gift of spotting the trusted figures and it was not to these college principals that he usually looked for support.

It was at about this time that I came across a gifted Afrikaner who had spent a year in Cambridge reading theology and had not met up with the CICCU men. In South Africa he had been a member of the Student Christian Association, which was an evangelical body but still affiliated to the liberal Student Christian Movement. Finding the SCM of no help to him, Norval Geldenhuys was very lonely. I was able to take him home for Christmas and eventually he became a founder member of the Biblical Research Committee.

I managed to get second-class honours in the theological tripos at the end of the academic year, which was some improvement on the maths and geography. But before the academic year ended, IVF had to elect a new Executive Committee and to my shock and surprise I was pushed into the chair, with the job of leading both the committee and the annual conference. The matter was complicated by the sudden death of my mother who caught typhoid in a Croydon nursing home after an operation. This left my undomesticated father on his own in the big house at Whyteleafe. I decided to pull out of Ridley for a year and to work in father's office as an accountant's clerk. So the student chairman of IVF turned up at committee meetings in London in a bowler hat carrying a rolled umbrella!

Ten

Accountant's Clerk — 1936/7

The change of scene over this year worked very well for me. My unmarried second sister, Susan, a graduate from Newnham College in Cambridge, kept house, and I commuted daily to London with my father. I worked in Wenham Brothers' office in High Holborn with the amazing head clerk, Mr Tarbath. He had a fearful stammer, but was completely devoted to the firm, his busy brain active day and night. He had a notebook by his bed in which he jotted memos with which he kept father informed and the office staff hard at work. I went on an audit to an East End furniture factory, whose dubious finances the Inland Revenue had commissioned us to investigate. I went on another audit to Bruges, where I enjoyed the beautiful old city and climbed the famous clock-tower of its Market Hall. But most of the work was more humdrum, for instance tidying up the books of the Cable Manufacturers' Association. I cannot pretend that this was anything like normal work experience but at least I valued a knowledge of what an office was like and what it was like to be a London commuter. Commuting for two and a quarter hours each day in the rush hour was more tiring than work at the desk.

On Sundays we worshipped at Chaldon church, unperturbed by the fearful hell-fire frescoes. Lay initiative had started some drawing-room meetings in the home of an elderly Mr Owen in order to reach outsiders. This led on to an invitation from the rector, Rupert Williams, to preach in church. I don't remember what I preached about, but I remember the comment of a gentleman (who I think worked for the Church Commissioners): 'That was *multum in parvo*' (a lot packed into a little). Doubtless I had a lot to say and had not yet learnt the lesson that the good communicator attempts less and gets across more. The rector asked me to take a leading part in an open-air play in the local chalkpit, which came to a most embarrassing end. I, who had never in my life flirted with a girl, had to act the romantic part, which I found impossible to do without getting very emotionally disturbed. On the day of the play I was running a high temperature and had to be confined to bed. I felt awful and presumably the show had to be cancelled.

As an unattached bachelor with few responsibilities at work and no professional exams hanging over my head, I was free to do a lot as IVF chairman. Douglas Johnson would share his enthusiasms with me. I can't remember at precisely what point his various schemes were hatched and how long they took to mature, but he had two schemes brewing up at about this time. One was the discovery of the Beddington Free Grace Library. This was a fine collection of Puritan books and books on Revival which had been brought together by Geoffrey Williams, a Strict Baptist, which were being loaned out mostly to his fellow Strict Baptists. To Douglas this was treasure-trove and he insisted that I come and see this great find stored in 'Noah's Ark' at the bottom of Mr Williams' garden. He conveyed his enthusiasm to Mr Williams and persuaded him that it ought to be more centrally located and be made available to a wider public. He got together a band of respected referees, including Dr Martyn Lloyd-Jones who became its president, and eventually the library was transferred to Chiltern Street in London where as The Evangelical Library it became a lending library for the whole world.

There was also much talk about the need for an interdenominational Bible college in London. He was concerned that any such college should be of a good academic standard, and he again got together the academics and business men who could make it such, and so London Bible College was founded. This was typical of D.J. – he got others working and then slipped quietly into the background. The vast work recorded in *Contending for the Faith* tells of the activities of thousands of people who managed to work together to achieve great things. What is easily overlooked, seeing it is nowhere stressed, is that much of the organization only worked because of the genius of this self-effacing man. People naturally divisive with their zealous narrow orthodoxies were brought together and kept together by the spiritual discernment and balanced theology of their inspirer. This cohesiveness lasted long after his retirement from the scene.

The enthusiasms of Douglas were shown both in committee and out. As chairman of the Executive Committee I had of course to take an interest in all aspects of a rapidly growing work: publications, travelling secretaries at home and overseas and planning for the annual conference, which I had to chair. This was all absorbing and enjoyable, but Douglas was particularly interested in the parallel movements springing up on the continent, especially those of the Dutch and the Scandinavians. With war clouds hanging over Europe, he wanted to bring them together for mutual strengthening while time allowed. He took me to Copenhagen to meet the Scandinavian leaders and begin to prepare for a big international student conference in 1939.

My deepest concern remained the theological students. I was getting plenty of time for reading and it was during this year that I recall one of my first attempts at 'trawling the gospels'. Rupert Williams and Christian preachers generally were continually preaching the love of God – an admirable topic which can never be preached too much if it is kept in balance. But I was conscious as I read the Bible and as I read the gospels in particular that there was another, and less comfortable, side to our Lord's teaching. I decided therefore to direct my Bible study before breakfast to the topic of The Hard Sayings of Jesus. I read steadily through the gospels in the Revised Version and noted every mention by Jesus of unforgiven sin or hell or eternal loss. These I recorded using single spacing with my Good Companion typewriter and found that I got fourteen pages of his sayings from the first three gospels alone. It confirmed for me something which I had read in Griffith Thomas: 'If we would preach less about the love of God and more about his holiness and hatred of sin, we should say more when we did preach about the love of God.' This, I am sure, remains true. To proclaim a God of love, who allows the sufferings of our present world, does not ring true, unless we also show him as a God of judgment, as our Lord undoubtedly does.

Another attempt at trawling the gospels was a more ambitious effort. It had become clear to me that we ought to have a conference for theological students, since the great majority were training in liberal theological colleges or faculties. I was aware of the fact that the assault on their faith was much more than simply an assault on the Bible. I was helped to see this by J.G. Machen's *Christianity and Liberalism*, in which he showed from his experience in Germany that liberalism is not only a different religion from biblical and traditional Christianity but that it comes in a different class of religions. (With its pantheising theology it is more akin to the Eastern religions than to the monotheism of Judaism, Christianity and Islam.) However, I felt that the assault on the Bible provided the main thrust of the liberal attack, and that we needed those who would come and help us defend the Bible. Initially just for my own edification I had been attempting another trawl, this time working through all the four gospels to determine how Jesus regarded his scriptures. This study was to prove invaluable to me for the rest of my life and much more immediately valuable when we found in 1937 that we could not get senior speakers to address our conference.

In spite of our efforts to find senior scholars to help us, we could find none. The best we could do was to get Canon S.M.

Warner, Vicar of Holy Trinity, Eastbourne, to come and act as housefather. He was a saintly old man who regularly read his Bible in the Hebrew and the Greek and who steadily gained converts and sustained a large congregation by his biblical preaching. He came to expound the Word to us and encourage us spiritually. We also had Jack Cobb who had been a CICCU president and was now a junior member of the London College of Divinity staff. I think that he, Leo Stephens-Hodge and I read papers to this, the first conference of the Theological Students' Fellowship. My paper 'Our Lord's View of the Old Testament' was eventually to become the Tyndale New Testament Lecture of 1954, which appeared first as an IVF booklet and later as chapter 1 of *Christ and the Bible*. We met at Digswell Park, north of London, in January 1937. There are twenty students in the photograph, not all of whom I can name. They include Denis Tongue, Tony Pouncy, Clement Connell, Digby Buxton, Rob Williamson, Raymond Fountain, Stanley Duthie, Joseph Parker, Eric Pitt, Jim Hewitt and Philip Seddon. It was a useful beginning.

Later in 1937 an international conference was planned in Budapest in Hungary, which contained the furthest outpost of Protestantism in Eastern Europe. I travelled out with the dynamic Howard Guinness whose medical career, like that of Douglas Johnson, had been cut short by his missionary endeavours. Guinness had stirred the student world by his second advent slogan 'Evangelize to a finish to bring back the King!' and later challenged students by the call to utmost dedication in his booklet *Sacrifice*.

We travelled as cheaply as possible on wooden third-class seats; we missed a connection en route and so had to spend an extra night of discomfort on the train, arriving in Budapest in time for service on the Sunday morning in a large 'Reformed' church. Magyar is nothing like the Indo-European languages and I recognized no word of the long sermon except 'Jesus' and 'Amen.'

But it was a big thrill to see Brethren (represented by F. Kiss, a medical professor who had suffered gaol for his faith) and Lutherans worshipping with a Reformed scholar like E. Sebestyen, a professor of theology. Friendships were formed, vision widened and zeal deepened.

Eleven

On to Ordination — 1937/8

About a year after my mother died, Father decided to marry again. It was to Ethel Good, the widow of an old tennis-playing friend who had three grown-up children, roughly the same age as our family. This was not a real love match and did not turn out altogether happily but must have seemed a sensible and considerate arrangement. It set me and my sisters free and the Good family moved into the big house and joined the daily commuting. Portley Wood remained my home during the vacations for another five years. Ethel belonged to the generation which did not think it odd to attend church but she never gave the impression of being a believer and Father's observances cooled off somewhat in consequence. I got to know the younger daughter, Mavis, best. She was tall, quite attractive and a good tennis player. One year we had the chance of entering a couple of open tournaments together, first at Reigate and then at Tunbridge Wells. We got knocked out in the first round in all the events till only the Tunbridge Wells mixed doubles handicap was left. She exercised her feminine charm on the referee and explained the situation to him, whereupon he gave us a good handicap, which enabled us to fight our way through to victory in the final – a happy end to an enjoyable fortnight.

I haven't many particular memories of my last year at Ridley, to which I had returned. It was busy as usual with much academic work and with IVF chairmanship carrying on right into the beginning of 1939. Lectures in the university included a course by Professor C.H. Dodd on Matthew, which resulted in a memorable incident. I had been quite perplexed about the Synoptic Problem – the question of how the first three gospels are related to one another. We were all being taught the B.H. Streeter line with Markan priority, the overlap of Mark and Q and the rest. But I was aware of the Alford-Westcott view, which held all three gospels to be independent, and of T.R. Birk's *Horae Evangelicae* (recommended by Basil Atkinson) which taught literary dependence in the Augustinian order: first Matthew, then Mark, then Luke. I chanced upon a big new book in Heffers by Dom John Chapman, Abbot of Downside, entitled *Matthew, Mark and Luke*, which I promptly bought and found fascinating. I was not convinced by everything in it but it seemed to me more convincingly argued than Streeter's book. So when Dodd on two occasions made a slighting reference to it, I thought to myself, 'I wonder what Dodd would do with the arguments?' I decided to go and ask him (he was a kindly little man). He received me courteously, but on hearing my errand said, 'As a matter of fact I'm afraid I haven't actually read the book.' From then on I became an undogmatic Augustinian, though eventually putting very little weight on literary dependence and moving nearer to Westcott. I think that Dodd may have had a slightly uneasy conscience about this incident, because several years later he recommended the Cambridge University Press to publish the better known book by another Abbot of Downside, B.C. Butler's *The Priority of Matthew* (see W.R. Farmer, *New Synoptic Studies*, Mercer, 1983, vii). The stock of Chapman's book was destroyed in the blitz and so is little known, but I prefer his to Butler's.

The syllabus to be covered at Ridley was the Cambridge Ordination Course which filled in some of the gaps in the tripos. I received possibly my only theological distinction when doing the exam! One of the subjects was doctrine, in which of course I was particularly interested, since it seemed to me vital to my

ministry that I should know what to believe, so that I could
preach it accurately and with integrity. One of the exam questions
was on Augustine and Free Will. I did not know much about him,
but I knew that all the Reformers were Augustinians and I had
taken quite a lot of trouble to understand the Calvinistic writers.
So I gave an explanation of Calvinist doctrine and pinned it on
to Augustine and, lo and behold, they gave me a distinction! By
way of Anglican preparation I read most of W.H. Griffith Thomas'
exposition of the Thirty-Nine Articles, fairly carefully. His *The
Principles of Theology* on the whole satisfied me well. Thomas,
sometime Principal of Wycliffe Hall, Oxford, was *au fait* with
modern thought; yet he seemed to me to have remained in tune
with the articles and the reformation theology from which they
came. E.J. Bicknell on the Thirty-Nine Articles I also used but
found it less to my liking. At this time I was not contemplating
any serious adjustment to my theological or ecclesiastical stance.
It was filling gaps, enriching knowledge, trying to put myself into
the position where I could justify my beliefs and practices to other
members of the church.

I was always on the look-out for light on the areas which
biblical infallibilists found difficult. At this time P.J. Wiseman,
father of D.J. Wiseman who was later to become an eminent
Assyriologist and who republished his father's books, produced
a lively book called *New Discoveries in Babylonia about Genesis*.
This book made one feel that the world of Wellhausen's J E and
P was quite anachronistic and that in the early chapters of
Genesis we have written records antedating the time of Abraham. S.M. Zwemer's book, *The Origin of Religion* of 1935 leads
one back even further. He takes his cue from Wilhelm Schmidt,
the great Roman Catholic anthropologist of Vienna, who produced a multi-volume work on the origin of religion which
denied an evolutionary derivation. I had been taught that our
ancestors, hearing the wind in the trees, had come first to a belief
in spirits, then to polytheism, then to henotheism and finally to

monotheism, and that traces of this process could still be seen in the Old Testament. Schmidt, followed by Zwemer, showed that in all religions there was a belief in the Sky-god or High-god above and behind all the lesser deities and that this belief could not be explained on evolutionary lines but required a common primitive revelation. Unfortunately, but understandably, modern Christian anthropologists have been disinclined to espouse such wide-ranging theories, which are felt to be the province of the philosopher rather than of the scientist. But eventually Christian thinkers have got to bring the sciences into their world view.

An experience came my way at this time, which was to affect my whole life. Bash told me that the father of a boy in my dormitory at his camp was worried about his son now at Cambridge. He had found that he had a secret store of nudist literature. Would I keep an eye on him? I was woefully ill-equipped to proffer any help and did not even try. So what was my horror when I heard that he had committed murder. An eminent barrister pleaded mercy for him and he was committed to a criminal asylum, where he was kept for more than thirty years. At times when I lived within visiting distance I used to go and see him. Though he kept mentally alert and in touch with the outside world through his radio, I was very unimpressed by this form of 'mercy', shut up in a single-sex institution with all your companions either criminal lunatics or hard-boiled warders. When at last they decided to let him out my wife and I offered him a home. In the event he did not take this up because, thankfully, he was helped to a large measure of independence by a relation. Then came the difficulty of getting a job at sixty with a background which he couldn't explain. After a year or so a miracle happened. He applied for a caretaking job looking after some DHSS property – and they forgot to take up his references! After some months they realised their mistake but seeing his work had been perfectly satisfactory they had no grounds for dismissing a man who had been declared fit by their own service. He continued to work for them till he reached retirement age.

Affairs took an unexpected turn at the time when I would normally have been looking for a curacy. Relying no doubt more upon my standing in the student world than upon my academic qualifications, Dr T.W. Gilbert, Principal of The London College of Divinity, invited me to join his staff as a junior tutor. I welcomed this opportunity of continuing work with theological students and of further study. I went on retreat at Fulham Palace during Munich week, when Neville Chamberlain was negotiating peace with Adolf Hitler, and was made deacon in St Paul's Cathedral by Dr Winnington-Ingram, Bishop of London, on Michaelmas Day 1938, the very day when 'peace' was announced.

Twelve

College Tutor — 1938–41

The next three years passed very rapidly, being years of intense activity in college and years of absorbing interest in a world plunging into war. Ordination to a junior tutorship at St John's Hall, Highbury (which was the other name for the London College of Divinity) meant coming under the principalship of the formidable Dr T.W. Gilbert. Gilbert was a good church historian with an Oxford DD, who took over the college when it was in financial difficulties and proved himself to be also a good financier. The college playing field had just been sold to the Arsenal Football Club, which raised a big sum and gained him a permanent seat in the Arsenal manager's box; and he continued to watch the expenditure of every penny. He was a tight-lipped martinet who ran the college like a Victorian headmaster, keeping in check a violent temper. Only once did I see him lose it but it was a frightening experience. Four Cambridge graduates had decided not to go to Ridley or Wycliffe Hall but to try Highbury instead. They found the college discipline irksome and showed a measure of independence which the principal did not appreciate. I happened to be in the anteroom of his study waiting my turn to see him, when suddenly the door was flung open with a terrifying crash and these four men came out, pale faced and bewildered, followed by the principal's denunciations. He died shortly after I left the college, the senior student climbing in through the bathroom window to find him dead in the bath after a heart attack.

The question was: What did they want me to teach? The answer seemed to be: A bit of everything – some Old Testament, some New Testament, Roman History (about which I knew almost nothing) for the London BD, Beginners' Greek, some doctrine. Fortunately not very high standards were expected and I was encouraged to use my predecessors' lecture notes. Somehow I managed to scrape through without too much angst. As far as the Greek was concerned it was a matter of keeping ahead of the class. I had learnt from H.P.V. Nunn's *The Elements of New Testament Greek* enough to get me through the tripos but much of the book I had not mastered. Not having any ability at languages, I sympathized with the difficulties of the novice and came to enjoy trying to help the beginner over the stiles. Doctrine I also enjoyed – I earned the nickname 'Warfield' after the eminent American whom I was fond of quoting. For doctrine I had the use of the lecture notes of Dr Harold Smith, a former teacher of the college who was a patristic scholar of distinction, being author of the six-volume *Ante-Nicene Exegesis on the Gospels*, which had earned him his London DD. He was sympathetic to the notion of conditional immortality and I was glad of his support when it came to lecturing on eschatology.

Highbury was very convenient for IVF work which was based on Bedford Square, London. Preparations were going ahead for a large international conference in Cambridge in June and July 1939. This was a remarkable occasion with eight hundred overseas students in residence celebrating together the theme of Christ Our Freedom. There was a unity not based on indifference to doctrine but on a warm and whole-hearted devotion to the Christ of the historic creeds. It was to leaders at that conference, like Professor Hallesby the Lutheran from Oslo and Professor Aalders the Calvinist from Amsterdam, to whom we were later to look for help in building up our evangelical literature. 1939 was also the year for the launching of the Biblical Research Committee from which eventually the Tyndale Fellowship was to emerge.

War was very much in the air but we took our family holiday at Vos in Norway nonetheless. The schoolmaster in Vos asked me to arrange an English service for his pupils and for the tourists (many of them Americans). This I was keen to do but it occupied a great deal of the holiday getting the service worked out and advertised and printed. But a good crowd came and they joined in well and seemed ready to listen. As we set sail for home news on the tannoy told us that the Mediterranean was closed – we all knew that we were fleeing from the wrath to come.

At the outbreak of war I and some of the students were moved out to Oak Hill College on the North London fringe where we joined Prebendary Hinde's dwindling flock. In November 1940 the college was severely damaged by a parachute mine and the whole college was evacuated to Wadhurst School for Girls in Kent. So began the long trek which was eventually to land it up as St John's College, Nottingham. When Donald Coggan took over in 1944, he had just three men living at Oak Hill. In 1947 he moved the college out to Lingfield in Surrey, where it stayed for ten years, before moving into a fine new college at Northwood in Middlesex. But after a time the church authorities decreed that it ought to be located further north and near a university faculty of theology, which meant another expensive upheaval.

At Portley Wood, the family home, we had an Anderson shelter let into the ground in the garden to which we could escape during an air raid; this was safe from everything short of a direct hit. But it was not comfortable turning out ill-clad on a cold night and we soon found an inviting alternative indoors. There was a full-sized billiard table in the house which provided excellent protection. It would have been even more comfortable to me if I had understood the distinction between sexual attraction and lust more accurately, for I found myself lying beside Mavis. This aroused me and disturbed my conscience, but I should have been horrified at the suggestion of having sex with someone to whom I was not married and who was not a believer – and I was not in fact guilty of lustful intent. This did not prevent me from trying to present the gospel to her. When asked to preach at Christ Church, Purley, I had her in mind when I prepared a sermon that tried to set out the two ways with clarity – the narrow way that leads to life and the broad road that leads to destruction. The vicar was evidently a universalist, for in the vestry afterwards he looked glum and simply said, 'Till he find it!'

I saw a more human side of Dr Gilbert while at Wadhurst. I was not at all immune to the attractions of the other sex, very much the reverse; but I remarked one day on the awful prospect of being irrevocably tied to someone for life. He said, 'You won't feel like that when you fall in love.' How right he was.

Thirteen

Parish Work and Marriage — 1941–43

With the student intake of the college dwindling, it was necessary to think about the next step. I had fallen in with a remarkable man. Frank Food, who was only about ten years my senior, had recently been made incumbent of St Matthew's, a parish in the back streets of Cambridge. He had been in industry, then an evangelist in the Young Life Campaign, where he had felt the serious deficiencies of interdenominational work, whence he had moved on to be the first secretary of the Young Churchman's Movement, a specifically evangelical Church of England work. He was not an intellectual and always felt himself uneducated, but he combined thoughtfulness with zeal, and was persuaded to go to Wycliffe Hall to train for the ministry. After one curacy, he was now in charge of a parish.

We managed to persuade the powers that be that I might join him as part-time curate. It was arranged that I should give some of my time to working for the London BD. This enabled me to learn Hebrew and read some philosophy of religion, two big gaps in my theological armoury. I lived in the vicarage and we were more like brothers than vicar and curate. St Matthew's is probably the ugliest church in Cambridge, which must have been painful to Frank who had a great sense of the dignity of prayer-book worship and a love of fine organs. He had a passionate concern for servicemen and the vicarage was constantly visited by bomber crews from the East Anglian RAF stations. I think that the parish sometimes felt that servicemen held a higher place in his affections than his parishioners.

There was plenty of work to do even though the parish was not over-large: baptisms, funerals, an occasional wedding, visiting the sick and the elderly, two preaching services on Sunday (including a children's slot on Sunday morning) and youth work. It was at this stage that I began systematically to keep my sermon notes, so that I have a fairly full record of what I talked about. It was all biblical stuff; but it covered a wide range. I did not attempt the exposition of lengthy passages in sermons, though we worked through 1 Corinthians in the youth group. My preaching was rather the exposition of texts or the treatment of topics. I tried to make as simple and interesting as possible the things which interested me. What thrilled me was the Good News; so my preaching was about God and fallen man and the Saviour Christ. I approached it from many different angles – from the calendar, e.g. Advent (and Missions), Christmas, Good Friday, Easter, All Saints' Day, New Year, Harvest; from doctrine and apologetics, e.g. the evidences of the Resurrection, the authority of the Bible, the sacraments; from the point of view of ethics, Sunday observance, gambling, giving, freedom, spiritualism; from the point of view of Christian graces, joy, humility; I did a course on Morning and Evening Prayer, explaining their structure by five Ps: Penitence, Pronouncement of Forgiveness, Praise and Meditation, Profession of Faith, Prayer. Giving the children's talk was an excellent exercise. In fact this whole period spent with non- academics encouraged a concentration on fundamentals.

My reading at this time included some of the masters of modern exposition. C.S. Lewis was beginning to make himself felt – his *Mere Christianity* was a marvellous evangelistic statement. D.R. Davies, *Secular Illusion and Christian Realism* brought home the reality of original sin, Dorothy Sayers proclaimed Jesus through *The Man Born to be King* and showed the thrill of Christian dogma. ('The dogma is the the drama,' she said.) William Temple made Old Testament ethics highly relevant with his *Christianity and the Social Order*. I was moved by books on Shaftesbury and Wilberforce and by William Booth's *In Darkest England* and *The Way Out* and Wesley Bready's *England Before and After Wesley*. An imaginative and practical grasp of the faith seemed more important than a grasp of theoretical minutiae.

But my thoughts were about to take another turn. Though physically attracted by many girls, I had only met one who had attracted me as a possible prospective wife. That was Grace Isaac, sister-in-law of my sister Eleanor. Back in 1934 Eleanor had married Bryan Isaac; I was an usher at the wedding and found myself paired up with his bridesmaid sister, a shy and attractive girl with beautiful eyes, a lovely complexion and a tip-tilted nose. Eleanor had sung her praises as being the saint of the family, totally reliable, exceedingly practical, always ready to help her hard-pressed mother. She was not an intellectual. Indeed she had some difficulty in passing her London BSc in domestic and household science. She was a good games player, especially at hockey. Nearly eight years had passed since that wedding, eight very busy years during which I was glad to have had no matrimonial entanglements. Grace had reached the stage where she believed that God was not going to give her a husband and she had wrestled to a point where she had told him she was willing if that was his will.

She now had a job, teaching cookery in the Cambridge Technical College, living in digs in St Barnabas' parish next door to St Matthew's. I had once or twice bumped into her fleetingly in the city centre when we had exchanged slightly embarrassed family greetings. Then one day I kicked myself and said, 'Why don't you do something about it?' I forthwith sent her a note, asking her round to tea to give me some advice about running the youth club (which was mostly girls). In no time I was madly, head

over heels in love. Grace kept all my letters (we wrote daily); so I
have a blow by blow account of all that happened. She did not at
once give in to my whirlwind advances, but when at last she said
'Yes' she was soon as deeply in love as I was.

We were itching to get married as soon as possible, but we
knew that her father would counsel delay. So before going down
to ask his consent, we agreed that we would not discuss the date
of the wedding. It turned out as expected, and so we waited till
we had got back to Cambridge, where we brewed up a reasoned
letter arguing that we would settle to work better married than
enduring a pointless long engagement. The wedding was fixed for
July, only four months ahead. Our engagement was received with
general approval except by one girl in the youth group who was
quite upset. In retrospect I blamed myself for male insensitivity,
for though she did not attract me at all, I had talked to her on an
outing (as I thought in an objective way) about Christian marriage ideals. This had evidently raised hopes in her, of which I was
quite unaware.

There was much to do in those four months and it was quite
unclear right up till the time of the wedding where we should live.
We felt it wise to ration the frequency of our meeting, so great
was our desire to be with one another. By way of preparation we
both read the same book: Helena Wright, *The Sex Factor in
Marriage*, thereby each knowing what the other knew. We were
married at St Saviours's Church, Battersea, where Bryan Isaac
was vicar, on 28th July 1942; Frank Food was best man.

We had planned our honeymoon at Salcombe on the South
Devon coast but we broke our journey for the first night at Bath,
so that we could call on Uncle John. I had visited him less than a
year before to celebrate his centenary. At that time he was living
in a small house at Combe-Down cared for by his housekeeper.
He had all his faculties and was forward-looking in outlook. He
wanted to know what the younger generation was thinking and
said at the age of 100: 'I think we need a great new experience of

the Holy Spirit!' When asked what he did during an air-raid, he said: 'We men prefer to stay in bed.' But in the intervening months he had been transferred to a nursing-home which, while he was there, had suffered a near miss. The home had two sections, one for the aged and one for maternity cases, and after the raid his picture appeared in the local paper nursing one of the infants. It was perhaps unfortunate that we let him know that we were coming, because he kept ringing his bell during the night asking whether we had arrived. But I was glad that Grace met this delightful and saintly man before he died.

Our first day at Salcombe was beautiful sunshine and I stripped to the waist as we walked the cliff paths, only to find that my fair skin had become quite badly sunburnt. This folly resulted in discomfort and a humiliating need to avoid further sun, but Grace cheerfully put up with it. On our return to Cambridge the train was delayed and we arrived after dark at a flat which had been lent to us by Tom (T.H.L.) and Mary Parker, who were on holiday. We could not turn on the lights, not knowing how to fix the black-out. So we entered by torchlight into a flat smelling of wet plaster. The water tank at the top of the house had overflowed and the water had dripped its way through every floor. Fortunately it had missed our bed, so that we could creep between the sheets and await the morning.

We then had to find out whether a house was becoming available for us in Silverwood Close, which was a small private housing estate. One fell vacant before the Parkers returned and we started our married life together in earnest. Grace almost at once discovered that she was pregnant. (She always became pregnant immediately – she had four babies and two miscarriages – if we did not take contraceptive precautions.) I learnt how pregnancy itself is a natural cement to marriage; she was prone to tears and I realized how much she felt she needed me. The birth was exceedingly difficult. She had been brought up not to make a fuss and was determined not to do so now. The result was that the medics did not recognize when she was in heavy labour and they left her many hours with the baby unable to emerge. When at last they realized the situation and delivered our firstborn by forceps, she was utterly exhausted and baby Gordon suffered permanent injury to his eye. When our second child, David, was born in Oxford, Grace was mercifully in expert hands already forewarned: the specialist's note said, 'Expect difficulty at all stages,' and she had her easiest delivery.

Grace was not only a wonderful wife, she was also a wonderful mother, having a fine combination of firmness and tenderness. I often feel that the contest of wills between mother and baby seems evenly balanced. The mite has power to make life almost intolerable to the parent by stubbornness or by yelling the house down. But I clearly remember her saying when Gordon was in a tantrum, 'I'm not going to be beaten by a thing that size!' She made the home a haven of peace and we all knew that as she went about her work she was habitually praying for us. It was almost unthinkable to let our standards down, knowing how it would hurt her. I am afraid that I was often insensitive to her feelings and probably never more so than when I announced to her without carefully preparing the way that I thought I should offer myself as a Royal Air Force padre. This was a great shock to her.

But there was one other shock before I left St Matthew's. I had continued to work away at the London BD and had sat the exam. Admittedly I had had a good many distractions, but I had read a lot of theology and much of the work was a recap of tripos work and I felt that by now I should have a good chance of getting a first. What was my horror when I heard that I had only earned a pass. Trying to analyse the reasons I came to two conclusions. First and foremost I believe that it was due to a poor memory which makes me weak on history and languages. I thought that early church history, which I had read some eight years before and had enjoyed, would come back without much work. But in fact it did not and I am sure that that was a bad paper. I was also probably unwise in espousing some unfashionable views such as the Pauline authorship of the Pastoral Epistles and the apostolic authorship of the Fourth Gospel. I came to realize that I work best with the facts before me in writing. I can assess them and come to informed conclusions, but I find that while the conclusions may remain most of the detail soon slips away. When it comes to writing a book I have to rework the detail and reassess the conclusions, which means that I am a slow worker. I can only hope that this laborious process leads to well digested results.

Fourteen

Air Force Padre — 1943–47

I had expected my time in the RAF to mean a deepening of my understanding of the real world but I had not expected it to mean a significant deepening of my understanding of the Bible and Christian theology. It was both. My training consisted of three weeks at Cranwell living alongside an established chaplain. I was then sent up to Arbroath on the east coast of Scotland to a recruitment centre, to which came men from all over the country straight out of civilian life just like me. At this stage in the war the call-up age was quite high; thus many of them were not young. They came for four weeks; each week they had one 'padre's hour' and one compulsory parade service; so I had them for eight sessions.

I concentrated all my efforts on making the faith relevant. One of my sermons was on the new birth. It had four propositions: 1) There will be no better world without better men and women. (There was considerable hope that a better world would emerge from the war.) 2) At present we have an in-born bias to evil. 3) We cannot change our own natures. 4) Therefore our only hope is if a power outside ourselves changes us. Once a month the whole station including commandant, officers and NCOs came to the parade service. On one such occasion I decided to preach on The Rich Man and Lazarus. I said that a padre is often thought of as a subsidiary entertainments officer but his proper job was to teach the teaching of Christ, particularly his unpopular teaching if it was being ignored. So I preached the Two Ways – you could hear a pin drop as I unequivocally declared that those who chose their own way and refused God's way would wake up to face the pain and horror of God's consuming wrath. I then issued an invitation to an Answer Back Meeting in the NAAFI.

I valued these compulsory sessions. Many who would never have come on their own felt them worthwhile. On my next posting the situation was reversed. I was sent further north to Alness on the Cromarty Firth, where they were training for anti-submarine warfare on Sunderland flying-boats. The chaplains' department was in consternation. My predecessor was an alcoholic who had been found drunk in a ditch. Everyone seemed to know about him except the commandant and the station adjutant. One of the airmen was so disgusted that he had brought the matter up when the unit was visited by the Inspector-General. I found the Church of Scotland padre, John Nelson, and the tiny band of faithful Christians, who met in a Nissen hut, quite dispirited. The station had a monthly parade service which in the circumstances was resented and badly attended. When I faced the aggrieved commandant, I found that he greatly admired a chaplain on one of his previous units, Gerald Gregson by name, who was a friend of mine. This softened him and, when I requested the abolition of the parade service, he readily agreed and remained co-operative thereafter.

Then John Nelson and I set about repairing the damage. John was a great colleague, theologically well read, yet down to earth. We did everything in common apart from Anglican communion services, and attendances built up from a dozen to ten times that number with the hut packed and a great atmosphere. I am afraid I was not a very good chaplain to the officers. They spent their evenings at the bar drinking huge quantities of beer and I thought my time better spent visiting the other ranks. I did however sleep with them in a sort of dormitory and one night one of them in his stupor peed an unbelievable flood all over the floor. The chaplain thought it a necessary service to mop up.

It was a great joy to get a pleasant bungalow and bring Grace and baby Gordon up for the last months before I was posted overseas. Then *SS Carthage* took me out to Egypt (very seasick) in slow convoy. I arrived at the transit camp on VE day, the day when victory was declared in Europe, the personnel understandably being somewhat the worse for drink. From there I went to Fayid in the Suez Canal zone, where I stayed till after the war with Japan had ended.

The station at Fayid was comfortable with fans to keep the heat down and Arab servants to do most of the hard work. The station church, built by Italian prisoners of war, was of excellent design and pleasant to worship in. After lunch we betook ourselves to our beds and either slept or read under our mosquito nets. When the greatest heat of the day had passed a lorry took us to the Great Bitter Lake for a swim. The Suez Canal links up one arm of the Red Sea to Lake Timsah and the Bitter Lakes. In Moses' day the Yam Suph, the Sea of Reeds, was probably permanently linked to these lakes in one continuous stretch of water which was very shallow in places. It is easy to see in the Exodus account how at the right moment a strong cyclic storm traverses the area, first driving the water back to open up a passage-way and then dropping down as the centre of the storm passes and finally it blows in the opposite direction. The passage-way disappears and the sea lashed by a violent wind prevents the Egyptians finding a shallow way of escape. The story only loses historical realism when the 'wall' of sea is pictured as a literal wall; the metaphorical use in Nahum 3:8 gives a better understanding of what happened.

RAF Fayid provided the last stage of training for fighter pilots. Shortly before I arrived the station had been badly shaken by a grim accident when three Thunderbolts flying in formation had plunged straight to earth. The difficulty and danger of passing through the sound barrier had not yet been understood and in a dive the aircraft had failed to respond to the controls. One day a pilot offered to take me up 'aerobatting'. He did his level best to make me sick and nearly succeeded – I took no lunch that day. On another occasion I got a lift to Heliopolis in a dual control plane and the pilot invited me to have a try at flying her straight and level. He flattered me at my success, on the strength of which, when I related it to my friend the pilot instructor, he offered to teach me to fly. In my daily letter to Grace (who had just given birth to David) I asked her whether she was agreeable. She wrote back warmly and I had half a dozen lessons before being whisked off to Jerusalem, unfortunately before I had ever flown solo.

In spite of our preoccupation with fighting a war, those of us who were in the forces were still in touch with the concerns of civilian life. Preaching the gospel to servicemen did not dampen our interest in the strategic needs of the church. Though I was not near at hand I was enthusiastically in touch with the founding in 1943 of Tyndale House, Cambridge, as a residential library for the pursuit of biblical research. In 1945 I published two articles, one for the Victoria Institute which was properly entitled 'The Intellect and Christian Progress' and the other 'The Authority of Christ as a Teacher – Does Incarnation Involve Fallibility?' in *Evangelical Quarterly*. The latter was essentially a trawl through the gospels, which eventually became Chapter 2 of *Christ and the Bible*. I regard this chapter as my most important piece of writing.

During the Fayid siestas I remember reading Dante's *Divine Comedy* and I remember also rewriting a book for my South African friend, Norval Geldenhuys. It was a shockingly badly written book advocating birth control by the natural rhythm method. I didn't know whether this method was satisfactory and I strictly forbade the use of my name in any preface, but I reckoned two things. First, it was essential, if the method was to be used, that it should be expounded clearly and accurately (it was neither). Secondly, it seemed likely that Norval would be a prolific writer and therefore it was desirable that his style should be improved. I cut the text down to half its length and, sticking largely to his wording, I ironed out the inaccuracies and obscurities. In 1950 I received a commentary by him on the Gospel of Luke. I was amazed, it was beautifully written; I thought my efforts had been well spent. Sometime later I learnt the truth. The publishers had received the Luke manuscript which contained much good material but was badly written. They asked F.F. Bruce to rewrite it, which he did, making useful additions and emendations, which were gladly accepted by the author. All went out in Geldenhuys' name and with his approval. One wonders whether Silvanus did something similar to Peter's first letter.

I spent just over a year in Jerusalem, including two Christmases. The adventures and lessons of this time would fill a book. The purpose of this posting was to participate in a Moral Leadership School which the chaplains' department was setting up. This was a twelve-day Christianity course which could rightly be thought to offer some boost to servicemen's morale. But there was a three-month delay before the school started. I was given the use of a Humber Snipe in order to familiarize myself with the Holy Land, with its places and its people. Here in Palestine many kinds met together: Jews of all types (including those fleeing Hitler's holocaust), Christians (Greek, Russian, Armenian, Syrian, Coptic, Ethiopian, Franciscans, Dominicans, Jesuits, Anglicans and Protestants of many kinds) and Moslim Arabs. There were archaeologists and biblical scholars galore. I was also flown out to Rome to see its Moral Leadership course in action (and on the way back I was allowed to pilot an aircraft full of brass-hats for twenty minutes over the African desert). From Jerusalem I went also to Damascus (experiencing a thunderstorm when it was snowing), to Jordan and to Cyprus. I was in Jerusalem when the Stern Gang blew up the King David Hotel, and part of my own ceiling came down when Archdeacon Campbell MacInnes' car had a collision with one of their lorries outside the ML School. It carried explosives which the police decided to detonate.

These three months before the school began were a marvellous time of learning. I was full of energy with virtually no duties except to get to know the Holy Land. I had the vision of an international Christian institute in Jerusalem that would be a natural development of the work established at Tyndale House, a work based on a believing approach to the Bible which would provide the intellectual backing to all the non-Roman churches and agencies operating in the country. I produced a fifteen-page memorandum which generated a big correspondence with Douglas Johnson, Norman Anderson and others. It was a magnificent vision, but 'the mills of God grind slowly' and it was not God's will that the work should go on expanding at the rate envisaged. The Tyndale Fellowship was to have great struggles and many set-backs in its attempts to work out a satisfactory theology.

When the school began I found myself with three or four colleagues, all but one being of a Catholic persuasion. Men and women came from all over the Middle East and we gave them sixteen lectures and showed them the main sites (this included a night in a convent on the Mount of the Beatitudes in Galilee). At the end we asked them their reactions. The lecture most appreciated by these people sent us by the chaplains was the first: 'Why Believe in God?' Asked why he chose this lecture one airman remarked: 'Well, sir, we do need to be sure about that, don't we?' This working closely with Catholics fundamentally affected my life. From believing theoretically that some of them might be real Christians, I came to know and love them as brothers in Christ. One such colleague was Evelyn Dunford – he reminded me that these Eastern Christians, whom many Protestants despise as ignorant and superstitious, had in fact survived many centuries of Moslim oppression and should rather be held in honour.

Another such was Bill May, chaplain-in-chief in the Middle East. He came to listen to me giving the lecture on the Old Testament. Afterwards he wrung my hand and said, 'How magnificent to hear someone defending the Word of God.' He then told me how he had read theology at Oxford. At first he was commended, but as he defended conservative positions his tutor became more and more annoyed and said, 'If you go on like this you will not only fail to get a first, I doubt if you will even pass.' This High-Church 'fundamentalist' was far from being a Roman Catholic or an extreme Anglo-Catholic; he was a diligent Bible student and well versed in the traditions of the undivided church. I was privileged to be best man at his wedding.

Protestants have rightly contended that all our acts in worship should be expressive of truth and traditionally they have held that eucharistic vestments (the chasuble in particular) express the doctrine of the mass. What was specially objected to was the notion that Christ's sacrifice on the Cross was not a finished work, but that he must be continually reoffered as a propitiation for our sins at every eucharist; so to wear vestments was a denial of the central truth of the gospel. I found that my colleagues when asked the significance of vestments never answered in these terms, they said that they demonstrated continuity with the early church. I knew also that to most churchgoers they were nothing more than the customary, colourful way of doing things. When, therefore, the school had the opportunity of taking a service of Holy Communion in the Chapel of Abraham in the Church of the Holy Sepulchre, I consented to break with Protestant tradition and allow myself to be dressed up for the occasion, a decision which I have never regretted since all traditions need honest reassessment in the light of scripture and contemporary realities. I also got used to incense and to the frequent use of the sign of the cross, which no longer suggested to me something heretical.

I came home to be demobbed, unchanged in my beliefs but widened in my sympathies.

Fifteen

Hadley Wood — 1947

I arrived back in England early in 1947 and was met by Grace looking radiantly happy, and I saw David for the first time, now well into his second year. I had had some correspondence about a possible curacy under B.C. Hopson of Cockfosters on the northern fringe of London. He had a daughter church at Hadley Wood, near Barnet, which needed a curate-in-charge. His churchmanship was quite different from mine, he being a member of the Modern Churchmen's Union which (as its name suggests) was thoroughly modernist. He was also a pacifist, which had earned him some unpopularity during the war with a congregation of largely self-made people. But he was a fine man with the courage of his convictions, a tall, striking figure and a good preacher. I went to see him, dressed in uniform, and he took me on for what was virtually an independent charge. I was encouraged to do this because Cockfosters church had evangelical patrons and I knew that their next appointment would be an evangelical and that it would be easier for him if the same tradition as his had been established at the other end of the parish.

Before ever we had moved to Hadley Wood I found myself in the midst of controversy amongst IVF graduates. Evidently other servicemen had come to question the worldliness taboos which they had learnt in their Christian Unions, and this had worried the senior leadership. So they invited certain stalwarts to write articles in the newsletter on 'The Minister's Attitude to Worldliness', reaffirming the old standards. They seemed to me to be erecting various arguable ethical self-denials into criteria of sanctification. So I wrote a letter pointing out that our Lord was not a teetotaller, that dancing was very biblical, that some good-living Christians were on the stage and that many of our Dutch and Scandinavian leaders smoked. Response was invited; one person supported me and ten opposed me. Basil Atkinson was most vehemently against me and (in another correspondence) was searingly rude. Actually I had no desire to lower standards. Later, my children would sometimes embarrass me by saying to a smoking visitor: 'Daddy says it is a dirty, wasteful habit!' I merely wanted evangelicals to live by their biblical principles and not cut themselves off unnecessarily from their neighbours. I think it is quite a good thing to draw a line between right and wrong and then add a margin as a safeguard for one's frailty and to help the weaker brother. Nowadays separation from the world is not taken seriously enough.

Hadley Wood provided a lovely pastoral charge with a small-ish congregation to be taught morning and evening Sunday by Sunday and a smallish area to be evangelized. I taught from the Bible and laid rather more stress on Holy Communion than is usual with Protestants – which made one or two of them suspicious. I thought that the Lord's Supper should be the focus of the family life of the church and that therefore there should be only one such service on a Sunday. So we alternated between 8 a.m. and 10.30 a.m. except on the fifth Sunday of the month when we had it in the evening. This displeased one or two high church people and was discontinued after I left. We had a memorable contact at this time with my wife's High-Church uncle, Brother Edward. He had been brought up in evangelical circles with a profound knowledge of the Bible and come to a Bible-centred type of Anglo-Catholicism. He felt called to give away all his possessions and devote himself to itinerant evangelism, not even

seeking the security of a religious order. So began the Village
Evangelists. He went mostly to High-Church parishes preaching
salvation by faith and emphasizing the Second Coming. He
stayed a night with us at Hadley Wood and preached at the
morning service, making a profound impression.

Another contact was with the Booths of the Salvation Army,
whose family home was only a stone's throw from the church. I
regret that I did not get to know them better but doubtless I
reckoned that they needed my ministrations less than any other
family in the parish. The matriarch of the tribe, Florence Booth,
widow of Bramwell Booth, the Army's second general, gave me
a copy of her daughter Catherine's biography of her father. This
book of 540 pages went to its seventh impression in its first month
of publication. It was a truly wonderful family used in a wonderful work of God. The Booths and Brother Edward both show
what God can do through totally dedicated servants, and they
show how differently he sees fit to use us.

Our time at Hadley Wood enabled us to re-establish a pattern
of prayer in the home which we continued without drastic
change for the rest of our lives. When we first got up we would
both read and meditate on the Bible and pray on our own. At
breakfast I would lead family prayers: again a short reading,
brief extempore prayer, the collect for the day and the Lord's
Prayer. Then at night Grace and I would kneel together at our
bedside, rehearse the specially urgent requests for prayer, then
read the texts for the day from *Daily Light* (later on we discovered Scripture Union's *Every Day*, which we much preferred,
being less fanciful in its arrangement of the biblical material)
and then give ourselves to vocal prayer. I never found the
recitation of the daily offices on my own very helpful. I found
that the basic pattern learnt from George Müller of gaining food
from the Word and then pouring out one's heart in prayer
remained very satisfying. Of course the number of people and
causes needing prayer quickly multiplied and topics for one's

regular intercession had to be spaced out according to a daily, weekly and monthly scheme.

I had been less than a year at Hadley Wood when an awkward decision was thrust upon me. I was offered the living of St Nicholas, Durham. It seemed to me that my stay in the parish had been too short to justify a move so soon, yet St Nicholas looked to be a sphere of work suited to my gifts. It was a fairly small parish in a city with a long-established residential university, whose students came to the church in considerable numbers. I felt that the move would be justified if I could get a successor at Hadley Wood without a long gap. The pay was rather inadequate; so I introduced an envelope scheme which raised the salary considerably for my successor, and (as if in divine confirmation of my move) a good man moved in to take my place the day after we moved out. Meantime Peter, our third son, had been born and the five of us headed north for Durham.

Sixteen

Durham — 1948–53

Grace and I regarded our five years in Durham as the happiest period of our lives in spite of many ups and downs. The Archdeacon of Durham claimed that the view of the cathedral and castle from St Nicholas' vicarage, looking across the Wear when the pear blossom was in flower, was the most beautiful prospect in Europe. But the vicarage with no central heating was damp and cold. The north wall of the house had been built straight into the side of the hill, so that earth several feet high was piled against it. We reckoned that on average it was even chances whether one or other of the four boys (Michael was born soon after arrival) would be ill at any one time. Even with some help in the mornings from Norah Moore, one of the fine women from the congregation, it was very hard work for Grace. I also got plenty of exercise since we had no car and I had to pedal my way up and down the hills of the city. Eventually on my days off I decided to cut a passage-way on the north side of the house to lessen the damp.

The population of the parish was fairly small, most of the people having been moved out to slum-clearance estates. The church had had a long tradition of good evangelical clergy going back at least to the nineteenth century. A curate from the church, Alfred Tucker, had the distinction of being the first curate in the Church of England to be raised direct to the episcopate. He did a remarkable work as Bishop of Uganda laying the foundations of the church in that country. When he returned to Durham as a member of the cathedral staff he ate his heart out at the pettiness of life there, which seemed to have so little relevance to the great movements which were sweeping society at the beginning of the century. Further distinction was given to the parish when my successor but one, George Carey, was made Archbishop of Canterbury.

There were clearly two sides to the job at St Nick's – there were the local people who resided permanently in the city and the students who came and went during term time. My predecessor, Hugh Evan Hopkins, was an outstanding man, who had been president of the CICCU in Cambridge, a missionary in the Dohnavur Fellowship in India and a travelling secretary of the IVF. He had gained a reputation (maybe entirely unjustly) that the students were his first love, a reputation which I wished to live down. Looking at it from a distance in Hadley Wood, my first anxiety, as a young man coming into his first living, was the knowledge that there was a lay-reader in the parish, William Craggs. How would I get on with him? I need not have worried; he proved to be one of the saints of the earth. When my church-warden resigned, just after my arrival when I knew none of the people, he was a father to me. I could always turn to him for advice as he knew everyone. He was chapter clerk and I was told that Michael Ramsey (then professor of divinity) had said that he was the man he would like at his bedside if he was dying. Mr Craggs said, and really meant, 'Vicar, I'll do just what you want – anything or nothing.' He was a beautiful reader of scripture and a fine preacher. Baby Michael had the good fortune to have him as godfather. He said a wise word to me when I once apologised in a sermon for repeating something I had said in an earlier sermon: 'I don't think there is any need for apology – people do not take in as much as we think.'

There had been a long interregnum after Evan Hopkins left, ably filled by an elderly clergyman, but church finances were in low water. I did not wish to get embroiled in money-raising efforts and have in principle always believed in direct giving, so I persuaded the church council to launch a gift day. The sum required to set things right was forty times an ordinary Sunday's collection. When this was pointed out in the parish magazine, I had my first taste of the local press; the headline ran 'Vicar says we must increase our collection forty times' – which made me look rather ridiculous. On another occasion they initiated a discussion of sex education and gave me a headline suggesting the precise opposite of what I had actually written.

Children's work in the parish was quite well cared for. The diminutive Willy Wilson was totally devoted to running a boy's club. I had been warned to be wary of him – I think he had been seen kissing one of the boys. I disregarded the warning and found him a wonderfully loyal friend and an indispensable worker. The Sunday School was run by Hetty Bulman (of the rattling dentures!), another tireless worker who loved the children and was loved by them.

A job which fell to me ex officio as vicar of St Nick's was chairmanship of the governors of the Blue Coat School, a task for which I felt little qualified. I had on my council the Dean of Durham, Dr Cyril Alington, sometime headmaster of Eton College, Councillor Ferens, mayor of Durham, the Vice-Principal of the teacher-training establishment (Bede College) and Professor Heywood, Professor Emeritus of Mathematics in the University of Durham. (Heywood was a remarkable man. He had just published a paper on the Four-Colour Problem which was the fruit of a lifetime's work. The problem is how to prove that four colours are sufficient in all circumstances for a map so that the same colour will never occupy adjacent spaces. His paper had nearly proved it! He was also a competent Hebraist, who took his Hebrew Bible to cathedral services. (When a distinguished canon preached from the psalms, Heywood was heard to say on one occasion, 'He didn't get that out of the Hebrew!') So this assignment brought me into touch with city, cathedral and university. Mrs Alington, incidentally, was a delightful, and a delightfully independent, person whose husband I always assumed was a staunch Tory; she said, 'I have voted socialist all my life; one half of the world doesn't know how the other half lives.'

Grace looked after the women's work admirably. How I feel for the clergy who have no wives or who are not supported by their wives. Intimate dealings should normally be men with men and women with women. I could entirely trust the women to her. I too was fond of the old ladies. Mrs Graham had the most shocking cough, which did not stop till she had 'bottomed it'. This had affected her heart and she had to sit on her bed for twenty minutes after climbing the stairs before undressing. I measured up her room and showed that there was just space for her bed downstairs and at last she consented to let us bring it down.

I tried to visit everyone in the parish, but made it a rule that if I did not get anywhere in the first ten minutes I would move on. I found that I had a strange reluctance to get up and go out visiting, but I usually came back exhilarated. Sometimes I would visit a home and have a good time talking about the faith and would feel that if I could come back once a fortnight there was hope of real progress; but such were the calls on my time that the interval before the next visit tended to be more like six months. One regularly went to bed with a sense of the Great Undone.

Visits were of many different kinds. Some visits were happy. I visited the daughter of a widow in the congregation who (I understood) had probably only a few weeks to live. She was in her twenties and was a believer. I talked to her about James 5:14 with its injunction to the sick to 'call for the elders of the church and let them pray over (her), anointing (her) with oil in the name of the Lord, and the prayer of faith will save the sick.' I could see no reason why this should apply only to the first century and she wished it done. So Mr Craggs and a praying older lady from the church and I prayed and anointed as instructed. I cannot say that

I had any inner assurance that faith had been granted to us, but we had obeyed as best we could, and in fact the patient lived on for seven years. Another time I was asked to cleanse a public house near the vicarage. It had an evil reputation and had been newly acquired by a Christian Science lady, who seemed quite sincere in her desire that it should become a good house. I gladly went and prayed in the bar parlour that this might be so, and that prayer was apparently answered.

Some visits were sad. One was to the home of a young man in the congregation who had been reported dead. While in the house a policeman arrived and announced to his parents that it was suicide. Another visit was particularly painful. It was to the mother of two of our Sunday school children. She began to tell me about the misdeeds of her husband and said, 'If he were to come on bended knee and ask forgiveness I would never forgive him.' The words of Christ came to mind, 'If you do not forgive men their trespasses, neither will your Father forgive your trespasses.' I felt that I had in front of me a damned soul. I solemnly quoted the words to her, but whether she ever changed her mind (i.e. repented) I do not know.

I also received visitors. One was an old lag who was a brilliant actor; he persuaded me to obtain a small sum from an ex-servicemen's organization for him. A couple of nights later with cold rain pouring down I had a phone call from the police saying that he had given himself up. In court he had a hangdog expression which suggested that no one would be deceived by him; the magistrate looked pityingly at me. This man had been making quite a good living mostly off the clergy and was given seven years preventive detention.

There were three regular services on a Sunday: an early celebration of Holy Communion, which I did not encourage, since it had a tiny congregation and could never conceivably become the central Sunday service which I wished it to be. (I argued the centrality of our God-given Lord's Supper, not as something High-

Church – it was central to Plymouth Brethren – but as something biblical, primitive and historical.) Then there was a mid-morning service, which was matins with or without communion, also somewhat sparsely attended. I found this rather hard going with poor singing in a large church, though I was amazed on one occasion when two complete outsiders began to attend. One of them was a miner whose dialect I had great difficulty understanding. But they stuck it out and were eventually confirmed, proving to me that the Holy Spirit could take a most unpromising situation and work in it. The evening service was well attended with a great influx of students during term. When Michael Ramsey came to preach he could hardly believe his eyes, that one of these ghastly evangelicals could attract such a congregation, though he came reluctantly to admit that there were 'intelligent infallibilists'.

I was a strong believer in preaching courses of sermons. It is a great saving to the preacher knowing well in advance what he has to preach about, and it is satisfying to the hearers to know that topics are being systematically covered. In 1951/52 we had a card printed, giving forty-eight sermon subjects covering the Sundays of the academic year. In the morning it was A Simple Course in Basic Christianity – What to Believe and What to Do. In the evening two terms were given to The Letter to the Romans and one to The Fascination of the Books of Moses. Christmas, Good Friday and Easter of course fell outside term.

There were special services. A particularly memorable one was a Battle of Britain service, at which I knew that there would be many ex-RAF personnel. On this occasion I had flu and was running a temperature, but was most anxious to be there and preach my heart out. I promised the doctor that I would go back to bed immediately after the service – which I did, but my temperature would not come down for a week and I was shunted off to hospital. This did the trick almost at once.

Another special occasion was the Lightbearers' Service, which fitted St Nicholas' particularly well, since it was a church with a strong missionary tradition, having sent missionaries to half a dozen different parts of the world. I got the seed-thought from some publication and worked it up into an exciting drama in which many members of the congregation had an active part. The basic idea was showing the spread of the Christian faith by the reading of a script which was illustrated by the lighting of candles. Evening Prayer with appropriate readings and hymns was first said, then instead of a sermon came the lightbearers' story.

The story starts in the lighted church with me in the pulpit and my wife at the lectern reading alternately. The creation is recalled when God says 'Let there be light'. Then comes man's fall and the church is plunged in darkness. The Old Testament preparation is briefly recalled. Then John the Baptist appears from the vestry with a lighted taper: 'He was not the Light but was sent to bear witness to the Light.' He proceeds to light a large candle in a large candlestick (kindly lent by St Oswald's church) which was set in the chancel – The Light of the World. The good news goes from Judaea to Samaria and Galilee and thence throughout the empire till it reaches Rome. (Candles are being lit on the holy table and throughout the chancel and eventually two are lit in the body of the church.) These two represent the Celtic and Roman strands of Christianity coming to our islands.

These strands are joined together by the lighting of another large candle at the foot of the chancel steps, which is the candle of the English Church united at the Synod of Whitby. From this candle the lectern, the prayer desk and the pulpit are lit up, representing the translation of the Bible into English, the creation of the vernacular Prayer Book and the revival of preaching. The evangelical revival produces more lights and the St Nicholas' missionaries go off to Persia, India, China, Japan and Africa lighting candles in the remoter corners of the church. Finally we are asked what we should do. The first thing is to train the children: children light candles on the font and sing, 'Jesus bids us shine'. Further practical steps are suggested; then the service ends with 'God is working his purpose out' and a missionary blessing.

This service had great advantages. It drew a large congregation and then gave them a lengthy, concentrated and inspiring course of instruction. It put the missionary task in the context of God's purposes from creation to the final consummation. It took about forty minutes and all the lightbearers had not only read the script but had attended two complete rehearsals. It also helped the Our Own Missionary project. I thought that the best way of sustaining missionary interest was to take responsibility for the partial support of a particular person. My old Pembroke friend Kenneth Kitley seemed just the man, athletic, brainy, humble, charming, now working in the Ruanda Mission. I set great store by his furlough when we hoped to build up a firm link. Unfortunately it was disappointing, for he didn't seem able to pass on the blessings of the East Africa revival to us. He didn't quite click with either the adults or the children. After he had talked to the children he said to me, 'Before the meeting I asked the Lord whether I should talk to them about Ruanda or about Jesus. The answer seemed to be: Jesus.' Though he carried a native drum he didn't beat it and what he said about Jesus didn't interest his young audience. An experienced teacher said, 'We teach them about Jesus fifty Sundays in the year. He alone could tell us the things we wanted to hear, that is, what Jesus is doing in Ruanda.' There are weaknesses as well as strengths in charismatic Christianity.

We attempted to co-operate with the other churches. I argued to myself that the Methodists, Congregationalists, Salvation Army and some of the High-Church Anglicans were all being influenced by the biblical theology movement and that we ought to have enough in common for a united mission. They made me chairman of the mission committee. The first two attempts to get a missioner were men who I knew would preach the gospel: Bryan S.W. Green and George B. Duncan. But neither could come. Then my colleagues recommended highly a Methodist preacher.

Working under the slogan 'Our City for Christ' we visited the whole city door to door twice. The town hall was packed and the missioner was a capable orator, but as the days passed the St Nicholas people and the Salvationists got more and more miserable. What he was preaching I cannot remember, but it was not what we understood by the gospel. Fortunately the children's missioner spoke excellently, but the whole experience taught a painful lesson. Supposed interest in 'biblical theology' may not be a sufficient basis for evangelism. It reinforced the William Nicholson stand: we are not passing on Good News unless the doctrines of the Creed are preached in a way which demands decision.

A more successful united effort was an open-air service one summer's evening when we assembled in the market place and then headed off in procession to the racecourse with the Salvation Army band leading and the cathedral canons in their cassocks bringing up the rear. Michael Ramsey spoke with great skill and warmth. The boats on the river came to a stop. His voice rang out from the loudspeaker: 'Prepare to meet thy God. Where do we meet our God? In the Cross of our Lord Jesus Christ!' His address was being discussed in the pubs that evening.

Preaching to the St Nicholas' congregation was a continual exercise in trying to combine accuracy and simplicity. Though we had no dependable support from teaching staff of the university we had many lively-minded students, and at one time we had regularly in church at the same service Mrs Hamilton, who left school at the age of twelve, and a young lecturer in philosophy, who was an atheist. I did not talk about 'epistemology', but 'how we know things'! The Durham Inter-Collegiate Christian Union was particularly flourishing under the leadership of Peter Dawes (later Bishop of Derby), who met his wife Ethel in Durham. She was marvellous with children and was the one person in whose hands we could safely leave the four little boys. Iain Murray (later a prime mover in the Banner of Truth Trust) was also around, challenging us with five point Calvinism. Mike Wilcock (later to be vicar of St Nicholas) was a shy young undergraduate. Hamilton Carleston, a double first in classics and till recently in the Indian Civil Service and now secretary of St Cuthbert's, attended the church with his family. I prepared him for lay-readership, and he and his wife invited me to be godfather to their daughter Marian.

St Nicholas provided one opportunity for a more academic presentation. An ancient worthy called Callaghan had left some money to fund an annual lecture which had to be given on a certain day or the bequest would cease for ever. I used these occasions to try out chapters of my proposed The Christian View of the Bible. 'Our Lord's View of the Old Testament' had another airing. (I was to give it again as a Tyndale New Testament Lecture in 1953 in Cambridge. On that occasion I showed it to Henry Chadwick, then chaplain of Queens, Cambridge, not knowing that he was a big brain destined to be Regius Professor in both Oxford and Cambridge. He entirely approved the thesis but remarked that it left big questions unanswered.) He was thinking no doubt especially of the question whether the incarnation made Jesus subject to the ignorance and errors of his times. This question was dealt with in another Callaghan lecture, which became chapter two of the book.

A third lecture dealt with the moral difficulties of the Bible, which was eventually to blossom into the book *The Enigma of Evil*. On that occasion Canon Alan Richardson took the chair for quite a distinguished audience which included R.R. Williams, principal of St John's College, and my lodger, G.E.L. Owen. At that time Owen was a research fellow in philosophy, but was later to be professor successively in Oxford, Harvard and Cambridge. He had met his wife in Oxford when they were joint editors of *Isis*. She had become a Christian but he had not. At one time he seemed very near the kingdom but he never took the plunge and sadly he and his wife lived most of their later lives apart.

Williams invited me to preach at Cranmer Hall, the theological college attached to St John's, on All Saints Day. I in effect took two texts: Romans 9:6 – 'They are not all Israel, which are of Israel,' and a passage from Hooker's *Ecclesiastical Polity*, Book 3, Chapter 1, which distinguishes between the mystical church and the visible church – a distinction very unpopular with modern theologians. The mystical church consists of those who possess eternal life, some of whom (like the penitent thief) may not have been baptised; the visible church of those who have been baptised, some of whom may have no faith and therefore no eternal life. I then urged the students not to be content in their ministry with outward conformity but to work for life-giving faith. Williams was thought by some of the students to covet the gaiters and to be inimical to this sort of doctrine and one of them said to me, 'You'll never be asked to preach again.' When Williams did become bishop, his clergy in fact found him a very helpful pastor.

A more direct effort was made to reach the dons and their wives with a series of four meetings in the vicarage drawing-room. The general title was Christian Fundamentals and Their Relevance Today. The most memorable was the second one chaired by J.B.S. Kemp, Professor of Greek, at which Norman Anderson spoke on the Evidences of the Resurrection. This developed into a heart to heart discussion between Winston Barnes, Professor of Philosophy, and Anderson. Barnes, who had already shown profound concern (if not disgust) over what he had seen in his own heart, said eventually: 'This is not an academic debate, it is a question of what you will do with your life.' The third meeting was chaired by Frank Rhodes, a nonconformist lecturer in geology, who was eventually to become head of Cornell University. He was an ardent evolutionist with whom I was to go geologizing in the Avon gorge – looking for conodonts, often supposed to be worms' teeth! I spoke at the last meeting, which was on Human Destiny, stressing the awful alternative of acceptance to heaven or rejection to the consuming fires of hell.

I had made it my steadfast aim to put the claims of the residents of the parish before the claims of the students, and the claims of all who attended the church before outside interests or my own private concerns. But undeniably I was still deeply interested in the proposed book on the Bible and I gave time to extend my researches and try to get the results on paper. It was mostly at Durham that I wrote roughly a hundred pages on *The Pentateuch as History*. The more carefully I read them the more valueless all the J E D P arguments appeared to be. They did not seem to me in any sense to provide a cumulative argument, since $0 + 0 + 0 + 0$ still adds up to 0. I was discussing this one day with Douglas Jones, an Old Testament lecturer who later became professor, who thought the idea absurd. So I asked him for one good independent argument. He then proceeded to argue at length the lateness of the sin and trespass offerings, one of Wellhausen's key points. It came out so pat that I thought he must have been lecturing on the subject that morning. I didn't know the answer off the cuff, so I promised to write to him about it. I found that W.L. Baxter, *Sanctuary and Sacrifice*, demolished the argument in twenty-nine lucid pages, the gist of which I sent to him. He acknowledged that I had made some good points which he couldn't answer. So I asked him to produce a better argument. A long silence. When at last I taxed him he said that there was no point in arguing unless I would come out of my dogmatic castle. I said that I had come out of my dogmatic castle and was asking him to argue on his ground with the best arguments of his choice. We got no further, but it confirmed me in my belief that liberals are quick to see dogmatic bias in conservatives, but they are sometimes almost completely blind to their own, and often will not look at the books which argue a conservative case.

It was during this time that a move was made to close down Tyndale House in Cambridge. The businessmen said that money was given to IVF for the promotion of evangelism, not for academic study, which all too often damaged the faith of young scholars. John Taylor (later Bishop of St Albans) was working for Part 3 of the theological tripos at the time. He remembers vividly the dismay and anger of the residents when prospective buyers began to walk around the house discussing what they were going to do with it. I protested vehemently that it would be suicidal to turn back after having progressed so far. Mercifully the decision was overturned and the house saved.

Our time at Durham came to an abrupt end when Stafford Wright, recently appointed theological college principal at Tyndale Hall, Bristol, invited me to join his staff. As this meant New Testament work for both London and Bristol Universities, I felt the need to join the recently launched Society of New Testament Studies. I was sponsored by my old friend Fred Bruce and by my more recent friend Kingsley Barrett, who was a member of Durham's lively theological society. I left the parish in the care of Colin Craston, my very capable curate who had himself been trained at Tyndale Hall. He had retained the older evangelical taboos concerning worldliness and had even compelled me to veto a church barn dance on threat of resignation; so I knew that I was probably going into a tradition in Bristol which had been a little stricter than my own.

So ended five happy years. The final evening communion service was very moving, as I administered the bread and wine for the last time to those with whom we had shared so many joys and sorrows

Seventeen

Bristol — 1953–58

In our early days of marriage we seemed to be continually on the move; we saw ourselves as 'pilgrims and sojourners on the earth'. Coming to Bristol was to be the one exception to this pattern of life, for we were to stay here for seventeen years. It was an immense boon to the boys for we landed on the doorstep of one of the finest academic schools in the country, which was to enable three of them to get awards at Pembroke, my old college in Cambridge. We had started off intending to put them all through the state system, but the Model School in Durham had very large classes of children drawn from slum-clearance areas. The good little boys were stuck at the back of the class thoroughly bored, while the teacher wrestled with the difficult children in front. We had to take Gordon away and (helped by my father) send him as a day-boy to the choir school. David got pleurisy and we put him into the kindergarten of the Girls' High School next to the vicarage where he was happy.

When we arrived in Bristol, Clifton College had just started a half-fees scheme for sons of clergy, covering both the preparatory school and the upper school, and at the same time my father offered to help further with the boys' education. When we were allowed four places on the scheme, I felt it was hardly fair to accept so much, but the headmaster said: 'This scheme is not just for the sake of the clergy, it is for our sake too. So many of our boys come from broken homes, we want boys from homes like yours.' Gordon got a major science scholarship to Cambridge, but against everyone's advice except his father's he opted to read theology. I knew that he had already fought difficult theological battles at school, being in a sixth form all the other members of which had declared themselves atheists. One day when he was ill, my wife heard him say in his delirium 'How can I believe?' Though he felt no call to ordination, he wished to be a useful Christian and I told him that the best time to lay a good theological foundation was as an undergraduate. He is a good linguist and during the long vac he went to Alec Motyer, a brilliant Hebrew teacher, who set him on the path to a double first.

Tyndale Hall, as a set of buildings, was fairly shoddy – a group of large Victorian houses coaxed and cajoled by manifold improvisations into a college. There were four houses each named after a Reformer – Wycliffe, Cranmer, Ridley and Latimer – the student members of which formed natural tea-drinking fellowships based upon the respective bathrooms. There was a simple oak- panelled chapel and two hard tennis courts, and that was about all. Our part of Cranmer had students above and the long-suffering gardener and his wife below. Mr and Mrs Heath showed their Christianity by the excellence of their work and their uncomplaining patience even when we played indoor hockey above their heads. Our home kitchen facilities were quite primitive – no such things as fridges or washing machines.

Stafford Wright was a man after my own heart. When he retired in 1970, I wrote this of him in the college magazine:

> Stafford Wright is a remarkable case of one whom the world would not call a great man, yet through whom God has done great things. The thirties, forties and fifties were tough years for Bible-believing Christians. During those years Stafford Wright probably did more than anyone else to lay the foundation of the evangelical revival which is now

taking place within the Church of England. He remained
steadfast to the view of scripture held by Christ, and he
refused to flinch however great the scorn of the learned.

Stafford Wright was always most considerate to his
teaching staff, yet he was unsparing of himself; indeed he
seemed to drive himself to the limit, often devoting immense
trouble to individuals, but somehow he knew how to avoid
going beyond that limit. He ran the College on a shoestring;
but even at his busiest he was most loyal in his attendance
at Bible Churchmen's Missionary Society committees. To
me he was always a wise counsellor and an undemanding
friend.

What was the secret of his success? Firstly, I would
mention his happy home. He had the inestimable benefit of
a devoted family, and a wife who shared all the relentless
burdens that fall upon a principal. Then there was his sense
of humour. Many of us have sat listening to him at the
College concert with tears streaming down our faces. There
was also his width of interest. This was both his strength
and, in certain respects, his 'weakness'. He is said to have
lectured on every subject except Church History (though
even here he had a remarkable knowledge of the cults). In
his early days the Old Testament was his main interest; later
it was psychology (including parapsychology). I once heard
Professor Bruce say that his monograph on Ezra was the
most widely noticed of all the Tyndale monographs. Many
of us found his occasional lectures particularly intriguing.
He was interested in beasts, birds, bugs, photography – and
Lundy! His many interests meant of necessity academic
width rather than depth. He was suspicious of abstract ideas
and was happiest in the world of fact.

His approach was one of sanity and gentleness, just the
reverse of the narrowness and aggressiveness which is
supposed to characterise Fundamentalists. He could

nonetheless show great courage over unpopular causes. He had, for instance, considerable knowledge in the vast fields covered by evolution, and he remained a convinced Creationist. What is commonly understood by 'leadership' and 'drive' were not his characteristics – to some people's regret. But his great strength was that he was just himself. His piety was deep, but not 'pi'; he taught us naturalness in public worship; his clarity of voice, his clarity of mind, his fairness and sweet reasonableness were all of a piece.

I think Stafford's intellectual ability was sometimes underestimated because of his sheer lucidity; it was a lucidity which came from a theology well digested. By 1953 he had already served on theological college staffs for more than twenty years and had gained much wisdom in handling men from evangelical parishes. One of his wise dicta concerned speaking in tongues: 'Never let it become an issue.'

When I joined the staff, student numbers were small and we two were the only full-time teachers. I replaced as vice-principal Philip Hughes, who had been on the staff for six years. He was a good scholar with a lively mind though somewhat dull in presentation. This and his strong Calvinism meant that his real worth was not always appreciated. He left to become secretary of the Church Society. The part-time staff that I remember were all 'characters'. Denis Tongue, a Cambridge man with a strong Birmingham accent, claimed that intellectually he owed more to George Bernard Shaw than to anyone else, because he had made him think. He was at one and the same time both liberal (by BCMS standards) in his New Testament teaching and also very Protestant.

There were two very able Ulstermen, Richard Coates, who lectured in Prayer Book, who was a vicar in Weston-super-Mare. He had a fine mind and a wealth of parochial experience. He was one of the very few men in evangelical circles who could stand up to and usually out-argue the redoubtable Martyn Lloyd Jones, when it came to debating the doctrine of church, ministry or sacraments. The other was William Leathem, vicar of St John the Baptist, Harborne, who lectured more widely in worship.

Leathem had the wonderful good fortune to have found a benefactor who allowed him to go into the best bookshop in Birmingham and help himself to any theological books which took his fancy. He was a ravenous reader and so built up a magnificent library. Though a staunch BCMS man he was not temperamentally conservative. Evangelicals, partly for legal reasons, were much wedded to celebrating communion from the north side of the table. Leathem was anxious that liturgical practices should be thought out from first principles, and he adopted the westward position facing the congregation. Those who didn't like it complained that he (with his full form and florid countenance) looked like a butcher serving behind the counter! He expressed the view that the Lord's Supper need not necessarily be cast in a penitential form as in 1662; its motif could be primarily eucharistic, full of thanksgiving. Jim Packer went to him as curate before himself joining the Tyndale Hall staff in 1955.

My teaching responsibilities were fourfold, all prepared for by my previous experience, since my passion had been to try to find ways of making the Christian faith intelligible to ordinary people such as I had met in the RAF and in parish life. First, I returned to beginner's Greek and worked hard at improving Nunn's *Elements of New Testament Greek*. I must have spent many hundreds of hours working at points of detail and eventually I saw my way to rewriting the book completely. I myself have a poor memory and I reckoned that the average student needed a lot of practice if he was to get the language into his mind. I split the beginners' class into two or three groups and was careful not to go too fast for any of them. I set them exercises which they themselves corrected from the Key. They found that most of their mistakes were quite obvious, but if they couldn't understand why they differed from the Key, they raised the matter in class. In this way they taught themselves and I was spared needless correcting. All this was a hard grind but it was lightened from an early stage by the reading of easy New Testament passages, usually from the First Epistle of John. However, it worked, because most of the students really wished to understand their Bibles, and I was greatly encouraged when an external examiner from Oxford remarked how good their Greek was.

My second task was New Testament teaching. This was less successful, particularly for students preparing for the Bristol BA and the London BD. I think this had two reasons. Firstly, I was interested in the wrong things from the examinee's point of view. For instance, I wanted to know how one reconciled some trivial item of gospel harmony which the examiner would probably think futile and improper to discuss. I was not particularly interested in the endless stream of theories emanating from radical scholars about which the examiner wanted to know. Secondly, having a bad memory I could not quickly and accurately assemble what I had read. Given time I would gladly work at a problem which I felt important, but the material in my lectures was thin, which evoked a deserved complaint from one class of BD students.

My experience in the Society of New Testament Studies was of a piece with this. I went to the Ninth General Meeting of the society at Marburg in 1954 – the year when New Testament Studies first appeared. We were only forty-three members present, with Rudolf Bultmann acting as chairman of the conference. All meetings were officially trilingual and, since I could neither speak nor understand French or German spoken at speed, I did not feel really at home. In spite of efforts to improve my German progress was slow and for many years after this I did not attend the society's meetings.

My third task was to teach the doctrine of church, ministry, sacraments and eschatology, which I thoroughly enjoyed, finding

myself in warm sympathy with the authors of the Book of Common Prayer and the Thirty-Nine Articles, whose doctrine purported to be apostolic, Catholic and reformed. I of course wished
doctrine to be apostolic; I was also satisfied that the decrees of
the general councils of the church on the Trinity and the Person
of Christ up to Chalcedon in AD 451 gave a true representation
of the teaching of scripture – that is what I mean by 'the Catholic
faith', the faith of the universal church up to that point — and I
was very happy with the formulations which came out of the
Reformation debates. I was happy, that is, with its stand against
anabaptism, with its repudiation of Luther's doctrine of consub-
stantiation in Article 29, and with its gentle Augustinianism
which avoids double predestination. I was glad too that the
articles on eschatology which stood in the Forty-Two Articles
were omitted. Article 40, which is against the sleep of the soul
between death and resurrection, I should have found difficult to
subscribe to. It is remarkable, when the vast range of teaching
covered by the Prayer Book and Articles is considered, how few
and small are the items to which I do not wholeheartedly subscribe. I am in complete agreement with the body of doctrine as
a whole; difficulties are almost all peripheral and of a semantic
kind – verbal difficulties which can be easily explained.

My fourth task was to give some guidance in preaching and
the conduct of services. In their first year students conducted
services for old people in Manor Park Hospital. I counselled the
utmost simplicity and usually they worked hard to try to get over
something memorable and kindly. One student, well steeped in
the puritans, thought that he had not preached the gospel unless
he had included a strong word on hell. At the end of one term I
discussed this with him and asked him whether Jesus ever
preached hell to those who were down. I told him to work through
the gospels in the vac and find out. Unfortunately he did not do
so, but I did, and the result was as I expected – Jesus never spoke
about hell to those in trouble. I was very angry at his supposed

devotion to scripture and his unwillingness to follow it. (It was in 1954 that a Tyndale House Study Group tackled The Intermediate State and the Final Condition of the Lost. It had some very competent members including Fred Bruce and Basil Atkinson. It did not come to an agreed conclusion, but it confirmed me in my conditionalist views.)

For the final year we worked out an effective system of sermon classes. Small groups accompanied by a tutor would go to a local church where one of their number would preach. Sometime later the sermon would be discussed in the light of a demanding questionnaire which covered manner, orthodoxy, coherence and suitability. One of the key questions, which made me the butt of college jokes, was, What Was Your Aim? I maintained that if the aim was simple and clear and ruthlessly followed something useful would follow. An aim was to have two parts: What am I trying to Teach? and What do I hope they will Do? (This followed the Ciceronian pattern of oratory: *placere, docere, movere.* You must find a point of contact that pleases and so arouses interest; you must then teach something (biblical of course); then you must aim (in the power of the Holy Spirit) to move your congregation to action on the basis of what you have taught; this might be anything from saying a sincere 'Amen' after the preacher's prayer to the total dedication of life to a great cause.) I taught (and have adopted for myself ever since) that this aim should be written out at the head of every sermon. It was encouraging to find that students of modest abilities who followed these principles became very acceptable preachers.

Tyndale Hall was part of a lively theological set-up. There were four independent colleges working together with the university faculty of arts for theology degrees – the Baptist College was of long standing, Didsbury was a Methodist college recently built and Clifton Theological College was another Anglican evangelical college formed as a result of a split from the BCMS college in 1932. We worked together in setting and marking examinations and we also had a university theological society. I read a paper to the latter on the resurrection narratives, the fruit of my researches in Jerusalem, already tried out as a Callaghan lecture and since further improved. This was well received and was to see the light of day in my *Easter Enigma* of 1984. The society also initiated a debate between Rupert Davies (church historian of Didsbury) and me, which was published by Epworth under the title *Is the Bible Infallible?* in 1959.

During my time in Durham I had thought a lot about the suitability of Prayer Book Anglicanism for the needs of the mid-twentieth century. With some skill it was still possible to make it intelligible and relevant. The intellectuals appreciated the beauty of Cranmer's language and the depth of his devotion and the non-intellectuals, who had been brought up in it, felt at home in the familiar forms as their medium of worship. But I was very conscious that if I was to find myself pioneering some totally pagan area I might find it necessary to use different means. We couldn't use seventeenth-century language and wear medieval clothes for ever. Traditional evangelicalism had neither the colour of the Anglo-Catholics nor the liveliness of the Pentecostals, so it was difficult for it not to look dull and dated. Reforms were being suggested which were thoroughly Protestant in ethos, yet it was not evangelicals who were pushing them. Some of the best missionary thinking had come from a High-Churchman Roland Allen in his *Missionary Methods: St Paul's or Ours?*. Attempts to make the Holy Communion more suggestive of the priesthood of all believers were coming from the liberal camp. In view of all this, when I first arrived in Bristol, I asked whether any conservative evangelical group was working on prayer book revision. The answer appeared to be 'None'. A few years later the answer was the same.

So in my lectures I was hammering away at fundamental scriptural doctrine, but all the time urging students to make sure that they were not 'making the Word of God void by their evangelical traditions'. Of course what I was saying was already in the minds of many in the post-war generation; so it was not surprising that in 1957, when we organized a conference for former students under the title The Uneasy Conscience of the Modern Conservative Evangelical, a bumper turn-out resulted. We covered a great range of subjects; I was given the theme of Sunday Observance which helped me to crystallize thoughts which had been in my mind for a long time. (I had played a leading part in successfully staving off the opening of Sunday cinemas in Durham.) The question was whether all the ten commandments, including the fourth, were law for the church of the new covenant. All the other nine are confirmed in the New Testament, but is the sabbath law (as the catechism and the 1662 Communion service might suggest) also confirmed?

The main points of my talk were as follows:

Our unease stems from our lack of theological clarity.
Right conduct is doing the will of God as expressed in the law of God.
God's will in different times and places has not always been the same, e.g. circumcision was a solemn obligation for descendants of Abraham but not for Christians.
What parts of God's law written in the Bible are binding upon us Christians?
All are agreed: the moral law but not the ceremonial law.
There are two views of the moral law:

(1) It is the law of love together with the Ten Commandments.
(2) It is the law of love together with the Ten Commandments except the Fourth.

For the first view it is argued that we all admit the unique place of the decalogue in Israel's economy – it was written with the finger of God and placed in the Holy of Holies. It is arbitrary to extract one law only, and the decalogue itself bears witness that it was not a temporary command since it goes back to creation: 'Remember the Sabbath Day', 'in six days the Lord made heaven and earth'. It dates back before laws of diet and before circumcision and should continue after these have been abrogated.

The second view says that it is not arbitrary to exclude one law, since the New Testament specifically underlines the nine but appears to exclude the fourth – see Romans 14:5, Galatians 4:10 and Colossians 2:16: 'Let no one judge you in respect of a sabbath day.' It is not included among the necessary things to be laid upon the Gentiles in Acts 15:28.

A strict law of abstention from work would have been virtually impossible for Christian slaves and this was never an issue in New Testament times.

I then followed the article 'Sunday' in *Hastings' Encyclopaedia of Religion and Ethics*, which says: 'A simple service, before or after the day's work was the only observance possible.' Gentile Christians were anxious to repudiate any connection between Sabbath and Sunday; the identification of Sabbath and Sunday became established in the ninth century. The Reformers were not very strict Sabbatarians. It was the seventeenth century which saw the growth of intense Sabbatarianism, and in this tradition evangelicalism was largely nurtured, though the Plymouth Brethren broke with it.

If then there is no absolute divine injunction as to observance of Sunday, how should we regard it? Answer: a holy day and a day of rest is a wise provision based on the strongest guidance from the Bible, a provision needed by society and by individuals. I can see no argument for abstaining from all work or shopping in a country where Sunday is a work day; or for a complete ban on games.

So, the law of God is to love God and our neighbour; and the wisdom of God is faithfully each week to observe a holy day and a day of rest.

I have always felt the need as a parson of taking a day off in addition to Sunday as I tire mentally quite quickly and soon lose efficiency. I also find that by the time one has kept sabbath, done the job one is paid for, done one's duty to family, local church and individuals for whom one has special responsibilities, little time is left for wider interests.

I did, however, continue to take an interest in IVF publication and in my work on The Christian View of the Bible and in TSF, particularly the TSF in Oxford. Evangelical theological students in Oxford had very little senior help at that time and I used to drive over to guide and encourage them. I remember R.T. France and Gervase Duffield as student leaders in those days. I also spoke to the recently founded Bishop Jewel Society which was trying to promote Reformation Anglicanism in the university.

Jim Packer's appearance on the scene in 1955 was important in many ways. He had been trained at Oxford through classical Greats and a DPhil on the Puritan Richard Baxter. He had been bitten by puritan theology and was already working closely and effectively with Martyn Lloyd Jones for the revival of puritan and Reformed studies. I confess that I envied his calling. My calling was in a sense negative and defensive, trying to parry the myriad petty critical attacks on the Bible, which left me limited time to explore the doctrinal treasures of the Word. His calling was to wade deep into those positive treasures and to bring them forth for the nourishment of the church. Though I had read John Calvin and several modern Calvinists, I was very ignorant of the Puritans, but Packer's presence forced one to think again about the five point Calvinism of the Council of Dort. I was challenged but still not persuaded.

Of more immediate importance were the current attacks on fundamentalism by Michael Ramsey, Gabriel Hebert, Alan Richardson and others. Jim wrote a magnificent book *'Fundamentalism' and the Word of God* showing that what was being attacked was historic Christianity, including the historic Christian view of an inerrant Bible. The book had three printings in 1957 and created quite a stir – not least in Oxford, where a confrontation was arranged between Packer and Christopher Evans (at that time a lecturer in New Testament). Jim and I were driven over by Richard Coates for a meeting scheduled to take place in the University Union. It was evident long before the meeting was due to begin that the union debating chamber was not going to be able to hold the crowd and it was hastily transferred to the Wesley Memorial Church, which was filled. (Estimates of numbers vary between seven hundred and eight hundred.) The confrontation itself was a flop. Jim had decided to talk extempore and was far too long. After Evans had spoken there was a time of questions at which Jim's response was ineffective. Unfortunately he had never been subjected at academic level to current critical teaching on the Bible and he didn't think it very important. The best answer to it, he considered, was a good grasp of reformed dogmatics, along the lines of John Owen. His '*Fundamentalism*' opens with a Spurgeon quotation: 'Defend the Bible? I would as soon defend a lion.' Oxford theology assumed and argued in detail that the Bible was obviously not inerrant; so the weakness of the evangelical case at the confrontation confirmed some in the belief that Packer's book need not be taken seriously.

Sitting at the back of the church throughout the session I was struck by two things. First was the quite extraordinary willingness of so many to come and hear a conservative evangelical state his case. Second was the impossibility of any adequate follow-up of the occasion, for there were no theologians in Oxford representing this point of view. Basil Gough, rector of St Ebbe's, was a good preacher, but he did not profess to be well read in theology. John Reynolds, in a country parish near Oxford, was a good church historian able to give useful guidance to the Christian Union, but he was very restricted in the time he could give to promoting evangelical scholarship. Going home in the car and linking this thought with the long-felt recognition of the need for scholarly work on prayer book revision, we said: Oxford needs a centre for scholarly research similar to Tyndale House, Cambridge, but with emphasis on those things which Anglicans need but which Tyndale House could not provide. So the idea of Latimer House was conceived.

Eighteen

Bristol — 1958–63: Launching Latimer House

Jim Packer, Richard Coates and I returned to Bristol convinced that something must be done. Jim and I both put our thoughts on paper. Mine was headed 'Oxford Evangelical Research Centre', his 'A Strategic Priority'. I noted our weakness in the councils of the church, our lack of scholars and lack of organization and I stressed the needs of Oxford. I suggested that scholars be set aside to research and write, and to encourage others to do likewise and to strengthen witness in Oxford – this to be done by means of a centre complementary to Tyndale House in Cambridge. Tyndale House focused on biblical research; this centre should concentrate on doctrine, worship, church history and church polity. Jim wrote a fervent memorandum stressing the need to conceive the project in terms of the immediately pressing needs of the church, particularly the need to expound and defend evangelicalism within the Church of England. 'The present position is one of extreme urgency. Canon law revision is in progress; Prayer Book revision is promised; revision of the Articles is threatened.' Oxford must be the centre; the staff must have competence and a sense of vocation; there should be a five-year plan.

The obvious difficulty was how to raise money without a house and without a staff, and how to raise a staff when no firm job could be offered. We formed ourselves into an exploratory committee with Basil Gough, rector of St Ebbe's Church in

Oxford, as chairman and John Reynolds, rector of Dry Sandford, as two Oxford representatives, together with Malcolm McQueen, an experienced lay member of the Church Assembly, and we met for the first time on 29 December, 1958. We had one ray of encouragement; both Richard Coates and his close friend Philip Hughes had told us that they had often desired to work together, and we found that there was no particular difficulty in either of them giving up their present jobs. This seemed to us like a clear sign from God. We asked Philip to join the committee. We all listed people who we thought might be interested and wrote inviting their provisional support, to which there was a good response. By January 1960, with John Stott now chairman, we were able to invite Coates to become warden and Hughes to become librarian as soon as property could be secured. 131 Banbury Road (which was to become Latimer House) was then purchased and everything looked rosy: two full-time workers lined up together with Jim Packer willing to give two days a week to the project.

Then things began to go wrong. Richard Coates, who loved working with people, began (it seemed) to get cold feet about the whole project. Though a fine brain and an excellent speaker, he had an inferiority complex about writing, and also he had a shrewd realization of the difficulty of working under a committee. He felt that a parish was his sphere, not a research centre. However, it came out in a different way to the committee. He told us that he could not work with Philip Hughes. It became clear to the committee that it had to make a choice. Hughes was a fine scholar but he was dry as a speaker and did not seem to have the public relations' gifts to lead the work. The committee chose Coates, and Hughes (who had not a particle of blame) was eventually exiled to the United States. I did my level best to iron the matter out but all to no effect except to make myself very ill. It seriously affected my eyes and I was sent to hospital after hospital for tests but they found nothing. It was purely psychosomatic.

Coates stayed on and Jim Packer was brought in as full-time librarian, but this did nothing to solve Coates' problem. In fact I suspect that it made it worse. Jim was a highly competent writer, but in Coates' eyes he was young and brash with little experience of the real world. I am pretty sure also that he had long ago rejected Jim's brand of Calvinism. Anyway he told the council (as it had now become) that his concentration was ruined and that he must return to parish life. The council upgraded Jim to warden and looked for a new librarian.

Roger Beckwith was the man they selected, and he was to continue on the staff for more than thirty years. When I first knew him he was bursar at Tyndale Hall, though no ordinary bursar, since he had a passion for academic study. He had been converted through the ministry of the Oxford Pastorate, based on St Aldate's. He had then tasted successively the three wings of the Church of England: Ripon Hall, which was the foremost centre of the Modern Churchman's Union and liberalism; Tyndale Hall, the home of diehard evangelicals; and Cuddesdon, perhaps the leading High-church college. After a curacy he returned to Bristol as bursar. On paper his qualifications were not strong. He had read English at Oxford and had only got third class honours. This was due to a wayward streak in him: he preferred to read what took his fancy rather than what his tutor suggested. He used to tell a story against himself. He found it very difficult to produce the weekly essays which were required of him. One day his tutor in exasperation solemnly warned him that if he defaulted again he would be sent down. The next week he still did not manage to produce his essay; and after that he had no further trouble from his tutor!

We who knew him well realized that beneath his quiet exterior lay most exceptional gifts. Exaggerated stories about him circulated – he was said to have to sleep on the floor because his bed was covered with so many books. He would go to a football game reading a book, which he would put down to play a fierce game and then pick up to read on the way home. Shortly after I first met him, I was surprised to find that he knew things about pentateuchal criticism which were unknown to me, in spite of the fact that this was the field which I knew most about. His passion for study meant that he was always pursuing ideas down strange bypaths; he was never content with second-hand knowledge and was forever tracking notions to their sources. He had a highly critical mind, quick to find the flaws in any argument, and so had the makings of an outstanding scholar. He had been made tutor at Tyndale Hall in 1959 and had served four years on the teaching staff prior to his transfer to Latimer House.

It was shortly after Beckwith's appointment that I decided that something ought to be done about the totally unrepresentative character of the Church of England's commission which was charged with the revision of the Prayer Book. I wrote an article for the church papers in the following terms:

Liturgical Omission
There are sins of commission and sins of omission, and there also appear to be sins of omissions from commissions. At least I have been much perplexed about an omission from the Liturgical Commission.

The strange fact is this. There is not a single conservative evangelical on the Liturgical Commission, and this at a time when Prayer Book Revision is in the air, and permission for experimental services is to be sought from Parliament. It is not simply that a considerable segment of Church opinion is not represented. (Though at a time when the proportion of conservative evangelical ordinands is steadily growing, it seems strange that this school of thought should be ignored.) The serious thing is that the point of view closest to that of Cranmer should not be represented.

Anglicanism, it may be, is a curious phenomenon. But it is undeniable that the supreme factor in the making of

Anglicanism has been the Book of Common Prayer, and that the supreme genius in the making of the Prayer Book was Cranmer. Failure to appreciate the greatness of the Prayer Book could bring irreparable damage to the whole Anglican Communion.

Now there are two points at which the conservative evangelical and Cranmer are at one, in a way that no one else quite is, namely on the doctrine of the Atonement and on the doctrine of Scripture. It is doubtful whether anyone but a conservative evangelical is quite happy with: 'The offering of Christ once made is that perfect redemption, propitiation and satisfaction, for all the sins of the whole world' (Art.31). It is doubtful if any but a conservative evangelical is quite happy about Cranmer's acceptance of the whole Bible (imprecatory psalms and all) as the foundation of the liturgical structure. Yet these two doctrines answer the two most fundamental questions of theology: What is your gospel? What is your authority?

I realise that the Commission is an unofficial body appointed purely at the discretion of the Archbishops, but its importance in the work of Prayer Book revision is great. It is pertinent (and, in all sincerity, I trust not impertinent), therefore, to speculate as to why the devoted Cranmerites are left out.

It can scarcely be maintained that there is no one adequately qualified. There are certainly some well informed people available. There seem to be two possible reasons for the omission. On the one hand the Archbishops might feel that these people represent 'The Menace of Fundamentalism', and must therefore be given no scope for the exercise of their baleful influence. If so, that's a pity. But are they really as dangerous as all that?

On the other hand, the Archbishops may feel that the distinctions between liberals and conservatives are not very important, and that the evangelical point of view can be perfectly well represented by those who don't hold to the extreme positions, such as propitiation and the infallibility of Scripture. This is plausible, but it doesn't quite bear examination. On theological grounds it is demonstrably untrue. The cleavage in theological principle between liberalism and the old orthodoxies is greater than that between orthodox Protestantism and orthodox Roman Catholicism. And in practical experience, liberals and conservatives don't always feel very close. Those who aren't at one as to the nature of the gospel and as to the principle of authority tend to disagree about most things!

I wonder which is the real reason. I feel pretty certain that the Archbishops would sincerely argue the second reason. Yet it doesn't argue well. The human mind plays strange tricks and we rationalize without realising it. I wonder whether the Menace theme is still at work in the subconscious?

This article was written more than a year ago, but was never published, because of an innate dislike for beating the party drum. But recent developments seem to make the matter more urgent. The names of the commission dealing with Roman Catholic relations have not yet been published. It would be a pity if those who are at the same time nearest to, yet most sharply separated from, the Roman Catholics were not represented. It is increasingly clear that it was a mistake that there was no conservative in the Methodist Conversations. It is even possible that the presence of one might have rendered the publication of a dissentient view unnecessary. If a further commission is to be set up, their contribution could be valuable.

But the prayer book is the most crucial field of all. I earnestly pray that lovers of our Cranmerian heritage may be allowed to make their contribution at the highest level, and that Anglicanism may not lightly throw away its most priceless treasure.

I sent this article to the two archbishops as an act of courtesy. I received a prompt reply from Donald Coggan the Archbishop of York, saying that I had made a valid point and asking whom I would suggest for the commission. In a letter in April 1964 I made two suggestions: first choice Beckwith, second choice Colin Buchanan. Colin was a Mods. and Greats man from Oxford, who was both athlete and scholar – he ran three times in one day against Cambridge in the university relay team. He came to Tyndale Hall already possessing a quite remarkable knowledge of liturgy and when it came to the official examination in Christian worship he was awarded a mark of ten out of ten by an experienced examiner. This must have been equivalent to at least 96 per cent, which I can only think meant that in some parts of the paper the examinee knew more than the examiner. Colin was duly appointed, with far-reaching results for English liturgy – and the article was never published.

William Knight and Evelyn Wenham,
the author's parents, with their
children, John, Nora, Susan and
Eleanor.

Alfred Ebenezer Wenham, the
author's grandfather.

The author as a pupil at Uppingham School.

In charge of the books at Scripture Union camp.

Tennis player at Portley Wood.

Wedding to Grace Isaac, 28th July 1942. Frank Food (best man) on extreme right of back row.

Royal Air Force chaplain 1943–47.

Teaching New Testament Greek evening class, Bristol.

With family, David, Peter, Grace, the author, Michael and Gordon, Bristol, 1965.

Warden of Latimer House, Oxford.

In his Oxford study, overlooking St John's playing fields, aged 80.

Nineteen

Bristol — 1963–65: Disaster

In the mean time things in Bristol were gaining momentum, not only at Tyndale Hall but also at the other Anglican establishment, Clifton Theological College. The existence of these two evangelical colleges, only a mile distant from one another, was an anachronism stemming from a split which had taken place in 1932. The Bible Churchmen's Missionary Society had set up its missionary and theological college in Bristol in 1925 through the initiation of Dr Daniel Bartlett, a missionary statesman who recognized clearly the necessity for sound theology as a basis for effective evangelism. He believed the crucial issue to be whether all Christ's utterances should be accepted as the truth of God, including his teaching about scripture. This was accepted by all members of the college staff, but differences arose concerning 'worldliness' and college discipline, in which the principal Dr Sydney Carter and the BCMS committee took opposite sides. As a result Dr Carter, who was a good church historian and a doughty controversialist but (it is generally thought) not a good judge of men, headed a new college on the other side of the Clifton Downs, no longer tied to BCMS but governed by an independent trust. This left both colleges in low water. But with the increase in the number of evangelical ordinands and the advent of good principals and good staff they both survived and were now beginning to prosper.

The Tyndale staff after the departure of Packer and Beckwith was reinforced by several men who like them went on to gain international reputations. Colin Brown came to the college as a student well equipped with modern languages. After completing a BD and an MA he returned to the college as tutor in 1961. He published a book on Barth in 1967, followed in 1969 by a remarkable book *Philosophy and the Christian Faith: A Historical Sketch from the Middle Ages to the Present Day*. Philosophy was a field in which few evangelicals had any expertise, yet Colin surveyed the scene from Aquinas to Wittgenstein and Barth with great competence and assessed their contributions from a Christian point of view, showing already his powers of understanding and organization.

Richard France, having completed classical Mods. and Greats at Oxford, came to Bristol in 1960 to do a London BD. He stayed in the college as part-time teacher while he worked on a Bristol PhD which resulted in a useful book *Jesus and the Old Testament* (1971). After a spell in Africa he returned to England to head the teaching of New Testament at London Bible College and then to become Principal of a flourishing Wycliffe Hall in Oxford.

Tony Thiselton (who had apparently been provoked by a talk which I gave stressing the need for big books – a need which he has fulfilled in a literal way!) joined the staff in 1963. Owing to eye trouble and to his dual interest in both philosophy and New Testament, he was a late developer. He was not greatly excited by the old theological controversies but he was profoundly interested in hermeneutics for which he was ideally trained and which made him a first-class teacher. I was delighted to become godfather to his son Martin.

On the other side of the downs Clifton Theological College was also building up a notable staff. Alec Motyer, the vice-principal, was a quite exceptional Old Testament tutor – not only a brilliant Hebrew teacher but also an excellent expositor, who firmly repudiated the fashionable disintegrating criticism which he considered ruinous of sound exegesis. Peter Dawes, a most lively character whom I had known well in Durham, came to teach church history with much wit and sparkle. Jim O'Byrne and Mike Farrer were two other capable tutors.

The two staffs were working together in the closest harmony; much of the lecturing was shared and the two libraries were being co-ordinated. The vision was growing of a possible reuniting of the two colleges. We even got to the point where the two vice-principals met the members of the two college councils in St Ebbe's Rectory and urged this upon them. We were most warmly received and we left believing that in principle the case was won. All the members of staff (and this was being strongly voiced by Packer in Oxford) realized that the growth of the work and the rising academic standards of staff were making changes in constitution desirable. The traditional concept of an Anglican theological college was that of a vicar running a parish helped by young unmarried curates. Those who were seeking passionately to raise theological standards with a view to the reform of the church felt that a college should be more like a scaled-down version of a Christian university. Room should be made for members of staff who felt that theological teaching was a life's vocation. It was not easy to share this vision with councils which had long thought along quite different lines.

What happened behind the scenes probably no one now knows, but suddenly in 1965 disaster struck. Motyer, Dawes and Farrer were sacked and two of their colleagues resigned in sympathy, while we at the other college protested vigorously. In a moment, the reputation of Bristol as a centre of training was destroyed and numbers slumped catastrophically. After the damage had been done and driven by expediency, moves were made to merge the devastated colleges, but on a doctrinal basis looser than that of BCMS and excluding from the staff Colin Brown, who had strongly criticized the sackings. This seemed to me an intolerable way to begin a new institution and I resigned my vice-principalship, though continuing to tutor at the college.

It was during this period as semi-tutor that I was able for the first time to work through the whole Gospel Synopsis, making up my mind about synoptic relationships. It was then that I made a big step forward in thinking. I came to the conclusion that the relation between the wording of the synoptists was not that of literary redaction but that each evangelist wrote in the way in which he was accustomed to teach. As far as I knew I was the only scholar in the world who believed this; so it was a matter of great cheer to me when the Society of New Testament Studies announced a forthcoming monograph by J.M. Rist, *On the Independence of Matthew and Mark*, which appeared in 1978.

The disaster which had overtaken us made me ponder deeply Article 9 on Original Sin, which says: 'This infection of nature doth remain, yea in them that are regenerated.' It was shocking that Christians could behave like this to one another, but I remembered how Samson with all his glaring and shameful sins could be numbered among the heroes of faith in Hebrews 11. The sermon which I preached at this time on 'By faith . . . Samson' was appreciated more than almost any other which I have given. Ever since I have not only ceased to look for perfection in keen Christians (which I had done long before), but I have learnt sadly not to be surprised if occasionally they are guilty of quite hideous wrongs.

Meanwhile the normal work at the colleges had been going on. My toil on Nunn's *Elements of New Testament Greek* was reaching a new stage. I had unashamedly made use of all the best ideas which I could garner from other writers and I had rearranged the material in a way which enabled the elements of the language to be learnt in an easy and logical manner. I tried to cut out all unnecessary learning and decided to take the bold step of cutting out all use of accents except in four instances where differences of accent were of help in distinguishing one form from another.

I took this step partly because I knew that an accented text would be a fruitful source of mistakes and partly because I knew that a full-scale accentual system came into being long after New Testament times and so was in a sense anachronistic. There was one snag about this policy – it made no provision for the high-flyers who wanted to go on to doctoral work or publication where accurate accentuation is expected. The tiny minority that has linguistic flair can take this considerable extra load in their stride, and I had planned to provide an appendix which would enable them to learn to do this. I intended that they should be able with its help to take their clean unaccented text and fill in the accents as they went along. This came to nothing and I was delighted when Donald Carson produced *A Student's Manual of New Testament Greek Accents* in 1985 which fully covers the ground.

The time had come to tell the Cambridge University Press that the manuscript was available should they ever want a new edition. I was aware that Mr Nunn in his old age was not interested in a major revision but I thought that the press should know that the new script was available. Before the year was out Mr Nunn had died and CUP was quite enthusiastic about getting the book into print for the 1964/5 academic year. They fell behind schedule and thereupon provided me with thirty copies of the complete manuscript for use with my classes – this in the days when photocopying had not yet become cheap and routine. It was in fact a godsend for it enabled me to test the whole book in class and make many improvements before it saw the light of day. I was grateful to the press for producing a beautifully printed book, but I was later on tempted to feel that what was advertised as 'the oldest press in the world' was also the most inefficient. Year after year this textbook was out of print at the beginning of the academic year. Several times they forgot to incorporate emendations in reprints. Once when I wrote to try to ensure that this would not happen again I got a letter back asking me what I meant. I had to send them some fifteen pages of correspondence which they had somehow lost.

The book proved its usefulness and versions have appeared in French (a beautiful edition), Welsh, Brazilian Portuguese, Indonesian and Swahili. Numerous rival books have appeared but *The Elements* continues to sell well. It is not a particularly good book for those who want to scrape through an exam with the least possible work, and I often shock people by discouraging a waste of time on a half-hearted attempt on the language. Unless you can plan so that your learning rate is substantially above your forgetting rate, you will waste a lot of time. There are fine translations and good commentaries in your mother tongue. I would much prefer that it were required of an ordinand that he should have read his Bible carefully from cover to cover than that he should have learnt a smattering of Greek. Martyn Lloyd-Jones was a good exegete and a superb preacher with virtually no knowledge of the original. Of course one would expect an exponent of French literature to know French, and ideally a Bible expositor should know Hebrew, Aramaic and Greek. But nearly all Christians find that in practice it is the Bible in their mother tongue which becomes the Word of God to them. In Oxford theology there is some disquiet at the present low level of Greek in 'schools'. It seems to me inevitable that this must remain so for most non-classicists unless it is clearly known that, say, there is an assured fifty per cent mark in one paper simply for a basic knowledge of Greek. I found in Bristol that the average arts student could master the elements in a year if he or she gave ten hours a week to the subject. An enormous boost would be given to biblical studies if some examination board would offer New Testament Greek as a subject for GCSE. There would, I know, be a good response and it would incidentally do something to halt the decline in classical studies. It would give all the would-be theologians a valuable start.

When *The Elements* was published half the royalties went to the Dean and Chapter of Ely Cathedral – for rather an amusing reason. Mr Nunn was an elderly bachelor who used to teach

Greek at St Aidan's College, Birkenhead for the sheer love of it. At the end of one long vacation the vice-principal, who was editor of the college magazine, said to one of his colleagues, 'Didn't I hear that Mr Nunn had died?' He replied, 'That seems to ring a bell, I think I heard that too.' They looked through the church papers to check their memories but they couldn't find any mention of it. But since they hadn't a complete set of papers, they thought that their common recollection must be correct, so the vice-principal wrote a short obituary. When Mr Nunn read it, he was not so much annoyed by the mistake as by the fact that so little was said in his praise! In his will he had left his literary remains to St Aidan's. He promptly rewrote it and transferred his bequests to Ely Cathedral.

With my reservations about the unsatisfactory way so much Greek is learnt, I have tended to bemoan the fact that *The Elements* sells so much better than the volumes of The Christian View of the Bible. A better understanding of the New Testament is of course valuable, but Greek provides only a peripheral refinement of one's knowledge, whereas the whole question of Christ's authority is fundamental to all our theology. However, when it came to the publication of *Redating Matthew, Mark and Luke*, I found that nearly all the reviews were respectful and that many of them started with some such words as 'We have all been brought up on Wenham's *Elements*.' And for this I was very thankful.

My Greek teaching at this time gave me an interesting contact with the Roman church. One of the BA students was a Catholic who had been working in an ecumenical centre in Edinburgh and was obviously enjoying her contacts with non-Roman Christians. Charles Davis, a teacher at Heythrop College who was reckoned to be one of the church's most orthodox theologians, came to Bristol for a meeting and Florence organized the tea. Charles had firm convictions that 'the dogmatic principle' was essential to the church and he was becoming increasingly unclear that all the dogmas were true, but to take the plunge and repudiate the faith which he had so long believed and taught was terribly difficult. Florence provided the catalyst. He fell in love with her, married her and then wrote an interesting book, *A Question of Conscience*. He has remained a fringe member of the church and has written a large number of rather radical books.

This period was a time of intense ecumenical activity into which evangelicals were drawn. I wrote up some of my experiences in a little book commissioned by SPCK, which was intended as the first of three in a series *Towards the 1980s*, the other two to be written by an Anglo-Catholic and a liberal. *The Renewal and Unity of the Church in England* was published in 1972 but sadly contributions from the other standpoints did not reach publishable standard. A quotation from the first chapter will show how deeply concerned I had become.

Nottingham Madness
On 18 September 1964 a large proportion of the Christian leadership of Britain went mad – or so it seemed. At Nottingham the First British Conference on Faith and Order was drawing to a close. Among its five hundred members were representatives or observers from all the main Christian groups in the country, including a galaxy of distinguished theologians, hierarchs, and bureaucrats, long inured to the penitential discipline of endless committees and conferences. One might have expected, if not a measure of quiet cynicism, at least an attitude of caution. But instead the atmosphere was that of a revival meeting. This resolution was put to the conference:

> United in our urgent desire for One Church Renewed for Mission, this conference invites the member churches of the British Council of Churches, in appropriate groupings such as nations, to covenant together

to work and pray for the inauguration of union by a
date agreed among them. We dare to hope that this
date should not be later than Easter Day, 1980.

I sat in my seat spellbound. I had come to Nottingham
reluctantly at the request of my bishop, Oliver Tompkins,
who was chairman of the conference. I had expected to find
myself as a conservative evangelical ploughing a rather
lonely furrow, expending a lot of effort with very little
result, but in the event I had found the proceedings moving
and spiritually rewarding. There was a sense of the hand of
God upon us. But my head told me that this resolution was
a lot of nonsense. The one truly significant reunion in
Christendom – that in South India in 1947 – had taken
twenty-eight years to consummate, and had then been twice
douched in cold water by the Lambeth Conferences of 1948
and 1958. In addition the current negotiations between the
Church of England and the Methodist Church appeared to
be heading for the rocks. I was being asked to say that I
dared to hope for a massive reunion within sixteen years.

My head said that it was a nonsense, but my heart said,
'This is of God.' The whole conference had been planned
with immense care and much prayer. For a year groups all
over the country had been engaged in preparatory study,
and from the start there was a sense (with one noteworthy
exception, which will be mentioned later) that the conclusions of the conference had not been predetermined, but
that we were seeking guidance and renewal from the Holy
Spirit. Quite outstanding were the daily Bible Studies conducted by Father Paul Verghese. Father Paul is a priest of
the Syrian Jacobite Church of India (incidentally he had
been private secretary to Haile Selassie, Emperor of Ethiopia, before ordination), whose education has been largely
western. He brought out and brought home the meaning of

four great New Testament passages with a spiritual power
which nourished the soul. We knew that day by day the
Word of God was being spoken to us. Then, quite unfore-
seen, rumour began to circulate of a hair-brained notion
which was under discussion by some members of the conference. There emerged this extraordinary resolution – winning its way first in one of the subsection study groups, then
in a full section, till finally it was commended to the whole
conference with reasoned passion. A large majority, perhaps five-sixths of those present, voted in favour. Fifty-
three voted against. I managed to keep my head and, along
with seventeen others, abstained from voting.

But when I went to bed that night, something happened
to me which has never happened before or since. I did not
sleep at all. Yet I was not restless or unhappy. I was simply
saying to the Lord, 'If you can use me in any way for the
unity and renewal of the Church, here I am'. For some
weeks I was like a man in love, full of goodwill even towards
Christians from whom I most profoundly differed, and with
the thought of renewal continually recurring to my mind
and with the word renewal repeatedly on my lips.

To many others Nottingham seemed to be a mountain-
top experience, but the high hopes of those days were
rapidly and cruelly eroded by the bitter realities of the
ensuing years. Opposition to the Anglican-Methodist
scheme seemed to increase rather than diminish in both
Churches in spite of the Herculean efforts of the top brass
to get it through. Attempts to get the Church of England to
'covenant for union' evoked no enthusiasm and were soon
up against a brick wall. In an attempt to learn from Nottingham, exposition of Scripture was introduced as part of
the business of the Convocation of Canterbury. This made
a good start, but after some deplorable failures the will to
persevere was lost. Evangelicals seemed to be showing signs

of new life. At Keele in 1967 they gave an impressive call to one another to a more active involvement in the life of the Church and the world. But the enthusiasm of Keele too began to fade. With half the time to 1980 already gone the euphoria of Nottingham and the heady stuff talked there seems to have come to less than nothing. Was it a chimera or did God give us a glimpse of what he intended to do?

This euphoria underestimated how much needed to be done for the renewal of the church, but I thought then, and I still think now, that God is doing a profound work of demolition, showing the unreality of our divisions, yet preventing us from uniting without a renewed understanding of the gospel. By Easter 1980 the Church of England had decreed that members of all Trinitarian churches were welcome at our communion services. Generally the feeling was abroad that sincere faith in Christ was what united us, but movement towards a common understanding of the gospel remained slow.

Twenty

Bristol — 1965–70: Convocation

With our zeal for the reformation and renewal of the church it was obvious that its governing bodies must occupy a strategic place in any plans that we might make. I therefore stood as proctor for the diocese of Bristol in the Convocation of Canterbury (predecessor of General Synod's House of Clergy) and was duly elected in 1965. It was quite an experience finding oneself in this archaic assembly, with its Latin litany and cumbersome procedures, modelled partly on the procedures of Parliament. Looking over the Proceedings of Convocation of 1965–70, I can see that my deepest interest was in the restoration of biblical doctrine and spirituality. At my second synod, still full of Nottingham euphoria, I proposed that each session of convocation should be opened with an exposition of Scripture. This was adopted and the next two sessions were opened first by Archbishop Ramsey and then by Archbishop Coggan. Both were biblical scholars with spiritual priorities, who did very well. But after that the supply of people who understood biblical exposition seemed to dry up and later efforts were largely valueless and the practice was eventually dropped.

In January 1966 I was asked to act as chaplain to a theological students' conference sponsored by the British Council of Churches. I gave three Bible studies on my favourite themes: the first showed that Jesus did not claim omniscience, but he did claim trustworthiness in all that he taught. The second showed how he taught that there were two, and only two, ways through life. (I quoted the thirty-two ways in which he expressed this.) The third showed how Jesus' mind was steeped in Scripture, the prerequisite to effective evangelism. Almost immediately after this conference I spoke in convocation about the confusion among theological students and the need for the recovery of an agreed doctrine of revelation.

At the next session in May the new experimental Holy Communion services were being debated which included the introduction of petitions for the well-being of the departed. I had gone through the whole New Testament looking at all the references to life after death and I attempted to boil this down to one speech. I argued that the church had for many centuries been imbued with a doctrine of the soul which appeared to be Platonic rather than biblical – the view that the soul was a separable, inherently immortal, entity – and that nowhere in the New Testament was there any sign of petitions for these departed souls. Rather there were two streams of pictorial teaching, one which represented the dead as corpses awaiting resurrection and the other which represented death as departure to be with Christ. If these two streams are mixed up an intermediate state is called for, but the New Testament nowhere depicts such a place. I urged that we continued to bear witness to the Christian triumph over death by remembering the departed only with unashamed thanksgiving.

This plea did not win approval and the subject came up again in October when burial services were being discussed. I elaborated further, according to the Proceedings of Convocation, as follows:

> The debate since their first discussions had in fact brought out some new and interesting points which raised in a very searching manner the Christian doctrine of death and of

heaven. Two arguments had been used in favour of intercession for the dead. One argument ran, 'I shall not be fit
for heaven when I die. It will take a long time before I shall
be wholly pure. I need your prayers.' Another argument
was, 'You pray for Christian friends on earth, although you
know that it is God's will to grant the blessings you pray
for. Why not do the same for the friends who have passed on?'

Dealing first with the second argument, it seemed to him
[Wenham] that when they prayed for their friends on earth
they were praying for those who were engaged in a deadly
struggle. They prayed that their friends might withstand the
temptations of the world, the flesh and the devil, and in
some mysterious way they joined with their friends in the
battle. Surely the glory of death in Christ was that they were
delivered from the clutches of that trinity of evil for ever and
no longer needed that help.

To deal with the first argument, it seemed to some people
to be mere magic to suggest that in death people were
suddenly changed, that the evil in them was destroyed. But
was not that just what the New Testament taught? In the
coming of Christ sinful beings like themselves would be
changed in a moment, in the twinkling of an eye. To him
[Wenham] it was a doctrine full of godly comfort that his
Creator and Redeemer had promised to destroy the evil
within him.

What was really at stake, he believed, was the Christian
doctrine of heaven. In this matter they were completely
dependent upon revelation. It was either the biblical picture
of heaven or the fruitless gropings of the natural reason.
Heaven was to enter into the joy of the Lord, to partake of
the inheritance of the Saints in light, to sit in the heavenly
presence of Christ, to enter the place into which naught that
defiled could enter, the place where sin and sorrow and tears
were no more. It was a wonderful picture. But if they denied

sanctification at death or rising, what happened? They must either invent a doctrine of purgatory in order to preserve a perfect heaven, or, if they repudiated purgatory, as the Report of the Liturgical Commission did, they must give up their perfect heaven. This seemed to him to be the logic of the position.

If they went a stage further and added to the notion of an imperfect heaven a universalistic doctrine – and admitted the unrepentant even – they would convert heaven simply into another stint of that same struggle that they endured here on earth. They would arrive at the other side to continue a limitless struggle between good and evil or, if they followed Hindu speculation, perhaps to face many reincarnations.

It still seemed to [Wenham] that there was much at stake. He hoped and prayed that intercession for the dead would not become a permanent part of the Anglican liturgy.

In the May debate there was a most important turn of events. The proposed communion service contained in the eucharistic prayer the words 'We offer thee this bread and this cup.' These words were very dear to those who thought that the Reformers had been wrong to delete this type of wording from the medieval mass. Colin Buchanan in the Liturgical Commission had argued unsuccessfully against their reinsertion. He felt so strongly about the matter that he hastily wrote a booklet which was put into the hands of every synod member. This was a field in which I did not feel sufficiently at home to be able to debate nor did the other conservative evangelicals. But to our delight and surprise a number of speakers of different points of view got up to say that they thought Colin had a point. When the *Alternative Service Book* was published these words were dropped and we felt thankful that we had been saved from something which would inevitably have been interpreted by some as a return to the repeated offering of

Christ in the mass. In 1978 Colin produced a Grove Liturgical Study entitled *The End of the Offertory – An Anglican Study*, a forty-page booklet into which is packed a mass of evidence showing how misguided was Dom Gregory Dix, *The Shape of the Liturgy*, the book which had so largely popularized the notion of offering at this point in the service. Petitions for the dead were also reduced to the innocuous 'We remember those who have died in the faith of Christ . . . according to your promises, grant us with them a share in your eternal Kingdom.'

At this time there was much cordial interchange between evangelicals and Anglo-Catholics, and I was invited to St Michael's College, Llandaff, the high-church theological college of the Church of Wales, to give a series of addresses during Holy Week. I expounded the whole of St Paul's Epistle to the Romans and finished up celebrating the Lord's Supper in the manner envisaged by Cranmer, showing how it depicted with great power the once-for-all sacrifice of Christ and the sinner's justification by grace through faith alone. Many seemed moved by the uncluttered simplicity of the reformation rite.

Another invitation was to the shrine of Our Lady of Walsingham in 1967. This shrine had been famous in the Middle Ages and many of the crowned heads of Europe had come barefoot to make their devotions there. These practices were stopped at the Reformation but were revived by Anglo-Catholics in the nineteenth century. Apparently a Spanish Roman Catholic monk had visited the shrine and had said to Colin Stephenson, Master of the Guardians of our Lady of Walsingham, 'What do you people believe about the Blessed Virgin?' Feeling somewhat put on the spot, he said to his friend, Hubert Box, I think we should have a Mariological Conference which should include some evangelicals.' As I often sat beside Box in Convocation he suggested that I should be invited to speak. For most of the conference I was the only Protestant present amidst the Anglos and the Romans and the Eastern Orthodox and I felt like a fish out of water with all the chantings to the Virgin Mary. But they listened extremely well as I expounded the Reformed Anglican doctrine of revelation and then applied it to the Mary of the New Testament.

I reckoned that the two solemnly promulgated dogmas of the Roman Church, the Immaculate Conception of 1854 and the Assumption of 1950, both stemmed from a belief in the sinlessness of the Virgin. If she was sinless from birth, why not from conception? If she lived and died sinless, was it not to be expected that her body would not see corruption? I majored therefore on the question, Does the New Testament teach the sinlessness of Mary? Clearly it teaches that all have sinned except Jesus. That Jesus had no sin is said three times but no such exception is made of Mary, indeed there are several indications to the contrary. I then went on to try to expound the natural meaning of what the New Testament had to say: Mary blessed among women to all generations, Mary trainer of the child Jesus, Mary mother of a big bouncing family, knowing all the joys and trials of womankind – in childhood, adolescence, courtship, marriage, pregnancy, childbirth, married life and love, and the toils and exhaustion of managing her many children. She knew what it was to be a great-hearted mother, a devoted wife and a lonely widow. She knew what it was to see her most precious son hideously crucified. To her, as to us, death was a falling asleep to awake with us on the resurrection morning.

One of the staff at the shrine said afterwards that he had probably listened to more addresses on the Blessed Virgin than most men alive but that he had seldom been more moved than by my discourse. So I was very thankful both to have cleared my own mind and to have had the opportunity of tackling an ecumenical fundamental. The paper was printed in *Churchman* of spring 1972.

Important debates were going on at the same time amongst evangelicals. I was asked to go to a theological students' meeting at Tyndale House to debate the question of inerrancy with Jimmy

Dunn (Professor James Dunn) and Ralph Martin. Though from the evangelical stable they did not want to affirm the doctrine of Warfield and Packer. In 1967 I published in *Tyndale Bulletin* the fruits of some research which I had been doing in connection with my big book on the Bible. I had already got some good ideas about the huge numbers of the Old Testament but I decided to spend about ten minutes each evening working systematically through its books. When I had got to the end, I felt that I had made good sense of nearly all of it except for the genealogies of the patriarchs in Genesis 5 and 11. The study gave credence to the idea that important corruptions of the original text had taken place but that when these had been detected there were very few serious difficulties left which could be properly attributed to the original text.

In 1969 the evangelical world was struck by what seemed to many of us a quite bizarre event. An English edition of the American book *The Genesis Flood: The Biblical Record and Its Scientific Implications* appeared. Its authors were J.C. Whitcomb, a well-qualified Old Testament scholar, and H.M. Morris, a well-qualified water engineer. This book of five hundred pages is regarded as the Creation Scientists' Bible. They argued that a straightforward interpretation of Genesis required three things: (1) that the flood literally covered the whole earth; (2) that the age of the earth, though rather longer than the date suggested by Ussher's 4,004 BC, was of that order and not the thousands of millions of years required by modern geology and cosmology; (3) that the creation took place in six days much like our present twenty-four hour day. They thought that these requirements could be met by the abandonment of conventional geology with its assumption of unchanging physical laws throughout the whole process of rock formation – catastrophism being called for rather than uniformitarianism. They thought that almost all the world's sedimentary rocks were laid down in the single year of the flood, and they suggested that the vast amount of water required to submerge the earth came from a huge 'vapor blanket' which had hitherto surrounded the earth. All was backed up by lucidly expressed scientific arguments which are well documented, some six hundred authors being referred to.

This book was the principal foundation of the creation-science movement which has gained many adherents, particularly in the USA. Societies which required a second degree in science as a condition of membership gained hundreds of enthusiastic members. The book was a shock to the evangelical world because the difficulties in Genesis 1–11 had been well known for more than a hundred years, and, though not fully and unanimously solved, they had seemed to pose no insuperable objection to biblical infallibility. Indeed the profundity of the early chapters of Genesis had always seemed to me a strong argument for divine inspiration. As far as I was concerned I was a great admirer of the science of historical geology, which had painstakingly unravelled the story of the rocks, and I regarded the thesis of Morris and Whitcomb's book as a load of dangerous nonsense – dangerous because naïve students embarking on a study of geology would be told that they must choose between believing the Bible or believing this science. This would create an intolerable tension in the minds of conscientious students, leading many to reject the Bible.

This movement creates a serious problem for those who wish to adhere to the view of Scripture which Jesus taught. Its strength lies in its epistemological starting point. It believes (quite rightly) that the Word of God should be the primary authority in all our thoughts. This is the genuine Christian position and wherever it is held with conviction it generates power. So it is to be entirely commended when Christians value the teaching of the Bible far above that of scientists who are suspected of unbelief. If an interpretation like that of Morris and Whitcomb is commended to them which seems natural and is itself supported by scientific arguments, it is not surprising if my views on historical geology are greeted with some scepticism. To me the geological record is remarkably clear – the hundreds of links between the phyla, classes and orders are as missing today as they were in Darwin's time; but this is a technical matter concerning which the layman is in the hands of the expert and he may find it difficult to know which authority to trust.

Another element in the strength of the creation-science movement is the sheer weight of common sense arguments against macroevolution. To think that the marvellous mechanisms all around us happened by chance is fantastic. The double helix of DNA is beautiful in its simplicity and awesome in its complexity. How did it begin? Are all the developments in evolution the result (as is generally supposed) of chance mistakes in the copying of DNA? What was thought of as a 'simple' cell is now known to be a highly automated factory. Wickramasingh said something to the effect that the likelihood of the human species happening by chance was less than the likelihood that a hurricane hitting a scrapyard might produce a Concorde. There are a million good reasons to encourage the fundamentalist to reject modern evolutionary science, such as those set out in Michael Denton's *Evolution: A Theory in Crisis* (Hutchinson, 1985) or Alan Hayward's *Creation and Evolution: Facts and Fallacies* (SPCK, 1985). The tragedy is that Christian scientists by and large have gone along with the evolutionary consensus and this has played into the hands of the creation-scientists. If we are to get a convincing Christian philosophy of life we need better exegesis than they are giving us and better science. Without it creation-science will continue to be an embarrassment to conservative Christianity.

Twenty-One

Summer Interlude — 1966

Life wasn't all heavy theology and tense ecclesiastical politics. In 1966 we had the opportunity of a wonderful family holiday. Although I had learnt to drive at the age of twelve I had never possessed a car of my own till I had reached my forties. In Bristol I had a good friend, Peter Wyatt, who was in the motor trade, whose help in buying a second-hand car was invaluable. My first car cost £40 and lasted three years. In 1966 we had a good solid Ford Consul which had already done a big mileage but was still trouble free. We found that the whole family was able to meet in Palestine in the summer. Of our sons, Gordon, the eldest, was just finishing his first year of post-graduate study which had started in Arab Jerusalem in the École Biblique and was ending in the Hebrew University on the Israeli side of the divided city. David at Cambridge had a long vacation. Peter was out in Iran gaining splendid first-hand experience of surgery helping in the CMS hospital in Isfahan. Michael was enjoying his school summer holiday. We decided to go out by road, all to meet up in Jerusalem.

Gordon and David had a friend from Pembroke College, Cambridge, Peter Warren, who was doing aerodynamics research in Bristol. He was quite handy with cars and we invited him to join us and share the driving. We loaded the car up with primitive camping gear and a massive supply of food so that we could do the trip economically. When we started off on 21 July there was an ominous bumping caused by the car being very low on the springs bringing the exhaust into contact with the bodywork. We planned to make our first stop at Cudham in Kent at my brother-in-law's vicarage, there to have supper before going on to Dover to catch the night ferry to Ostend. Worried about the exhaust, someone hit on the bright idea of bandaging it up with some heat-resistant cloth used for ironing. We set off and were cruising merrily along the main road when we were assailed by a terrible smell. We stopped the car and found that our 'bandage' was smouldering and then almost immediately it burst into flames right under the petrol tank. We managed somehow to stifle it with a newspaper (of all things) and then to cool it off with a little water. We breathed a sigh of relief, thankful for 'journeying mercies'.

We travelled on through Belgium and Germany greatly enjoying all the new scenes, until one evening near the Austrian border our worthy Consul just stopped. At first Peter couldn't find what was wrong; so David went off to summon help in the form of the German AA. While he was gone Peter discovered a loose lead to the distributor – which was embarrassing. However he left it disconnected and when the expert arrived Peter tactfully coaxed him towards the point of trouble. We unloaded the remains of our German currency on him and then sailed off, everyone happy. We had intended to camp near Salzburg, but it began to rain heavily and we knew that it would be hopeless to try to pitch tent; so we crossed the frontier heading for Vienna. We had become rather edgy about the car and heard above the sound of the rain an intermittent ticking noise which we thought must be something wrong with one of the wheels. We slowed down and opened the window and had a good laugh when we realized that it was only a chorus of noisy crickets along the roadside uttering their short, sharp bursts of sound in unison. So we pressed on, snatching some fitful sleep in a lay-by.

Vienna early on Sunday morning was almost completely dead. A little hotel, the Roter Hahn, was loath to take our bedraggled party in, but after a shower and breakfast and changed into some Sunday clothes we looked quite respectable. We enjoyed a siesta and a good night ready for the next day's drive to the Yugoslav border. A Yugoslav boy astonished us, seeming to know more about Bobby Charlton and the World Cup than we did. When we had passed through Bulgaria and arrived in Ankara in Turkey, needing to replace the car's exhaust, we found the British Embassy distinctly unhelpful as all the staff were listening to the final – which of course England won!

We spent our second Sunday in Ankara. The weather had now become hot – we had struck the hottest day of that year so far. Ankara was marvellous for its aggressive traffic and for its wonderful Ford repair workshop. We were guided to the latter by a kindly accountant. We were regaled with tea while a team descended upon the car, replacing the exhaust and repairing the horn with great expedition, and making only a modest charge before sending us on our way. We had some beautiful scenery, some terribly hot mosquito-ridden camp sites and eventually reached Syria and Lebanon. In Lebanon we passed an airfield which had parked on it an antique Italian trimotor biplane. Peter Warren, a connoisseur of such things, said, 'I would like a photograph of that.' So, slightly reluctantly, I pulled in to the side. No sooner had he taken his snap than a military policeman rode up on a motor- cycle and said, 'Follow me.' We drove into the airforce station; Peter was taken off for questioning and we were left in the blazing sun wondering what was happening. Grace was in tears; we foresaw great difficulty for an aerodynamics researcher hoping, in due course, to cross the border into the territory of the hated Israelis. We needn't have worried; they were entertaining him very pleasantly in the officers' mess and merely confiscated his film. But it was a salutary warning to us.

Arab Jerusalem had to be approached from the east. So we went through Amman and down to the stifling heat of the Jordan Valley; then up to Bethany on the other side for our last camp

before taking up residence for a few days at St George's hostel in
the city. Gordon in Israeli Jerusalem was cut off from us as traffic
was only allowed one way across the border. He had, however,
made good friends with a seventeen-year-old Arab youth called
Issam and his family. We did all the usual tourist sites in Jerusalem, as well as Bethlehem, Hebron, Jericho, Qumran, the Dead
Sea, Samaria, Sychar and Mount Gerizim. These had lost much
of the carefree pleasantness of the days before the post-war influx
of Jewish refugees and the division of the land into hostile camps.
Jerusalem itself had one specially interesting venue: Hezekiah's
tunnel which runs under the old city of David and which supplied
water to the people in times of siege. Gordon had arranged that
Issam should lead us through the tunnel but when we arrived
there we found that there was an official guide in uniform ready
to do the job. Issam asked to be allowed to sit in the car while we
waded, torches in hand, down to the Pool of Siloam which
provided the lower exit. When we had emerged we returned above
ground to the car park, but to our horror there was no car! We
hastened back to Siloam and down the road beyond the pool to
find the old Consul crashed at the roadside smothered in white
limestone dust. The naughty lad, whose father was a taxi-driver,
had obviously been overtaken by the temptation to drive the car
down to meet us. He had driven down to a turning-point and on
his way back to the pool had crashed the car. A wheel was
damaged, also the inside mirror, a bumper and the radiator. After
changing the wheel and tidying up, we tried the self-starter – and,
lo and behold, it purred into action as though nothing had
happened!

The MacInnes family took us in hand. Archdeacon MacInnes
was now Anglican Archbishop in Jerusalem and he arranged for
a garage to repair the car, which was again done amazingly
efficiently and cheaply. Mrs MacInnes was a qualified doctor and
she came to our rescue in a more serious matter. Peter, our third
son, had arrived from Iran on the Sunday quite unwell; by Friday

his temperature was 104.4 F, sandfly fever being suspected. Eventually jaundice was diagnosed and he was admitted to the Augusta Victoria Hospital which looks down upon the Old City. There he had to end his Jerusalem visit. Grace stayed behind to look after him, while the others of us went to join Gordon on the Israeli side. We had a further week's sight-seeing based on Haifa, by which time we were ready to head for home. I personally felt just saturated with experiences, feeling as though further adventures would merely drive out some of the memory of what had gone before. In addition, Michael was suffering from gippy tummy and I was not too happy at having deserted Grace and Peter.

So we took a boat of the Epirotiki Line to Piraeus. It was a real shocker, overcrowded, stinking, run by a grossly overworked crew. The passengers got up a protest to send to the management – it did nothing to endear Greek shipping magnates to us. We 'did' Athens before nightfall! The next day we had an unhurried visit to Delphi and then camped at the foot of Mount Olympus. After that it was full speed for home. The marvellous old Consul covered 450 miles a day without a murmur. We arrived at Venice overnight and 'did' it before breakfast! We had a beautiful run over the Simplon Pass and down to Lausanne. Next day we pressed on and crossed the Channel by a night ferry and so to Bristol in time for breakfast, delighted to find Grace and Peter, who had flown home, in good form. A truly wonderful family holiday!

Twenty-Two

Warden of Latimer House — 1970–73

In 1969 Stafford Wright retired from the principalship of Tyndale Hall and Jim Packer was invited to replace him. This left Latimer House without a warden, and I who had been secretary since the foundation of the original exploratory committee was invited to take over. This I accepted with a good deal of diffidence knowing that my academic gifts did not match those either of my predecessor or of my prospective colleague, Roger Beckwith. Both of these were quick workers with a prodigious range of interests, whereas I was slow with a limited focus of expertise.

In its decade of existence the tiny staff had done a remarkable work reinforcing the growing band of evangelicals in many directions. They had set up fifteen study groups which had been working on publication in the fields of Liturgy, Patronage, Missionary Theology, Church and Ministry, Tradition, Law and Morality, Ecclesiastical Polity, Preaching, Church and Community, Pastoral Reorganization, Church and Sacraments, Ecumenism, Sex and Marriage, Race Relations, Roman Catholicism and Eastern Orthodoxy. Philip Crowe, who was also part-time editor of the *Church of England Newspaper*, was giving half his time to pushing the groups along.

Roger Beckwith had written many articles and some books (besides working on a *magnum opus* on the Old Testament Canon) and had carried on a world-wide correspondence, particularly with Anglicans in different parts of the world who were working on prayer book revision.

Jim Packer's influence had been quite remarkable. Before coming to Latimer House he had made a name for himself not only by his *'Fundamentalism'* book, but also by his association with Martyn Lloyd-Jones in the promotion of Puritan and Reformed studies. Lloyd-Jones was a man of fine intellect totally given over to the preaching of the Bible, which he believed best understood and expounded by Calvinist divines like John Owen. He was a classical Independent with some Baptist leanings, who had little liking for and no very great understanding of Anglicanism. Both he and Packer thought that a revival of Puritan theology and pastoral practice was the key to true renewal in the church. During his time at Latimer House (it seemed to me providentially) Packer was not much concerned about such questions as limited atonement, which had so endeared him to some evangelicals and made him so suspect to others. He plunged wholeheartedly into the subjects which were agitating the wider church – authority, inspiration, and the doctrine of church, ministry and sacraments. And it was in this field that, almost single-handed, he decisively changed the course of English church history.

Great hopes had been centred on the move to unite the Church of England with the Methodist Church, the biggest (and historically closest) of the free churches. Their commissions had produced a scheme, unanimously approved by the Anglicans and approved by eight of the twelve Methodists. At the heart of this was a service to reconcile the ministries. It was so devised by its use of words and actions that in the eyes of classic Anglo-Catholicism the Methodist ministers were undoubtedly given proper episcopal ordination. But it was explicitly stated that no Methodist minister need believe that he either needed or had received a fresh ordination. This was set out with all the obscurity and ambiguity of the best ecumenese. Four members of the Methodist commission, all good scholars, refused to sign, and they produced a minority report in lucid English. When the matter came before us in the Anglican synods, it had a mixed reception and it was agreed to send it back for clarification.

The first commission had had no conservative evangelical member, which was recognized as a defect. So Packer was summoned. As the Methodist dissentients did not feel able to join in discussions which were intended merely to clarify the scheme, it was realized that Packer alone effectively represented the historic Protestant position. The Bishop of London, who was Anglican chairman, said in effect: 'A reunion scheme which does not unite is useless. Dr Packer, you have got to be satisfied.' So Horatius was left to defend the bridge. He was made one of the secretaries and did most of the drafting, insisting all the time that differences be spelt out clearly, to the great delight of most of the Methodists whose views he expressed better than they had been able to do. By the time they had finished Packer was almost reconciled to the scheme, but not quite. He felt that in conscience he still could not sign and he wrote a one-man dissenting report. The revised report was no longer acceptable to either evangelicals or Anglo-Catholics and was rejected; and that was almost the end of fudged attempts at reunion.

When I took over from Jim Packer (who incidentally became the chairman of the council) he had been passing through a very difficult period in his career. He had been devoting his gifts and energies to the reform of the church to which he had conscientiously given his allegiance, believing that Reformation and Puritan Anglicanism represented a strain of scriptural Christianity which it would be hard to better. His exhortation to evangelicals was therefore to drop their ghetto mentality, to get alongside their fellow-Anglicans and to accept responsibility in the leadership of the church. He campaigned strongly for this at the National Evangelical Anglican Congress at Keele in 1967, which caused great offence to his Free Church friends. Packer had no intention of suggesting that evangelicals should compromise their principles in the process of becoming more fully involved, but to Lloyd-Jones dialogue and co-operation was already compromise and a sheer waste of time. We Anglicans, on the other hand, thought that schism was wrong unless forced upon us; following the apostolic example we thought that the time to leave the synagogue was when we were driven from it. The last straw came for Packer when the book *All in Each Place* was published. He, Michael Green and Colin Buchanan had found real rapport with Eric Mascall and Graham Leonard, high Anglicans who believed fervently in Christian unity and who believed that truth must have primacy. They devised a reunion scheme based upon a common acceptance of fundamental Christian truth. To some of us it seemed to over-estimate the degree of unity actually achieved, but to Packer's Free Church friends it seemed no less than a denial of the faith. It led to a most unhappy rupture of fellowship which was to last for a long while.

The Latimer House council had been worried for some time that the staff for all their productive energy seemed to lack a clear set of priorities. Jim kept on telling us that he was working on a history of the Puritans (which appeared in a somewhat altered form in *Among God's Giants: Some Aspects of Puritan Christianity* in 1991!) and Roger that he was producing a book on the canon of the Old Testament (which appeared – a great work – in 1985). They seemed to have so many projects of varying value all going at once. I with my slow and tidy mind felt that it was essential to try to get our priorities clear. The council reaffirmed our three aims: to provide facilities to enable the staff to write; to encourage others to write; to help the evangelical cause in Oxford. It seemed to me that a research centre must be concerned with strategy rather than tactics. I was clear enough about my writing priority. It had seemed to me all my converted life that Protestant Christianity was based on the authority of Scripture, and that the truth of Scripture needed to be both asserted and defended. I had already worked for more than thirty years on The Christian View of the Bible and my priority was to get this published. That satisfied the first aim of Latimer House but I was very conscious that there was nothing specifically Anglican in it. The second aim was being fulfilled to some extent by the study groups. The third aim had always been dear to my heart. Oxford had hundreds of able teachers and students from all over the world who were in some way interested in theology. They were strategic people and work amongst them, though not immediate in its results, was potentially most fruitful.

I immediately got down to a great sorting out and throwing out of the ten years' accumulation of paper-work. The library still had many books uncatalogued and I worked also on that. It was doing this that brought to my attention a totally unsuspected clue to the understanding of the synoptic problem. There was a book by G.R. Balleine, already well known to me as author of the lively *A History of the Evangelical Party in the Church of England*. It was a popular book, but quite scholarly, entitled *Simon Surnamed Peter*. In it he argued that when Peter escaped from prison in AD 42 and went 'to another place', that other place was Rome. I rubbed my eyes and read with astonishment. Here was I who had been reading and teaching the New Testament all these years and this idea had never come my way. I read it and got others to read it; I wrote a paper on it and eventually got *Tyndale Bulletin* (23, 1972) to publish an article 'Did Peter go to Rome in AD 42?' It threw a flood of light on the later history of Peter and it opened up exciting possibilities about the dating of the synoptics. I was immensely cheered when J.A.T. Robinson in 1976 quite independently came to the same conclusion.

We reviewed all that the study groups were doing. Some had completed their work and had produced worthwhile publications. Others were going very slowly, being led by busy people who hadn't the time to put real drive into them. I was anxious about the liturgy group led by Roger Beckwith because prayer book revision was coming on apace and I was afraid that our publications would not be out in time to influence events. Roger asked to be relieved of the chair and I offered it to Colin Buchanan, who had already shown amazing drive in the liturgical commission. Colin began to produce once a month his punchy and up-to-date Grove booklets. It was, I think, the deepest disappointment of my wardenship that Colin and Roger could never work really happily together. They were two superb brains fundamentally at one in their aims and complementary in their temperaments. Roger was not averse to change, but his instincts were conservative; he knew the arguments of the earlier theologians and armed with this knowledge his instinct was to think immediately of all the objections to any new idea. Colin, on the other hand, was bursting with new ideas and he was always ready to fly a kite whether it was well thought out or not. If only those two had worked together criticizing and challenging each other, Latimer House would have been a formidable force. As it was Grove publications came to be thought of as somewhat trendy, and Latimer publications as a bit out of touch.

As far as my *magnum opus* was concerned I was in a lot of trouble. I presented the whole manuscript to IVP and they came back with the altogether sensible comment that it was too ambitious for an unknown author and that it would be better broken up into (say) four volumes. I immediately accepted this and IVP was anxious to get its hands on the first volume straightaway. (This eventually appeared as *Christ and the Bible*.) To me the whole project was a single concept and I always felt that the whole added up to much more than the parts. Looking back now on the subsequent history I feel sure that I must have been guided by the Holy Spirit, for I insisted that they could have volume 1 – which covered Christ's authority, his view of Scripture, his authentication of the New Testament, the extent of the canon and the reliability of the text – provided they undertook to publish volume 2, which dealt with the moral difficulties of the Bible. This they agreed to do. Then trouble began.

To me the greatest moral difficulty in the Bible is Hell. That God should create beings capable of knowing and loving him and should then finally dismiss them from his presence for ever seemed to me more shocking than any of his temporal judgments. So when dealing with these judgments I said that, since as Christians we must accept Christ's teaching on hell, it is foolish to boggle overmuch with the lesser judgments. Then I set out our Lord's teaching on hell in the very words of Scripture. I knew that it was impracticable to develop the theme, which would require a whole book, so I thought it best to let the biblical imagery speak for itself. The IVP reader commented: I thought you would give us some help at this point, but you simply say, 'This is Christ's teaching, take it or leave it.' I saw at once that this was a valid criticism. I realized that it is all very well just to give the biblical imagery but none of us come to the Bible with blank minds. Our culture has been coloured by Dante, Milton, medieval paintings and by various non-Christian influences. Yes, people need some help. And I myself had had great help for many years from a belief in conditional immortality. I had come to question the immortality of man, seeing immortality as something which is acquired when we receive eternal life and become partakers of the divine nature – partakers of the nature of the one 'who alone has immortality'. Yes, I can certainly give some help. So I wrote three short pages advocating the ultimate annihilation of all evil. At this IVP were up in arms – 'We can't publish this, it will upset our supporters.'

This led to a lengthy correspondence in which I pointed out two things. (1) I was acting on the sensible suggestion of their own reader which they themselves had handed on to me. (2) The ultimate aim of all the work which we were putting into biblical research was not improvement in our understanding of archaeological and philological minutiae, but in deepening our grasp of basic biblical doctrine. In 1954 the Tyndale Fellowship had given a whole conference to the study of the fate of the lost, which had confirmed my belief in conditional immortality, a view shared by many of IVF's staunchest supporters, like Basil Atkinson, Harold Guillebaud, Stafford Wright, Robert Clark and Norman Anderson. It was outrageous that a view held by Bible students who were completely loyal to the IVF basis of faith could not even be gently mentioned as a serious possibility. It was putting expediency before truth.

Eventually we had a top-level meeting in London at which the whole matter was discussed. I was frankly amazed at how little these Christian leaders seemed to have thought about the matter. They believed that most of their neighbours were unsaved and heading, unreformed and irreformable, to an existence of everlasting torment; yet they had never seriously faced up to the horror of their beliefs and looked at alternative ways of understanding the texts. In the end I suggested that I should state the two views as clearly and forcefully as I could and leave it to the reader to make up his own mind. They agreed to this, and so a great watershed was crossed. I don't think that any evangelical publishers jealous of their orthodoxy had previously consented to do this at any time during the twentieth century. I was thankful that my own views were so firm and that I had been guided to insist that IVP could not have volume 1 unless they consented to take volume 2.

This lengthy palaver was embarrassing, because I, like the other members of staff, had been promising a major work which never seemed to appear. It was not till my third year at Latimer House was well advanced that *Christ and the Bible* saw the light of day. I had said that I had hoped to produce the four volumes in my first four years. In fact it was more than twenty years before volume 4 appeared. I did, however, produce one genuinely Anglican little book in 1972, *The Renewal and Unity of the Church in England* to which I have already referred. Unlike my laborious books on the Bible which took roughly ten years apiece to write, this was something which I wrote off the top of my head in about a month. It was commissioned by SPCK – I believe the first book on a controversial subject by an evangelical published by that society within living memory. Unfortunately they greatly overpriced it and a good many copies ended up as pulp.

In fulfilment of the third aim I gave a great deal of time to cultivating graduate and undergraduate theological students. I remember particularly Chris Sugden and Tom Wright, now back with us in Oxford. Tom Wright says that it was I who suggested that he should take up academic work – though I don't in the least remember the occasion.

Perhaps the most memorable of all my student contacts was Josif Ton. He was a pastor in the Baptist Church in Romania which had suffered much persecution. The church had, I believe, two hundred pastors only two of whom were graduates; these were trying to minister to a fairly well-educated population. Josif saw the need to get himself theologically trained so that he could give a better training to future pastors. The government for a short time eased restrictions on the churches; Josif saw his opportunity and got permission to come to Regent's Park College in Oxford during this honeymoon period to study theology. At the end of his first year he was ordered home, and he had to decide whether to obey the state or to obey God and see his course through. After he had got a good second class degree he was visited by his old friend Richard Wurmbrand, who had suffered terribly in Romanian gaols. Wurmbrand told him that it was no use his going back, it would only mean prison and torture; he would do more good staying in the West, telling the world what Communism was really like. I saw him the next day; he said that he had been through the worst day of his life. But he had wrestled it out with God and he believed that he should go back utterly defenceless – saying, 'You can do with me just what you like.' He went back and surprisingly had considerable freedom, getting large student audiences. The one part of the work which was not prospering was pastor training, because they had no adequate textbooks in Romanian. He began to feel the need to get out of the country, gather together a group of translators and get some seventy basic theological textbooks rendered into Romanian. But it was not easy to get out of a Communist country. However, the authorities began to be worried and started subjecting him to ruthless daily interrogations. When they threatened him with death, a threat which they would have had no compunction in carrying out, he said that he would count it the greatest privilege to die for the Master who had died for him. Furthermore, he said, his death would greatly strengthen the work, because his sermons were circulating on tapes all over the country, and their influence would multiply tenfold if they knew that the author had died for his beliefs. The authorities evidently believed him, for one day they brought him his passport and told him to go and not come back for a long time. When Ceauşescu was killed forty books had been translated in America and Josif returned ready to build on sound theological foundations.

The result of my frustrations at Latimer House was that when two and a half years had passed and the extension of my appointment came up for reconsideration, I did not have much to show for it. I hadn't even articles to my name. Nearly all my work was on some aspect of the Christian view of the Bible, which I did not wish to get lost in miscellaneous journals but preferred to keep all together in the one book. I had, as it happens, made one discovery at this time which threw light on a knotty Old Testament problem. It is very puzzling in 1 Samuel 17:58 that Saul does not seem to recognize David who had been both his lyre player and armour-bearer. None of the pre-critical explanations seem at all satisfactory; so there is strong temptation to posit two contradictory sources. One day Gordon and I – he with his Hebrew Bible and I with my English one – sat down together to look at the passage. Suddenly inspiration came. Saul does not say, 'Who are you, young man?' but 'Whose son are you, young man?' All that is needed to make sense of the passage is the supposition that Samuel's secret visit to anoint one of Jesse's sons had been reported to Saul in the form, 'It is rumoured that your old enemy Samuel anointed one of Jesse's sons as future king.' Saul realizes for the first time that the son in question may have been David when it is too late to do anything about it. The whole sequence from 1 Samuel 16 onwards makes wonderful dramatic sense. I passed this suggestion on to someone who was writing a commentary on the book. He said that it was ingenious but, alas, did not mention it when he came to expound the text.

The council had always thought of my appointment as short-term, and though they offered me an extension of one year, my time was effectively at an end. Both the Beckwiths and ourselves were quite hurt at this termination of our partnership as our working together had been most cordial. What disappointed me most was the fact that no one on the council as far as I knew had read *Christ and the Bible*. This to me was a strategic book but I knew that some members of the council did not really believe in defending the Bible. Shortly after I was offered part-time work in a country parish, which promised to allow me time for continued academic work, and the wardenship was put into the capable hands of my learned and well-loved colleague Roger.

Twenty-Three

Cottisford — 1973–75

We moved to Cottisford where I became officially assistant rector of the Shelswell Group. This group was on the northern edge of Oxfordshire. Our address was Cottisford, Brackley, Northants and the rector's address was Newton Purcell, Buckingham, Bucks, but we both lived in Oxfordshire. I had the care of two of the smallest of the five villages in the group: Cottisford and Hardwick. There were in fact four settlements: Hardwick church was in a tiny village in the parish of which belonged also the Tusmore estate, and Cottisford parish had in addition a hamlet known as Juniper Hill. The latter was famous as the home of Flora Thompson, author of *Lark Rise to Candleford*. Flora attended school at Cottisford in the 1880s leaving at the age of twelve with the sole distinction of having gained one prize for scripture. She lived in abject poverty owing to her father's drinking but read ravenously anything she could lay hands on. She wrote some articles recalling her childhood days, which came to the attention of Sir Humphrey Millford of the Oxford University Press. He encouraged her in her sixties to write up her memories in three short volumes. By 1954 they were all in The World's Classics – a wonderful bedside book: never exciting, never dull, often amusing.

My rector, John Sergeant, and his wife Amy were a brave couple, having suffered terrible family tragedies and yet remaining cheerful. Our paths did not cross a great deal, though I ministered occasionally in the churches for which he was mainly responsible and he in mine. Cottisford and Hardwick were beautiful churches with immaculate churchyards, and my total population was about 150 – I could pray for them all by name. Cottisford had Holy Communion every Sunday morning – this was a said service with hymns, an arrangement which I liked in every way. But I was soon faced with a dilemma: the small adult congregation was occasionally joined by a child or two for whom the service seemed rather meaningless. So I tried to find out what hymns the children knew and liked. I invited them to a hymn-singing tea party to which nearly all the Cottisford children came. I promised them that at least one of the hymns which they liked would be sung every Sunday morning. I encouraged those who played recorders to stand by the organ and add to the accompaniment.

The rectory was rather large and burdensome with a fine seventeenth-century barn and a large garden. We decided to try to make the best of this. The barn we made into a slightly undersized badminton court and we extended the lawn to make it into a tennis court. (The back netting posed a problem as hedgehogs got caught in it at night. I patented some 'edge 'og 'ooks for hitching up the net after play!) We had croquet and clock-golf, and indoors billiards and darts. (We had to watch the larder door with some care as one of the lads was light-fingered.) I think that at one time or another all the children of the village crossed the rectory threshold. But all this was not doing much to tell the children about Jesus.

I persuaded Stephen English of the Scripture Union staff to take an interest in the parish. He took a series of excellent meetings and led a holiday club one summer which drew in a number of older people from the parish as helpers. Eventually I had a small confirmation class, which I did not feel was very successful. One could only pray that some of the teaching would bear fruit in due course. The same applied to preaching. I preached once to a Cottisford evensong congregation of about four. An artist lady afterwards said, 'That was a magnificent sermon; it ought to have been preached in a great city church.' But she never came to church again except once when I inveigled her into church to judge some children's pictures!

Evangelism was fundamentally a one-to-one task. At Hardwick there was a fairly elderly bachelor called Ned. He was a good-living man who could not read; so one could not invite him to church. As his dialect was extremely difficult to follow, he presented a real puzzle to the evangelist. We asked him to come two afternoons a week to help with the rectory garden for a couple of hours. When he had finished work we would sit him down in the kitchen with a cup of tea for a chat. Then Grace and I would prompt each other when one of us followed his dialect and the other didn't. Ned obviously enjoyed coming. Then he was twice taken off to hospital with cancer. One day when I was told that he had been taken in again I drove straight round to see him. To my surprise he was sitting up in bed looking quite perky. I offered to read the Psalm of the Good Shepherd to him and afterwards prayed. That night he died happily and at peace with God.

At Hardwick also there was a mother with two school-age children, who nursed some great grudge against the rector. When I called she wouldn't come to the door; she would hardly speak to her neighbours; she seemed like a hunted animal. In the next village, Hethe, which was not under my care, lived a retired parson and his widowed mother, John and Mrs Westlake, who used to come to Cottisford church. I mentioned her to them. They said, 'If there are any matters about which you would like prayer, please let us know.' I gave them a little list and had a note in response, 'My mother and I are already at work.' This lady was taken off to hospital in Oxford also with cancer. There an Australian doctor did a wonderful job on her body giving great relief, while God did something wonderful to her soul. She came back to Hardwick a different woman, talking to her neighbours and waking each morning to read the Scriptures and to pray. I was much moved at her funeral.

Another character was an ex-prize-fighter. An illegitimate child, he had had to learn to use his fists. Happily I reminded him of a curate whom he had known in his youth who was skilled in the martial arts – little did he know what a coward I am! He had some deep-seated grudges which made him a most awkward member of the church – virtually the leader of the opposition. He read *Run Baby Run* by Nicky Cruz, the converted drug addict and gang leader of New York, and told me one night that he was burying the hatchet. After that he was a different man. Talking about cowardice, I had an amusing illustration of the difference between theory and practice when I preached one day at Hardwick. I have always been afraid of unknown animals – I cannot even cross a field of cows or meet a yapping dog without a sinking feeling in the pit of the stomach. I preached on the power of God, arguing that God's power was far greater than that of the forces he had put in the universe, which I illustrated from the forces of a supernova explosion and the Hot Big Bang. Why fear? It was stupid of us not to trust him implicitly. As I left the church a dog that had given my wife a painful bite in the calf the previous week came down the churchyard path. My immediate reaction was barely disguised terror! So much for our simplistic recipes.

I had another amusing incident at Hardwick, which reminded me of a saying of Keith de Berry (once rector of St Aldate's Church in Oxford) shortly after he was ordained. He said that the only useful thing he had learnt at his theological college was the correct way to hold a baby in baptism. The local squire's son had invited a well-known theologian to baptize his child. To my horror he held the baby along his arm so that its head dangled loose at the end – I was afraid it might do itself an injury. So much for theologians!

I was impressed by the general paganism of the countryside. There was a handful of churchgoers to whom the things of God meant quite a lot and of whom I became very fond, but I used to say sadly of Cottisford parish that there were only two homes bar the rectory where God was actually put first – and they were homes of Jehovah's Witnesses. I got on surprisingly well with them, because they recognized that I knew and believed the Bible. I even went to one of their annual communion services. The sermon was a genuine attempt to expound the epistle to the Romans but the promises of the gospel were said to be only for the 144,000. The JWs started as a small sect and they saw themselves as the 144,000 servants of God mentioned in Revelation 17 who were to be sealed with the divine seal. When the movement gained millions of members they thought that the promises must apply only to a core of the faithful who had an inner assurance of salvation. So when the communion bread was passed round, hardly anyone (if anyone at all) partook of it. It was sad. The Roman Catholics were also sad. There were more than a dozen of them in my parishes but, in spite of a church at Hethe nearby, I think only one of them went regularly to mass.

Another interesting contact made while at Cottisford resulted from a book entitled *God's Truth* (revised edition, Lakeland, 1977) which was sent to me for review. It was by Alan Hayward, an author of whom I hadn't heard, but I was impressed by his defence of the Bible, amongst other things skilfully negotiating the minefields of prophecy and also provoking my curiosity by his reference to biological journals in which evolution was questioned. He alluded to open-air preaching and confessed to having smuggled Bibles in behind the Iron Curtain. He was head of the National Physical Laboratory in Glasgow, so I wrote to him saying that I would like to meet him. He came down to stay with us and I was surprised to find that he was not very interested in talking about evolution but that he called himself an evangelical member of the Christadelphian Church and was anxious to widen his contacts with other Christians. Christadelphians believe in the whole Bible but disagree with traditional interpretations at a number of points. For instance they believe in the virgin birth, resurrection and second coming of Christ, but not in his pre-existence; and so not in the Trinity or incarnation. They believe in conditional immortality, which traditionalists use as an argument against the likes of me – we suffer by guilt of association with anti-trinitarians. Alan and I became and have remained good friends ever since, having much to discuss in common and little time to discuss our differences. There are grave divisions within the Christadelphian church, conservatives wishing to keep strictly to the old ways and progressives wishing to widen their horizons. Alan has written other books since: *God Is* and *Creation and Evolution: Facts and Fallacies* (SPCK, 1985). He belongs to the select company of those who reject macro-evolution and equally vehemently reject theories of a young earth.

The one really important piece of academic work completed was Volume 2 of The Christian View of the Bible, which dealt with the moral difficulties of the Bible and of providence. It came out under the title *The Goodness of God*, a title chosen because I wanted it to be seen as a positive rather than as a defensive statement. However it was later pointed out to me that this is not the place where Christians itch. We are all happy at the thought of the goodness of God. Where we itch is the problem of evil. So the title was changed in 1985 to *The Enigma of Evil*. In this book the question of animal pain comes in. My time in the country did little to change my views on this subject. I don't like the hunting of animals but I cannot get excited about the matter; it is too like nature, the supposed cruelty of which is greatly exaggerated. I think there is greater pain inflicted in shooting where injured birds get away. My deepest dislike is for factory farming – I am haunted by the sight and sound of battery hens dishevelled and moaning in their tiny compartments.

On the domestic front, the boys were all getting married and grandchildren began to arrive. David was married in Cottisford church and the reception was held in the beautiful setting of the rectory garden. Grace was a wonderful mother-in-law, amazingly sensitive to the feelings of the young couples. Her philosophy was that there are many different ways of bringing up a family and no one way is the right one. One of the boys paid this tribute to her: 'She never made any of us feel that she was criticizing the way we were doing things.' It was sad that she was not going to live long enough for her grandchildren really to get to know her.

My week-end job was threatening to become a full-time one with The Christian View of the Bible being the casualty. I felt I must decide whether to stay on and hope that Cottisford would become a strong rural centre to which people who wanted a vigorous ministry of the Word would come, or whether to retire and get on with the book. I reckoned that it must be the latter but I was loath to leave the parish without a strong successor. The diocese was busy selling vicarages and amalgamating parishes in a manner that looked to me like pure retrenchment. When I wrote *The Renewal and Unity of the Church in England* I had advocated moving towards a church which was self-propagating and as far as possible self-supporting and self-governing. That meant local churches which were neither dependent upon nor constricted by the central church but able to grow by generating their own resources. I thought that there might well be in Oxford (only twenty miles away) a 'live' young man who was doing theological research but was no mere bookworm, who would welcome a house to live in, a small part-time stipend and an outlet for active pastoral ministry. I asked the Cottisford people if they would be willing to support such a man. Enough promises were forthcoming to make it look quite feasible. But the diocesan authorities showed no real interest; they were intent on selling off the rectory. They opposed the idea 'because it might create a precedent'. I wrote an article for *The Church Times* with the refrain 'it might create a precedent'. I pointed out how marvellous it would be if all over the country parishes were saying, 'We will provide the cash, if you will provide the man.' This is a recipe for advance,

whereas centralized control financed by crippling parish shares
is a sure recipe for retreat. The diocese did not like the article very
much but I hope that some of our future leaders read it and will
in due course apply the lesson.

My sister Susan, who had retired to Allington near Salisbury,
found us a pleasant cottage in the village which she helped us to
buy. So after three happy years we said good-bye to our friends
of the Shelswell group and departed to start a hard-working
retirement.

Twenty-Four

Allington — 1975–80

Chapel Cottage and its garden were both small and easily managed. As its name might suggest, it was semi-detached from the
Methodist chapel, which was still functioning. Allington church
was one of the four churches which constituted the upper end of
the Bourne Valley group. The valley lay amongst the rolling chalk
hills north of Salisbury and the Bourne (an intermittent stream)
flowed behind our house in the winter months. Though it was very
pleasant countryside one was not allowed to forget the twentieth
century, for up the farm track to one side was the highly secret
Porton Down establishment, the centre for chemical and biological warfare; and on the other side was Boscombe Down, whence
Harrier jump-jets came over with shattering roars.

At the top end of the valley was Cholderton which had a
church like a miniature cathedral. Apparently a nineteenth-
century incumbent with more money than sense had got hold of
a fine roof which he transported to Cholderton. He pulled down
the little Saxon church which then existed and built this larger
structure for his roof. It was far too large for the needs of the
village, expensive to keep in repair and perishing cold in winter.
Heating was not the only problem; there was also considerable
difficulty in finding adequate organists in these village churches.
I remember being puzzled when a well-known hymn was announced and the organist appeared to be playing an unusual tune.

It turned out that the usual tune was intended, but was not recognizable! We normally attended whichever Anglican church had a morning service and then joined our Methodist neighbours in the evening. I felt sorry for a vicar from the East End of London who valiantly undertook the task of looking after these four churches. Trained by the Southwark Ordination Course he came with considerable zeal and with a sense of humour to this totally new experience. I did my best to back him up but I fear that my presence was as much an embarrassment as a help.

As with many villages today a large proportion of the inhabitants were not native to the district. I got particularly friendly with the Dawkins household from Northumberland. It was a case of a geriatric couple looking after a super-geriatric. Ralph and Rene Dawkins cared for Ralph's mother who lived to over a hundred years of age. They had had some Christian teaching when young but had turned against it seeing the injustices maintained by the privileged classes in their young days in the north-east. They came to church or chapel only on the rarest occasions. The old mother was very deaf and used to complain, 'Why doesn't God take me?' I told her, 'God knows best.' Ralph went down with cancer and while in hospital began to open up spiritually in a wonderful way. He clearly died rejoicing in his new found faith and I was privileged to take the funeral. At the house afterwards with all the guests chatting his mother looked very lonely. She asked me for her slate to write on. She wrote, 'God knows best.'

Another contact was an ex-army sergeant recently rescued from alcoholism by Alcoholics Anonymous. He was diligently following the AA routine: meditating, seeking the help of a power outside himself, working to help other alcoholics. We at once found ourselves on a common wavelength, though I was always sorry that he seemed to live on a thin spiritual diet and wished that he might know Jesus as Saviour and find the warmth of a live Christian fellowship. Some fifteen years later he wrote a letter full of joy to tell me that this had happened and that he was about to be baptized.

In 1976 Jim Packer, who had become associate principal of Trinity College, Bristol, and a member of the Doctrine Commission of the Church of England, lent his signature to the commission's report *Christian Believing*. The chairman in the preface calls it 'a joint report carefully worked out and subscribed to by all the members.' Then follows an account of faith and the Bible which seemed to me searingly liberal. For example, 'The men of the New Testament corrected or rewrote earlier histories; they denounced error with a violence of language that verged at times on the frenzied or the obscene' (p. 28). The historic view of Scripture nowhere comes over in the report except in contexts where it is criticized. I wrote to Jim in protest, it being so out of character with his '*Fundamentalism*'. I thought that he must have signed up because with his many commitments he had not been able to give enough time to the commission. But after discussing it with him I came to think that his background and interests made him unable to attempt a more effective contribution.

He was, however, shortly to show that his heart was still where it was in the early days. He was not altogether happy at Trinity College, Bristol, and found himself in considerable demand on the other side of the Atlantic. Thus when in 1978 he was offered a job at Regent College in Vancouver which promised him a sphere with no administration and plenty of opportunity for writing, he accepted. The North American conservative evangelicals were much concerned at the growth of liberal ideas in their ranks, so they launched the International Council for Biblical Inerrancy which held a big conference in Chicago in that year, which I attended and in which Jim played a prominent part. He was, I think, the main drafter of the pronouncement on inerrancy which came from that assembly.

Just before the Chicago conference there had been a great assault on the conservative position by James Barr, Oriel Professor of the Interpretation of Holy Scripture in the University of Oxford. The liberal theological leadership had long watched with frustration the steady growth of the conservative movement which they thought so wrong-headed and dangerous. Barr, who had come into conflict with the IVF leaders in his student days, launched his attack in *Fundamentalism* (SCM, 1977). It was a book of 379 lucid pages. I began reading it one evening and found myself hooked. The author clearly knew a lot about the subject but he seemed to get it just a little wrong at each point. I took the book to bed with me and then realized that I would not be able to sleep, so I read on until I had finished it next morning at eleven o'clock. This was the first of a number of books by Barr on the same theme and we were to have several amicable contacts later on. I came to the conclusion that he genuinely wanted to preserve the authority of the Bible but that his attempts to do so were totally unsuccessful, because he accepted virtually without question that modern critical methods were sound, whereas I was sure that they were unsound. I maintained that the doctrines of biblical authority and biblical infallibility came straight out of the Bible itself and could be satisfactorily defended in detail. Once this is accepted there is no valid objection to treating the Bible in the traditional way.

This led to one of several abortive attempts at publication while at Allington. I was frustrated by the fact that I had much useful research in the bag, garnered for The Christian View of the Bible, but I did not know how to present it in relevant publishable form. I thought that Barr needed answering and that part of the answer should consist of a repudiation of the critical methods on which he relied. 1978 was the centenary of the publication of Wellhausen's *Prolegomena to the History of Ancient Israel*, the book which has probably done greater harm to the Christian church than any book published in her long history. So in 1977 I wrote a book *Fundamentalism and Antifundamentalism* 'in which is celebrated the centenary of Wellhausen's *Prolegomena* and a fresh look is taken at the higher criticism of the Bible and the question is considered, Which side took the wrong turning?' The book was not a direct reply to Barr, but it consisted of five chapters on higher criticism together with a review of Barr's book and a chapter on the vexed question of inerrancy. The five chapters dealt with Daniel, the documentary theory of the Pentateuch, the role of Moses, gospel origins and gospel harmony.

IVP thought that it would not be possible to do an adequate job in time for the centenary, and they also doubted whether detailed consideration of critical problems was the best approach; Barr was better answered 'at the level of theological principle'. This was the old idea reasserting itself that you don't defend the Bible. The point about catching the centenary was certainly right, for correspondence and committee meetings dragged on and I had to drop the idea. The work on gospel origins and gospel harmony was eventually to see the light of day in fuller form in *Redating Matthew, Mark and Luke* and *Easter Enigma*.

On first reading Barr's book I was astonished that he entirely omitted his former Manchester colleague Fred Bruce from his assault on IVF scholarship. Bruce alone shared with Matthew Black the distinction of having been President of both the Old and the New Testament Societies, and he had played a prominent part in building up IVF scholarship; why not mention him? Barr reckoned that Bruce was a conservative liberal rather than a liberal conservative. In other words his thought was governed by a deep faith in Christ, which did not include belief in any clearly formulated doctrine of Scripture. As an IVF reviewer said of his big book *Paul: Apostle of the Free Spirit* (1977):

> There is a noticeable lack of any detailed consideration of such doctrines as the atonement, election, scripture and apostolic authority. He presents Paul's teaching as the developing thought of an apostle, formed out of his exceptional experience of Christ, rather than as the inspired truth

of God. Whilst for the most part reaching conservative conclusions, he appears to proceed on largely liberal assumptions.

I came to believe that Barr was right and I am sure that Bruce's influence on the whole evangelical constituency has been immense. So great was his scholarship and so clear his presentation that 'Bruce says' was inevitably to many a stronger reason for belief or disbelief than any particular arguments. The result has been a neglect of Christ's view of Scripture and a noticeable liberalizing of the Tyndale Fellowship for Biblical Research.

Another abortive effort concerned the relating of Genesis 1–11 to modern knowledge. I have long been impressed by the fundamental place of these chapters in the divine revelation. I have no doubts about their direct inspiration by God but they present considerable difficulties to those who are attempting a sound reconciliation of the two. In a sense I regard the scientific questions as quite peripheral. Most people are converted without the slightest thought concerning evolution or cosmology and most Christian scientists get along happily enough regarding evolution as God's method of creation. But when one tries to look at the total picture vast questions are raised: What are the credentials of science in general and of biology and cosmology in particular? Does the New Testament teach that Adam and Eve were figures in history? Was the Fall an event in history? What are we to think of the Flood? and so on. I was personally convinced that large scale evolution is a myth which we must reject if we are to get the total picture right. I did a lot of reading in this field and wrote eleven chapters of a book, *The God Who Made the Universe: An Exploration of Science and the Book of Genesis*. The chapter titles were The Coming of the Scientific Age, The Rise and Decline of Reductionism, Further Limitations of Reductionism, Uniformitarian Dogma and Christian Pliability, Towards a Christian Philosophy of Science: Some

False Trails, The Christian Faith-Way: The Primacy of Revelation, The Christian Faith Way: The Doctrine of God and Scientific Law, Bringing Science and Scripture Together, The Story of the Cosmos, Is Evolution a Fact?, Embryology and Vestigial Organs. And there, alas, the work came to a stop, never even to be looked at by a publisher.

I made good progress with the section on the harmony of the resurrection narratives and thought that the last piece in the jigsaw puzzle had fallen into place. But I sent it to IVP and they turned it down. I think this was at least partly because their theological advisers were no longer friendly towards the harmonizing enterprise. As a liberal reviewer said later on, 'You can't do your New Testament work that way; you must do the critical work first.' The book (which was eventually to appear as *Easter Enigma*) simply set out to examine the question whether the resurrection narratives contradicted one another. There was no endeavour to show knowledge of the mountain of modern literature on these passages; it was simply an attempt (assuming the stories to be true) to present in the most straightforward manner their natural meaning. The result was a book very unlike the typical modern New Testament study, but it was a valid effort at answering an important question.

My academic work did bear a little fruit. It was at this time that I began to have serious doubts about our current views on the text of the New Testament. I had assumed that the text which Westcott and Hort had bequeathed to the world and the eclectic texts which followed in their footsteps were basically right, and had said so in *Christ and the Bible*. Maybe the process of moving house had caused me to look at my books again. Anyway, there was one book which I had bought for 6d from David's bookstall in the Cambridge market-place as a student, which had long lain on my shelves unread. It was by George Salmon, the mathematician turned theologian of Trinity College, Dublin, whose *The Infallibility of the Church* and *A Historical Introduction to the*

Study of the Books of the New Testament were already well known to me. I had picked it up because I thought it had some interesting things to say on biblical inspiration. I hadn't taken an interest in its primary subject matter: *Some Thoughts on the Textual Criticism of the New Testament.* Salmon had followed the great debate between Burgon and Scrivener on the one side, who believed that the *textus receptus* which underlay the Authorised Version was basically right, and Westcott and Hort on the other side, who believed that Codex Vaticanus, the text of which so greatly affected the Revised Version, was nearest to the original text. Hort's theory won the day and was accepted nearly everywhere. Salmon, however, was not convinced by either side and thought at first that he would take his doubts with him to the grave, but then felt increasingly that Hort's complete victory was unjustified and unhealthy and that he should put his thoughts on paper.

I had long been interested in questions of gospel harmony and a hint from Salmon led me to write an article which was published in *New Testament Studies* (Vol 25, July 1979) entitled 'How Many Cock-Crowings? The Problem of Harmonistic Text-Variants', in which I argued that Mark's apparent mention of a second crowing was due to textual corruption. It was quite a good argument if one accepted the Hort text, since it owed nothing to a belief in the *textus receptus* (or to the Byzantine or Majority text).

Another question of gospel harmony was the problem of reconciling Matthew's account of the rich young ruler with that of Mark and Luke. In the latter the young man addresses Jesus as 'Good Master' and Jesus replies 'Why do you call me good?' Whereas in the former (according to the Hort text) he simply says 'Master' and Jesus replies 'Why do you ask me about the Good?' N.B. Stonehouse in his *Origins of the Synoptic Gospels* gives a whole chapter to the reconciliation of these two which I had found quite unconvincing. Salmon, however, shows most convincingly that the Hort text is almost certainly not the original text, which ran 'Good Master, what good thing must I do

. . .' and Jesus replies as in Mark and Luke, 'Why do you call me good?'

I saw at once that this had an important bearing on the synoptic problem, for there were at least four synoptic theories in current circulation. So I wrote an article, 'Why Do You Ask Me About The Good? A Study of the Relation Between Text and Source Criticism', which was also accepted for *New Testament Studies* and published in January, 1982. Then to my great surprise I received notice that the Society of New Testament Studies at its next meeting, which was to take place in Durham in 1979, was to debate this passage in its Synoptic Problem seminar. I knew that something like what did happen would happen: Margaret Thrall tried to explain why Matthew had so altered Mark and Bernard Orchard tried to explain how Mark had come so to alter Matthew. I realized that if I was right, they were debating a non-question because they had got the text wrong. I sent my article to Professor Bo Reicke, the chairman of the seminar, in Basle, who asked me to come and read it. I then fell sick, but I tottered up to Durham not long out of hospital and my paper was received without demur. I came back saying to Grace, 'This is the group I have got to satisfy if I am to do anything serious on the synoptic problem,' and I continued to attend the society's meetings till the seminar packed up in 1982.

At about this time I also read Wilbur Pickering's *The Identity of the New Testament Text* (Nashville: Nelson, 1977) – not a perfect book but sufficient to persuade me that the Byzantine type of text was better than the modern texts. I wrote a review to this effect which F.F. Bruce accepted for the *Evangelical Quarterly* (51, Jan 79) to the great cheer of the majority-text people in America. I later got in touch with Maurice Robinson, who to my mind is the ablest of the group, who answered my many questions with great patience and lucidity. When I had news that *Christ and the Bible* was being translated into Chinese, I modified the chapter on text and sent the new version off for incorporation in the

Chinese edition. This was also incorporated in the second English edition. By the time of the third edition in 1993 I was able to make a firmer and fuller statement.

It was while at Allington that Grace and I nearly became overseas missionaries. At Limuru in Kenya was a theological college serving Anglicans, Methodists and Presbyterians. It was the Anglicans' turn to nominate the principal and I was asked whether I was willing to allow my name to go forward. It was a daunting prospect (as the eventual principal was to discover), but we thought we ought to consent, and so mentally we packed our bags for Kenya; but providentially it was overruled.

My spell in hospital had been the result of two or three little strokes. I had gone to Salisbury to do some shopping but came over all queer. I groped my way back to the car and sitting down felt better and drove home. We rang Peter in Nottingham who promptly came down and took me to the University Hospital for examination. It was there surprisingly that I had a disturbing sexual experience. The lengthy examinations involved the testing of the functioning of various limbs. This was done in a private ward by a pretty young trainee doctor; she couldn't complete the tests on the first day and promised to return the following day. I was worried by the thought of another session with her pulling my limbs about and slept badly that night. Her conduct was impeccable and we got through the session all right with me talking to her about the Christian faith, but it was an unpleasant experience which I felt ill-equipped to cope with and which I discussed soon after with Grace and Peter. It brought home to me the difficulties which our western society with its enforced intimacy of the sexes thrusts upon those who wish to live by Christian standards.

Back in Allington I think I was rather more gaga than I realized. Susan suggested to the extramural department in Salisbury that they might put on some classes for beginners in New Testament Greek. These were successful and enjoyable and helped me to get back to normal, leaving me with little more than a slightly impaired circulation. My eldest son, Gordon, said at this time, 'Mum and Dad, have you ever thought what you would do if either of you were taken? Any of our four families would be happy to have you living with us, if you liked.' So we talked it over. Grace said that she would not want to impose herself on any of her daughters-in-law but she would like to move near to one of the families. I, being very undomesticated, said that I should be most grateful to be looked after by one of them.

Then came a surprise communication from SNTS. The society's meeting in 1980, which was to take place in Toronto, planned a new departure. In addition to the usual seminars and main papers, members were invited to submit short papers. I said, 'Stroke or no stroke, I'll submit a paper and if it is accepted I'll go.' Professor R. McL. Wilson, editor of *New Testament Studies*, told us to bring our papers ready for printing. He made no promise to accept all the papers, but he wanted to do a Toronto number. To my great pleasure F.F. Bruce took the chair for my effort on 'Synoptic Independence and the Origin of Luke's Travel Narrative' and all went happily. However when I brought my paper to Professor Wilson, he said, 'I have done two articles for you recently. I am not sure that it would be fair to do a third. Post it to me when you get back to England and I'll think about it.'

Back in Britain I had promised to talk to the Theological Students' Fellowship at Lampeter University on 24 October. It was a pleasant day and Grace and I had planned to drive over. An acquaintance had recommended that we take the Melksham-Devizes road – not much traffic. The previous day had been Grace's birthday and we had been in touch with all the family; she said, 'We must make this a real holiday.' In half an hour it was all over. We were passing through a village which had quite a sharp bend. As we approached it we noted a stationary vehicle on my right-hand side waiting to cross over to a farm entrance on my left. A furniture van came round the corner and promptly stopped behind it. It was followed by a twenty-ton lorry which found itself right on top of the stalled vehicle. The driver jammed on his brakes and skidded straight at us, killing Grace outright and knocking me unconscious.

When I began to come round the firemen were cutting me out of the wreckage – the car had been also smashed from behind. I had just seen Grace's hand out of the corner of my eye but I was too shocked to take in what had happened. They took me to the Bath United Hospital and wheeled me in with nurses standing round looking grave. The first thing they did was to hoover me down since I was covered with thousands of splinters of glass. After a time the chaplain Geoffrey Holden turned up. He said, 'You won't know me, but I know you. I sat at your feet in Jerusalem. I wasn't even a Christian then. After conversion I went to Oak Hill College to train for the ministry.' Then, when he broke the news of Grace's death, the words of Job came to me in great power: 'The Lord gave and the Lord has taken away, blessed be the name of the Lord.' I knew that in God's purposes this was no accident; Grace's work was done, but God still had something for me to do. On later reflection I came to see the love and wisdom of God in thus painlessly taking her to himself. For some ten years she had been troubled by sharp neuralgic head-aches and arthritis. An operation for prolapse repair had proved very trying. After my strokes she had been much exercised by the possibility of having me an invalid whom she could not nurse.

I was in a dreadful mess and they spent nearly all day tidying me up, but it gradually became clear that the injuries (fractured collar-bone and sternum, cuts and bruises) were not serious. My left elbow was also broken but I had evidently put my arm in front of my eyes, for I was cut on the forehead and lower lip but my eyes and right hand were untouched; the elbow remained wired up for six months. The accident was on Friday morning and they planned to operate on my elbow on Saturday. The chaplain asked me whether I would like communion on Sunday, if I felt up to it. He drew the curtains round and took a beautiful short service. On Monday my youngest son Michael came to see me. I said to him, 'That lorry driver at the other end of the ward must be feeling awful. Do go and tell him that there are no hard thoughts this end.' He came back with a deeply grateful message from Bob Jordan, who had been scarcely able to sleep for trying to think how the accident had come about. He said that his only regret was that when he heard me having my service he was not there with me. We had a service together later in the week and I said to him that it would all be worthwhile if it helped to bring us all to genuine faith and a happy reunion (with his wife and mine) in heaven. We have remained good friends ever since.

I have always been addicted to Christian 'thrillers' such as *The Hiding Place, The Cross and the Switchblade, Appointment in Jerusalem, Joni, Selected to Live, God's Smuggler, Sergei* and the rest, which provide a useful complement to one's theological reading. My time in hospital was definitely a spiritual 'high', which may account for the fact that I did not even want pain-killers. It was very easy to speak of one's faith. While there I read Jackie Pullinger's *Chasing the Dragon* on the cover of which it says, 'Love took her to the darkness of the Walled City.' The head night nurse had lived in Hong Kong as a child and knew the reputation of the Walled City. She said, 'Fancy you reading a book like that.' I said, 'It is not what you imagine it to be. I think you'd find it fascinating reading.' She walked off with it and returned it after a day or two deeply impressed.

I had a letter in hospital from Professor Wilson, which (unknown to him) meant a great deal to me. He said that he was publishing my paper. It was God saying to me that his hand was still on my work.

After twelve days in hospital I was fit to leave for the new home which God had prepared for me. Michael and Jane and their two children had just moved to New Marston, Oxford. The funeral had been kept till I was fit to attend. Grace was buried in Allington churchyard surrounded by many loving friends, her four sons bearing the coffin.

Twenty-Five

Oxford — 1980–93: On the Home Front

Michael (with Jane, Rachel and Paul) had moved to New Marston to become head of English at Cowley St John (comprehensive) school. I went to convalesce at their home, walking myself back to health. As I faced the prospect of continuing study on my own, I was most anxious that I should not dry up and lose living contact with Christ. When I realized that the apostle Paul (who was no mean theologian) thanked God that he spoke with tongues 'more than you all', I prayed (without any ifs and buts) that he would grant this gift to me. I was well aware of the potential dangers of so-called charismatic renewal – it can bring disunity, superficiality, naïvety, gullibility, anti-intellectualism, even heresy – and I didn't believe that there were any short cuts to spiritual maturity. But, providing we do not forget the lessons learnt by diligent study of the Word and by careful attempts at total obedience, I can see no necessary harm in seeking spiritual gifts. Jackie Pullinger showed how invaluable was the gift of tongues to converts living in the Walled City of Hong Kong, where quiet and privacy were unobtainable; and charismatics are doing wonderful work in getting the scriptures to the hard places of the earth.

There were three eras in Bible history when God, so to speak, drew back the veil which hides him from us and made his presence known by miracles: at the time of Moses and the founding of the nation of Israel, at the time of Elijah and Elisha

and the establishment of the line of prophets, and at the time of
Jesus and the apostles and the founding of the Gentile church.
Occasional miracles are recorded at other times but not in
profusion. In our own day there are many well authenticated
miracles, sufficient to make me believe that we may be living in
a fourth such era; perhaps we are in the last days of world
evangelism before the Second Advent. I should not have been
the least surprised if I had found myself speaking in tongues but
God did not grant this to me and I was content to recognize that
he grants such gifts to each 'just as he determines'.

I wrote a letter at this time to let distant friends know about
Grace's death and to thank those who had written in sympathy. I
had a letter in reply from my old Cambridge friend, Ian Douglas-
Jones, which prompted me to write to him personally – with a very
happy outcome. He had four daughters and I had always imagined
that such a good home would produce four particularly nice girls.
So I said to him that I was always rather sorry that none of my four
boys had ever met up with any of his girls. Then a thought struck
me (I wondered, Is this inspired by the Holy Spirit?) and I wrote:
One of my sons has a friend who badly wants a wife; you haven't
any daughters left by any chance? This was greeted by roars of
mirth – they had been earnestly praying that one of the daughters
would meet the right man! Both of them were working in London;
they met, fell in love and were happily married.

Michael and Jane invited me to stay permanently with them
but their house was too small for me and my books with them
and their growing family. (In February Jane had their third child
– a most exciting occasion. Labour came on unexpectedly quickly
and she knew that she couldn't get to the John Radcliffe hospital
in time although it was less than half a mile away. An urgent call
brought a midwife hurrying down to arrive in time for the last
contraction. It made her day, and ours.) We sold their house and
my cottage at Allington – Susan was glad to take it over – and we
bought a larger house in North Oxford. Except for tidying up, I

never had to return to an empty home. In Bainton Road I have a lovely study overlooking the St John's College playing field; it had just room for my books. The house has enormous roof space and we had a loft conversion which gave us two extra rooms, one of which became my bedroom. An advantage of moving to smaller accommodation is that you can get rid of the things you don't like and keep the things of which you are fond. Grace and I had already had a considerable turn out, including some silver which used to come out of the bank and go back in again at every move. We sent nearly all of it to a missionary auction and it has caused us no further bother. We decided to keep the ancient crockery and now I enjoy using it.

In due course there was the coroner's inquest into the accident. The lorry company's insurer hired in his defence someone whom I can only regard as a professional with questionable ethics. Bob Jordan was strictly enjoined to say nothing. This 'expert' with a lot of professional letters after his name told how he had examined the road three days after the accident and saw from the skid-marks that Bob had tried to control the skid. He also suggested there was a flaw in the lorry which could not have been detected. He said enough to confuse the magistrate who concluded a verdict of accidental death. My excellent lawyer, Edward Bradley, thought that the case for compensation should be fought. I was opposed to this, partly because Christians are discouraged from going to law, partly because I thought Bob had suffered enough already, partly because I did not want the hassle of a court case and partly because, if we lost, it could be wickedly expensive. Edward then suggested that he should say to the company that he was recommending his client to proceed (although he knew that I would not accept his recommendation). This I agreed to and said that any money coming from an out-of-court settlement should go to some Christian cause. I don't remember the amount but in the end they paid up quite handsomely and everyone was happy.

My nerve was remarkably unaffected by the accident but I had a sharp warning that I could not assume that I possessed a charmed life. Gordon lived only forty miles away at Cheltenham and I used to drive over in Michael's car. One day I was accelerating well to overtake a big vehicle and there seemed to be plenty of time. However, he flashed me to keep me back but I pressed on. The vehicle seemed unbelievably long and the road had barely room for three. I just squeezed through and found myself saying, '*mea culpa, mea culpa.*' I am not in the habit of breaking into Latin but I felt awful that by my own fault I had endangered the lives of those in both vehicles. I felt the worse because I could not apologize to either party. It was my worst error in fifty years of driving. I now say grace before driving – it seems to me more important than before meals: 'Lord, give us good driving and a safe journey.' I find cycling in Oxford more nerve-racking than driving! My sons gave me a fine Raleigh for my seventieth birthday, but at the age of seventy-eight after a very minor accident I was glad to give it up. With a good minibus service to the city centre I seldom need it.

We joined St Andrew's Church where we had worshipped in our Latimer House days. It was well attended, had a good ministry of the Word, and seemed to be dealing successfully with the problem of catering both for beginners and for the mature. One member of the congregation, Mrs Buxton, was an example to all the elderly who don't want anything changed. When nearly ninety years of age she said, 'What I like about St Andrew's is, it's so exciting, you never know what is going to happen next!' I told the vicar that I felt writing to be my priority but that I would be glad to help in any way if I was needed. They took me very literally and I think I was asked to preach less than ten times in ten years.

I have felt at times that I am a forgotten man and have been tempted to feel frustrated but again and again over many years dating right back to my Bristol days one verse of Scripture has kept coming back to me. It is the New English Bible translation of 2 Corinthians 12:10, 'I am well content for Christ's sake with weakness and frustration, for when I am weak, then I am strong.' I have a great sense that we are all part of a tremendous divine purpose and that all we have to do is to keep in touch.

> O let me see thy footmarks
> and in them plant my own

has been my constant prayer. It has become clear to me that the Lord does not wish me to spend a lot of time and energy on preaching but that my priorities are prayer, writing and counselling. One of the blessed things about retirement is that one is unlikely to be interrupted in the first hour after breakfast, so that this time can be given to chewing over the Word and intercession. One soon accumulates the names of hundreds of people and causes that need prayer, and intercession can often be no more than a 'making mention' of them. But our feeble prayers are to a Mighty God and therefore are not in vain. I remember Dr Northcote Deck, a missionary to the South Sea Islands (who incidentally spiced his deputation talks with lavish helpings of pidgin English), comparing the prayers of supporters to the input of many low-voltage sources which are transformed by God into high-voltage power in the ministry of the missionary who is prayed for. Oxford is of course an ideal place for the study required for writing, and it is perhaps the greatest mission field on earth. Gifted teachers and students from all over the world converge upon this city and counselling of such is abundantly worthwhile.

Adjusting to a single life produced some problems. I had loved working in harness with a Christian woman with whom I could share everything and it seemed the ideal way to do Christian work. Grace had said to me shyly in Allington, 'Don't feel you would be disloyal to me if I die and you want to marry again. I'd like to know that someone was caring for you.' I was quite strongly drawn towards a new partnership and had to think seriously about the matter. I knew that humanly speaking it would be a terrific gamble, as it would be hard to conceive of anyone coming up to Grace's standard. I prayed most earnestly, 'Thy will be done,' and God showed decisively that it was not his will for me.

But it raised a serious theological question. Gordon had written a book in collaboration with William Heth, *Jesus and Divorce* (Hodder, 1984) arguing most powerfully that Jesus and the early church totally forbade remarriage after divorce, (thus incidentally reconciling the apparent discrepancy between Matthew and Mark). While welcoming this statement I felt that it was almost irresponsible to put such theological dynamite on the market without dealing with the pastoral problems that it raised. This deficiency has, however, been splendidly remedied in Andrew Cornes, *Divorce and Remarriage: Biblical Principles and Pastoral Practice* (Hodder, 1993). In a footnote (p. 213 n. 28) Heth and Wenham raise the question of the right interpretation of *mias gunaikos andra*, 'husband of one wife', given as one of the qualifications of an *episkopos* in 1 Timothy 3:2. Should it be translated 'married only once', thereby forbidding an ordained man from remarriage, or does it mean only that his marriage must have been strictly monogamous. The argument that it is the former turns largely on the interpretation of the parallel phrase in 1 Timothy 5:9 where a widow is only to be enrolled if she is 'a wife of one man'. While polygamy was common in the ancient world, polyandry was not; so (it is maintained) it does not refer to it here. Once again the pastoral implications are most serious if it means that there is a different standard for clergy and laity. I am unconvinced that this is so but it is a matter which merits careful study. How much turns on how little when we try to obey Scripture!

In the early days of single life I tried to maintain something of the old standards of hospitality, laying on ploughman's

lunches for students, but I soon found that the time and labour
involved was out of all proportion to the advantages gained. In
fact the use of a kettle and a good box of biscuits provided all
that was necessary by way of hospitality. It is an illusion to think
that family hospitality is better than individual hospitality. Indeed it is one of the strengths of Cornes' book that he shows the
positive value of the dedicated single life. I in fact find endless
opportunities for evangelism. It is easy for a Christian writer,
because people ask you what you do. 'Write books.' 'Books
about what?' 'The gospels. . . .' And so one launches right into
the heart of the matter. I had one six-hour coach journey from
Cornwall to Oxford with an artist girl who had tried most things
and was now living in poverty. We talked the whole way and I
ransacked my total armoury of theology, apologetics and aes-
thetics. Another day I met a Chinese economist on Port
Meadow; I happened to know a Christian from his home town
Shanghai and we found ourselves talking about Christianity
almost at once.

Another contact was a more frustrating one. St Andrew's
Community Care Committee was interested in a young man with
multiple sclerosis, so they asked Michael (who was about his age)
to visit him. He lived in a flat on his own, visited four times a day
by the nursing services. His lifeline to the outside world was the
telephone and he often used to ring Michael up. Frequently it was
I who answered the phone and I began to realize that I had more
time to spare than Michael; so I started to visit him nearly every
day. I kept off religion almost entirely because he was quite anti.
He was a difficult patient and complained bitterly one day that a
nurse had arrived and had collapsed on the floor in his kitchen.
He thought it disgraceful that they should send someone in that
state. I said, 'You don't know that woman's condition. She was
probably not feeling too well, but for your sake decided to carry
on.' The next day he repeated the same charge. I said, 'Tony, if
you are so completely self-centred, you are going straight to hell.'

'How do you know?' 'Jesus said so.' 'I don't believe in your Jesus; I gave that up as a teenager.' 'You've had twenty years' experience of life since then; it's time you thought again.'

I contemplated giving up my visits, remembering that Christ had said 'Cast not your pearls before swine.' But, though I cut down my visits a great deal, I continued to keep in touch. During the summer I thought of him in terms of the prodigal son and prayed much that he would come to himself and say, 'Father, I have sinned.' Just before Christmas, apropos of nothing in particular, he said, 'I am a horrible person, I am a horrible person to live with.' I didn't really know what to say; so I just thanked God inwardly. For Christmas itself, to allow his nurses a break, he was sent off to hospital, which he usually loathed. I visited him on Christmas day and one of the nurses remarked, 'What has happened to Tony? He's different.' Tony in fact seemed to have quite enjoyed his stay. When back home he said to me, 'I've made a New Year's resolution – I am going to try to be nice to people.' I had no chance to talk to him about his new-found faith and a few days later he died in Sobell House with his ex-wife at his bedside. The funeral was in her village at Stanford in the Vale where Michael was one day going to be vicar. I preached on the prodigal son, pointing out how Tony had had nothing to live for in this life or in the next, but that the Father had embraced him and welcomed him home.

Another interesting St Andrew's friend was Moses, the first of a number of Chinese and Japanese contacts. He was a schoolmaster from Shanghai, who had come to Oxford ostensibly to improve his English. He said that he wanted to learn about the Bible and Christian theology. As a teenager he had lived through the Cultural Revolution and had seen his Christian grandfather crippled by torture and his father giving up overt Christianity. He was terrified lest he be sent back to China. We got him a place at the Birmingham Bible Institute, where he did well. He married a keen Christian Chinese midwife from Indonesia who had long been resident in this country, and he is now safe from deportation. They work steadily among Chinese students. I met weekly for about a year with another Chinaman who was financed by Glaxo seeking an antidote to Aids. We read large parts of the Bible together but whether he has come to personal faith I can't say. More recently I have had close contacts with two others straight out of Communist China, one who had already come to some belief in God (though not in Christ) and another who is reading a Good News Bible which she gladly accepted. I had the privilege of sponsoring the former for baptism.

I had interesting times with two Japanese professors. One, an economist, I overtook literally dragging an enormously heavy suitcase quite near my home. It was his second day in England and he was looking for an address in Bainton Road. We put the suitcase on the saddle of my bicycle and wheeled it round. Our Christian conversation began to blossom one day when he referred to the reproduction of a well-known picture which was hanging in his digs. He remarked, 'It is sometimes said in Japan that art has declined in the West, because the West has ceased to believe in God. What do you think?' We had several conversations. One day I invited him to a concert by Cherkassky, the pianist, in the Sheldonian Theatre. He accepted and then mentioned that he had another professor friend staying with him: Could he bring her too? I was quite troubled knowing that he spoke lovingly of his wife. Was he being unfaithful to her? When we met I could see no signs of the lady, only a male friend. The Japanese have trouble with the gender of our pronouns!

One day he called on me carrying an electric typewriter. He had an acquaintance who was suicidal and he had decided to cut short his time in Oxford a little, so that he could escort him back to Japan. Would the typewriter be any use to me? It did me good service for several years. I don't think that he has become a Christian but he wrote to me saying that the most important thing about his time in Oxford was his 'thoughts about the God'.

One Sunday evening I got home rather tired and Michael told
me that a professor (of international law?) in Wolfson College
wanted to see me. I went round somewhat reluctantly, only to be
greeted by the words 'Can you tell me just how to become a
Christian!' I did my best for a couple of hours; he left for home a
few days later. I put him on my daily prayer list, praying I fear
without much faith or fervour. Seven years later he reappeared
in St Andrew's very evidently a Christian! He left me a table-cloth
which I regularly use for my tea-parties and by which I remember
him.

Michael, after much heart searching, came to the conclusion
that he should train for ordination. He cycled into Wycliffe Hall
each day and also kept some educational ploys going. He was
grossly overworking and, on the morning he was to move out, he
and I were alone in the house. I heard a loud groan and found
him unconscious on the kitchen floor with blood on the tiles. It
was an epileptic type of fit which seriously hindered his first year
in the ministry as a curate at Norbury near Manchester. Coincid-
ent with Michael starting his training, David had joined the staff
at Wycliffe, teaching New Testament and living in a college
house. When Michael and Jane were ready to move out, David
and Clare and their two boys were ready to move in, and I stayed
put under new management. It was then that I came across
another Christian thriller: *The Torn Veil* by Gulshan Esther.
Gulshan had been brought up in a devout Moslem home in
Pakistan but was paralysed in her left arm and left leg and so had
been unable to walk for the first nineteen years of her life. She
had an encounter with Jesus during which she was healed. It is an
astonishing story and when I showed it to David, who is not
sceptical either about New Testament or modern miracles, he was
a bit incredulous. Then one day he discovered that one of his own
students, who was working in St Matthew's parish as part of his
training, was in the same house group with this very lady. I asked
for her phone number and rang her up. The reply was, 'Are you

free for lunch on Saturday?' I went round and have since introduced her to a number of Christians and non-Christians. I have bought, and passed on, more than sixty copies of her book.

At about this time Lynne and Gordon at Cheltenham suffered a great tragedy. Rather unexpectedly Lynne, who had had three successful confinements in Belfast, became pregnant again. The baby came too quickly with no doctor present and little Anne was badly brain-damaged. They kept her in hospital sustained by various unpleasant tubes for a fortnight and then the parents decided to take her home to die in an atmosphere of love. She at once began to improve and we hoped that the doctors would be proved wrong. For six months she was lovingly cared for and all seemed well but then rather suddenly she caught an infection which carried her off. Gordon and Lynne are vigorous anti-abortion campaigners and doubtless this hard experience of seeing themselves as parents of a child whose life (they were told) was to be that of a vegetable, greatly deepened their sympathy for those in similar situations.

Having worshipped at St Andrew's for ten years, I was somewhat taken aback when our vicar Colin Bennetts, who was about to leave us, preached a sermon about church-planting. He said, 'Three out of four of you here don't live in the parish. You might be more useful if you went to your parish church.' As I certainly did not seem needed at St Andrew's, I thought that I ought to try St Margaret's, a fine tractarian church, in whose parish Bainton Road is. I was warmly welcomed, the worship was reverent, the music was quite exceptionally good, there was a concern to serve the local community, the congregation was of a size where we might hope to get to know one another, and so I stayed. Its greatest weakness seemed to be the lack of a theology of the Word to give consistency and edge to the preaching but the desire for such seems to be growing. I was greatly encouraged at a time when one wanted to be sure that one was walking in the line of God's will in having (I think for the first time in my life) the

privilege of actually leading two people to Christ. One was a
research student whom I met at St Andrew's one Sunday evening.
I asked him whether he was a Christian. He said that he was not
but that he and his girl friend were interested. I tried to show him
the way and then invited him to come and see me on the Monday.
He arrived, still in the dark. We talked and then I suggested that
prayer might help. We knelt down, I prayed a prayer, then
haltingly he did the same. But he didn't get up, he seemed lost in
God for perhaps five minutes. When he did so, I told him to ring
up his girlfriend and tell her. Later, just as I was going to bed the
door-bell rang. There he was, 'so full of joy that I thought I must
come and tell you!' A happy Christian wedding followed. The
other was an undergraduate who had been unable to believe
because of the doubts sown in his mind by the philosophers, but
the Holy Spirit also brought him to faith.

Twenty-Six

Oxford — 1980–93: On the Academic Front

Looked at from an evangelical point of view how different was the theological scene in Oxford in the eighties from that in 1937, when we could find no senior speaker in the whole country who would come and defend the Bible for us; or from that in 1958 when John Reynolds was our sole Oxford academic left behind after the Packer–Evans confrontation. There were now fully thirty competent theologians who were from the evangelical stable who would not be ashamed of that label. There were flourishing churches like St Aldate's (presided over by Michael Green), St Ebbe's, St Andrew's, St Clement's and Woodstock Road Baptist Church, backed up by distinguished members of the theological faculty like Oliver O'Donovan and Tom Wright. Wycliffe Hall was the strongest evangelical institution, having Dick France, chairman of the UCCF Research Council, as its principal and Alister McGrath as its most distinguished theologian. Regents Park College (Baptist) had among its teachers Barrie White, Larry Kreitzer, David Cook and Tim Bradshaw (Anglican). New institutions had sprung up: The Oxford Centre of Mission Studies, presided over by Chris Sugden, which provides opportunities for research in theology and church history for students from developing countries without withdrawing them from their homelands for long periods. The Whitefield Institute, an arm of UCCF's research council, staffed by David Cook and Stephen Williams, set up its headquarters here in Oxford. One of its first public meetings was graced by Alvin Plantinga, the eminent philosopher of religion, who was here to deliver the Wilde lectures.

Not surprisingly considerable changes had come over evangelical leadership in a period of fifty years. At the beginning of the century they had felt acutely that the 'higher critical' assault on the Bible was a direct attack on the authority of Christ and therefore they had concentrated attention on these matters. With the growth of scholarship had come a great widening of interest. When Colin Buchanan began to pour out his Grove Booklets, he said that he thought it was time for us to take the truth of the Bible as read and get on with applying it. Some good work continued to be done in the field of higher criticism but no one mounted a really effective challenge to J E D and P and no one succeeded in putting Moses back in his place as possibly the most influential figure in the history of the world. The conservatives not only did not convince the world of liberal scholarship; they did not altogether convince their fellow-evangelicals, and so it increasingly became the practice to concentrate on the matters which seemed to be central to the Christian faith and to regard biblical inspiration as something slightly peripheral, not to be defined too closely. Criticism came to be thought of as something neutral. Barr's attack on fundamentalism was particularly an attack on inerrancy; on the idea, that is, that the Scriptures were the direct product of the God of truth and therefore to be accepted in their entirety. Dick France's response to this was that he hardly ever met a fundamentalist, which presumably means that few of his acquaintances would now defend inerrancy. They would advocate preaching of the Bible but it need not be the Bible as understood to be true throughout in its natural sense.

I got the impression, therefore, when I came back to Oxford that we had lost some ground as well as gaining some. We were a considerable army but we gave the impression that we did not quite know where we were going. We lacked cohesion because we lacked clarity. The effect on the students took two different forms: some saw the way of fruitfulness in charismatic experience; others followed the emphasis of the Proclamation Trust and saw expository preaching as the key to fruitfulness. Both were inclined to undervalue apologetics and theological study in spite of the fact that good exposition presupposes good commentaries and good commentaries presuppose accurate scholarship.

The institution in which I had a particular interest of course was Latimer House, only ten minutes' walk from where I live. I was elected to the council and saw a good deal of Roger Beckwith, who had been warden since 1973. Roger had maintained a prodigious range of interests and had gained greatly in skill as a writer. In 1985 he published his book *The Old Testament Canon of the New Testament Church* and put in for an Oxford DD. John Barton of this university, who had also written on the canon, says of it:

> This monumental work . . . is almost certainly the most detailed work ever written on the formation of the Old Testament canon. It is unlikely that any living scholar knows more than Roger Beckwith about the evidence . . . Unless archaeology . . . reveals fresh texts relevant to the formation of the canon, this book will remain a completely authoritative compendium of all the evidence we have on the subject. The labour it must have entailed is staggering; its meticulous attention to detail will command the respect of every reader . . . He has probably read everything ever written in major European languages on these questions and knows how to expound it.

He then goes on to say:

> It is a thousand pities, therefore, that such a book should turn out . . . to be essentially a very sophisticated fundamentalist apologetic . . . the alert reader will very soon spot . . .

within the first couple of chapters what the conclusion is going to be: that the Reformers were entirely right to accept only the books of the Hebrew canon as their Old Testament; and that in this they were true to the very teaching of Jesus himself.

The topic, he says, was however 'a matter of religious indifference to Jesus and the apostles'.

(*Theology*, 90 (1987), pp. 63–65)

With this prejudice to contend with and with James Barr's great influence, it is not altogether surprising that the degree was refused. But it is nonetheless deplorable that a work so learned and so lucid should be rejected because it was 'a fundamentalist apologetic'. A hundred years earlier this standpoint with regard to Scripture would have been orthodoxy, the position probably of most of the theologians of Oxford. It is much to his credit that George Carey recognized Roger's learning and awarded him a Lambeth DD.

Roger's personal influence as a scholar was great but Latimer House did not grow. It had a small band of supporters and was not well known even in Oxford. The house's librarians had found it a useful place in which to do some writing but they had come and gone without making a big impact. In 1992 the council appointed Martin Davie as librarian (initially for a year). I had known him for ten years; I was impressed by his spirituality and had the highest hopes for his success. Though he had joined the Quakers after his conversion and had written his DPhil thesis on Quakerism, he had come to hold firm Reformation Anglican views. He had read theology schools in a year when seven first class degrees were awarded and he came top. It was a remarkable achievement in an Oxford so prejudiced against fundamentalism, since he never in the least disguised his belief in inerrancy. He was at home in all branches of the subject – languages, history and philosophy – and was specially interested in a systematic theology that was strictly based on careful exegesis of Scripture. With a fine gift of lucidity I saw him as a person who could do great things for Oxford theology and for the evangelizing of the world from Latimer House. But sadly it was not to be. He went on to teach at Oak Hill College.

Finding myself back in Oxford I had to reassess my own position. My first five years of retirement in Allington had not been very productive – two rejected books, a half completed book and a tiny crop of articles. One of these was published in *The Journal of Theological Studies* (New Series 32 (1981) p. 150). Entitled 'When were the Saints Raised? – A Note on the Punctuation of Matthew 27: 51–53', it argued that Matthew understood the opening of the tombs to have occurred at the time of the crucifixion and the raising of the saints after the resurrection. My three articles in New Testament Studies had been partly on textual criticism, partly on source criticism and partly on the relation of the two. Professor George Kilpatrick, one of our greatest authorities on text, lived nearby and I frequently discussed matters of text with him. Though I did not find his overall approach convincing, it was helpful to find that he believed the Byzantine text-type to be much earlier than Hort's theory allowed and he believed that on the whole longer readings were to be preferred to shorter ones. But these questions were somewhat peripheral to my main interests, although I have come to feel more and more that text is an area in which useful progress is possible. What I was really anxious to do was to write a book redating the four gospels. Later on I came to see that this was too big a subject for one book and had to confine it to redating the three synoptic gospels.

The first step forward for me academically came from participation in a St Andrew's house group. This was led by Martin Brett, a medievalist. I gave him the manuscript of *Easter Enigma* to read, hoping for one or two intelligent comments from him. What came back was far better. I had gone through the resurrection narratives in turn in order to remind the reader of their contents and at the same time calling attention to the points of interest which would be of value when it came to putting them together. Martin said, 'I wouldn't like this to be said of anything I had written, but I think you need to stand the book on its head. You are letting the cat out of the bag gradually! You'd do better to present topography, actors and evangelists first and then look at the narratives.' At first this sounded somewhat daunting but it was solely a matter of presentation, since all the basic work had been done; the rewriting didn't take long and Paternoster warmly took on its publication. So that meant that three books in The Christian View of the Bible series had been completed.

I was seeing quite a number of theological students. Michael Green had a regular meeting for undergraduates, which I usually attended. We also started a Fellowship of Research Students in Theology through which I made many valued friendships and learnt a great deal. Dewey Ducharme convinced me that for understanding the human person one needed some sort of dualism and that Basil Atkinson's version of psychosomatic unity as I had understood it was not adequate. Steve Palmquist gave me a new respect for Kant. Alan Paget inveigled me into conducting a service for the renewal of marriage vows in Oriel College chapel on the tenth anniversary of his wedding. Later I had the happiest fellowship with Juan Chapa, a Roman Catholic priest from Spain who had strongly conservative views on the Bible. When we had extempore prayer together I led off; then he said, 'And shall we ask for the intercession of the Holy Mother?' I am afraid I was only able to offer a non-committal grunt.

I wished that I could do something more substantial and systematic for these students and for the great host of others whom we were not touching. Greatly daring and with considerable diffidence I offered the university a series of Speaker's Lectures on 'Objections to Fundamentalism'. This title was suggested by a recent series of books in which various writers who were known to be open-minded in their views nonetheless defended views which had come under attack e.g. 'Objections to Humanism', 'Objections to Roman Catholicism', etc. I thought that since Oxford had given so much publicity to attacks on fundamentalism it was only fair that scope should be given for reply. I knew that it was extremely unlikely that the proposal would be accepted but I thought I had enough unpublished material and material published but not widely known to make an interesting and informative series if the miracle of acceptance did take place, and I think there would have been a good attendance.

When this was turned down I was able to concentrate my efforts on *Redating Matthew, Mark and Luke*. I attended regularly the meetings of the Synoptic Problem Seminar of SNTS, trying out some of my ideas and getting useful come-back. I remember attending the society's meeting in Rome in 1981, to which I took two large visual aids. I had plotted Luke against Mark on a graph showing how consistently Luke follows the order of Mark in spite of omissions and additions. Michael Goulder believed that Luke was also following Matthew. This produces a totally different graph, no longer a steady gradient but more like that of a force-8 earthquake. At a gospels conference in Ampleforth in the following year, Michael took a different line, which he told me was the result of contemplating my visual aids.

I could see that with a rather technical book under construction I was likely to be in trouble over a publisher. If Cambridge were to accept it, they would probably give it a price tag of £40 and put it out of the reach of the ordinary buyer. If I gave it to an evangelical publisher it would be branded 'fundamentalist' and not read by the scholarly community for which it was written. I also thought timing important. Good books, even great books like those of Kierkegaard, have often been ignored because the climate of thought was not ready for them. I therefore prayed much about this matter. My experience in the SNTS seminar convinced me that the time was right. The members were all at sixes and sevens. It was decided after twelve years' work to disband but the chairman thought we should ask ourselves before we dispersed whether we had come to any common conclusion. The answer was that we didn't agree on a single thing. Yet as I had listened to all the discussions I had felt that my view met the objections of all the others. The time undoubtedly seemed right. Then something like a miracle happened.

I gave a talk to the TSF undergraduates outlining my new dating. A student, Andy Saville, who was in his last term said, 'That's the most exciting hour of theology that I have ever listened to!' He then got a job at Hodder and Stoughton. When my manuscript had reached its penultimate stage, I sent him a copy just for his interest and comments. Unknown to me he passed it on to his chief, David Wavre, who then wrote to me and said that he thought Hodders would be interested in it, if I could make it less technical. I thanked him for his interest and said that I had written the book for scholars and couldn't contemplate popularizing it. Then some weeks later he wrote again saying that he didn't often change his mind but that he had in this case. Could he come and see me? I didn't even have to go up to London. He came to Oxford and told me that he would be prepared to publish it at £10. At this penultimate stage Martin Davie read the script for me and sent me forty-eight A4 pages of useful comment. All the technical matters of Greek type-setting, graphs, diagrams and the rest were safely negotiated and handsome editions in both hardback and paperback appeared simultaneously.

But this was not the end of the story, for shortly after publication David Wavre had a difference of opinion with his employers whom he had served well and they gave him a golden handshake. This enabled him to establish his own firm of Eagle Books. He sent me his first list of publications and invited my comments. It was a list majoring on spirituality and practical Christianity. I said that it was a good list but that to get the best balance it needed a bit more theology. I was concerned that *Christ and the Bible* and *The Enigma of Evil* were out of print in this country and suggested that he might like to reprint them. He asked to look at them and then sat on them for six months. When I jogged his memory he replied that he liked the books but in these hard times he couldn't see his way to reprinting them. This was disappointing because to me they were the foundation volumes of one work, The Christian View of the Bible, all of which should be available together.

One day Gordon mentioned to me that a friend of his wanted a book reprinted and had discovered that it could be done for £1,500. I had tucked this bit of information into the back of my mind and had nearly forgotten it, when I found myself in a rather embarrassing position. I and an American whom I had never met had put up some money to help a Serbian student called Olivera Petrovich who was doing a DPhil here in experimental psychology. She was testing the theory of Piaget who taught that children did not begin to think abstractly until about the age of twelve. This theory was enormously influential, being used by Goldman and others to say that children should not be taught about God till that age. (As though God was abstract!) She devised simple experiments to show that at the age of three children are able, for instance, to distinguish between things (like chairs) which a man can make and things (like trees) which a man cannot make. Owing to a misunderstanding Olivera had managed to live very frugally and had paid her fees while we were expecting at any moment a swingeing bill from the university. In order to regain tax our American friend had paid the money through Latimer House, so when we learnt that the money was no longer needed we wrote to say that the money would be gratefully returned. He, however, said, 'No, let Latimer House keep it. Or, perhaps, half (that is £2,000) should go to John Wenham.' The thought came suddenly to my mind, 'Is this

the pump-priming to get *Christ and the Bible* back into print?'
So there and then I said, 'Thank you very much.'

I rang up David Wavre and said, 'Would £2,000 make any
difference?' He said, 'I'll do some sums and come and see you.'
He came to see me on my birthday and when I explained to him
my whole The Christian View of the Bible project, he went away
enthused by the idea that the out-of-print books could be reprinted (and if any of the other books went out of print they could
all be republished) as volumes of The Christian View of the Bible.
It was the best birthday present I have ever received.

There were three other matters of some interest during this
period. My son Gordon was prime mover in the launching of the
Open Theological College, which operates on the lines of the
Open University. This is offering courses of degree standard in
nearly all branches of Christian theology. It aims at an unim-
peachable university standard in the subjects which are of practical value for Christian workers. It should be a great value to the
whole Christian church. His college at Cheltenham and several
other well respected institutions are behind it.

My next door neighbour Danah Zohar and her husband
produced an interesting book called *The Quantum Self* in 1991.
She is a physicist who writes semi-popular articles for *The Times*
and other respectable publications. Quantum physics had entirely revolutionized her outlook on life and she was now definitely religious. I visited her one day about an Amnesty
International effort (in which one of my sisters was involved) to
get a Russian physicist freed from a Siberian labour camp. When
I asked her how the book was going, she said, 'It's going into
twenty-five languages!' She then told me about a debate in which
she was about to take part advertised as 'Science versus Religion'.
It turned out that it had been arranged by the Jewish society and
that three well-known Oxford atheists (including Richard
Dawkins) were to debate with two Israeli scientists (who were
Talmudic fundamentalists) and Danah. It was a poor debate and

inordinately long but something like six hundred (mostly students) had turned up to listen. I took issue with Dawkins on two points. He said first of all that evolution was incontrovertible, which was a plain misstatement of fact, which most of those present would not be in a position to recognize. Secondly, he and another speaker said that faith was a cop-out. I pointed out in a letter that he misunderstood the New Testament concept of faith; it was not a feeble substitute for reason when reason failed. In a serious quest for God the seeker will think as hard as he possibly can but is then likely to come to the conclusion that the mind is far too puny to get round such an enormous and complex phenomenon as the Universe, let alone the Creator of the Universe. It may then dawn on him that it is the pure in heart who are said to see God; this will make him add a moral quest to his intellectual quest. When he does so, the time will come when he knows that God is there demanding his allegiance. Faith is simply saying Yes to God who is known to be present, and faith results in a profound inner certainty.

A very different spiritual encounter was with Edward Greene (cousin of Graham Greene) who runs a well-known tutorial establishment in Pembroke Street. His outlook could scarcely be farther removed from that of Dawkins. He was an Etonian brought up in a form of traditional Anglican public-school religion. One of his sisters turned Roman Catholic, which set him seriously thinking about his own faith. A Scottish minister introduced him to Charles Hodge's three-volume *Systematic Theology* which led to his conversion and to his joining the Free Presbyterian Church of Scotland of which he became an enthusiastic member. As an undergraduate he and a friend founded the Oxford University Free Presbyterian Society which debated the motion: 'This house does not believe in religious toleration!' I found that I had much in common with him. He was an elder of the same church that my grandfather had been an elder in, we were both Bible-believing Protestants, we were both followers of the Byzantine text. He welcomed the idea of making a pilgrimage (is that the right word?) to my grandfather's grave at Rednal. We roamed the Lickey estate, had a splendid lunch and I was allowed to drive his Bentley (a Rolls-Royce in everything but name) on the way home. With Hodge as foundation and years of interest in the faith, he is no mean theologian and I fear is much saddened by my views on hell. Knowing the intellectual power of Hodge and of the other great Calvinist writers he regards the Westminster Confession of Faith, which is the secondary standard of his church, as almost faultless, which I do not. But I respect his faithfulness to the church when so much is against it.

Then, an invitation to return to Scotland arrived. Rutherford House in Edinburgh, which exists to promote sound theology and sound ethics within the Church of Scotland and in the wider Christian world, holds a biennial conference on Christian dogmatics. In 1991 the subject was 'Universalism and the Doctrine of Hell' and I was invited to offer a paper. So to Edinburgh I went to read a paper on 'The Case for Conditional Immortality'.

Twenty-Seven

Rutherford House — 1991:
The Case for Conditional Immortality

The Rutherford House conference was a select little gathering which took place at the time of the Edinburgh Festival in beautiful sunny weather. Its proceedings were lightened for some of us by a visit to Mozart's *The Magic Flute*. There were ten papers of varying difficulty and varying interest which have been collected together in *Universalism and the Doctrine of Hell*, edited by Nigel Cameron and published in 1992 by Paternoster of Carlisle and Baker of Grand Rapids, USA. I will recount at some length my own contribution and then comment on points of interest in the other papers. With small differences, I argued as follows (for fuller documentation see the original paper):

The Case for Conditional Immortality
This paper is deliberately restricted in scope. The presupposition on which it is based is an acceptance of the canonical books of the Old and New Testaments as divinely inspired and harmonious in their teaching when interpreted in the natural and intended sense. There is therefore no discussion of critical questions which see one part of Scripture in conflict with another.

By way of definition: belief in conditional immortality
is the belief that God created Man only potentially immortal. Immortality is a state gained by grace through faith
when the believer receives eternal life and becomes a partaker of the divine nature, immortality being inherent in
God alone.

It is a doctrine totally different from universalism, which
I have long believed quite irreconcilable with Scripture. It
shares the doctrine of judgment held by the upholders of
everlasting torment in almost every particular – except for
one tremendous thing: it sees no continuing place in God's
world for human beings living on in unending pain not
reconciled to God. The wrath of God will put an end to
sin and evil.

An Answer Awaited

I am grateful for the opportunity of expounding this case,
for it is seventeen years since I tentatively committed myself
to it in print. This was in my book *The Goodness of God*
where I dealt with the subject of 'Hell' in one short chapter.
I could do little more than outline the main points of the
case for unending conscious torment and for conditional
immortality (the latter in seven pages) as convincingly as I
could and leave the reader to make his choice. I said,
however, that I felt under no obligation to defend any
doctrine more shocking than conditionalism until the
arguments of L.E. Froom, Basil Atkinson and Harold
Guillebaud had been effectively answered.

I had learnt the doctrine from Basil Atkinson (as recounted in Chapter 8) in about 1934. When I left Cambridge
in 1938 I had to teach doctrine at St John's Hall, Highbury.
There till 1941 I taught conditionalism with much reserve
and restraint. After that I had twelve years out of direct
academic work, before joining the staff of Tyndale Hall,

Bristol. Here I taught with rather less reserve, particularly after a Tyndale House Study Group in 1954 which was devoted to The Intermediate State and the Final Condition of the Lost, at which some of the best brains in IVF studied the subject for (I think) three days. Though bringing home to me the great difficulty of coming to assured conclusions about the intermediate state, I was more than ever persuaded that the final end of the lost was destruction in the fires of hell.

Matters reached crisis point in 1973, when I presented Inter-Varsity Press with the manuscript of *The Goodness of God*, as recounted in Chapter 22. Their acceptance of the manuscript was a great step forward for neither Atkinson nor Guillebaud had been able to find a publisher for their carefully written books. I concluded the chapter on hell by saying, 'We shall consider ourselves under no obligation to defend the notion of unending torment until the arguments of the conditionalists have been refuted.'

So I have been waiting since 1973 for a reply to the massive work of Froom (2,476 pages), to Atkinson's closely argued 112 pages, to Guillebaud's 67 pages and (more important) to the one additional (excellent) book which has appeared on the conditionalist side: Edward Fudge's *The Fire That Consumes* of 500 pages (Texas: Providential Press, 1982.)

An Answer Attempted

To my knowledge there have been four serious attempts at reply. In 1986 The Banner of Truth Trust republished the work of the reformed theologian W.G.T. Shedd, *The Doctrine of Endless Punishment*, first published in 1885, which faithfully reasserts the doctrine of the Westminster Confession, chapter 32 of which says:

The bodies of men after death return to dust, and see corruption; but their souls (which neither die nor sleep), having an immortal subsistence, immediately return to God who gave them. The souls of the righteous, being then made perfect in holiness, are received into the highest heavens, where they behold the face of God in light and glory, waiting for the full redemption of their bodies; and the souls of the wicked are cast into hell, where they remain in torments and utter darkness, reserved to the judgment of the great day. Besides these two places for souls separated from their bodies, the Scripture acknowledgeth none.

In 1989 the same trust published Paul Helm's *The Last Things: Death, Judgment, Heaven and Hell*. In 1990 J.H. Gerstner, *Repent or Perish* (Soli Deo Gloria Publications) was published, which has four chapters directed specifically against Fudge. In the same year J.I. Packer published his Leon Morris Lecture, 'The Problem of Eternal Punishment', which he declares to be 'a dissuasive . . . particularly from conditionalism' (p. 25).

The extraordinary thing about these replies is that none of them actually addresses the arguments used by the conditionalists. Shedd, it is true, refers to the eighteenth-century Anglican Bishop Warburton, who 'denied that the immortality of the soul is taught in the Old Testament.' Shedd's reply is that it 'is nowhere formally demonstrated, because it is everywhere assumed' (pp. 50f.). He then proceeds to demolish views which as far as I know no conditionalist holds. Similarly I did not recognize the conditionalism to which Helm refers – he gives no references. He says annihilationists hold that 'when the impenitent die they do not go on to await the judgment, but they go literally out of existence' (p. 117). He does, however, acknowledge that 'Scripture does not teach the immortality of the soul in so many words' (p. 118).

When we come to Gerstner and Packer an important new factor has arisen: J.R.W. Stott and P.E. Hughes, two leading conservative evangelicals, have written sympathetically of conditionalism. In *Essentials*, his dialogue with David Edwards, Stott writes that he holds his belief in the ultimate annihilation of the wicked 'tentatively'. He also expresses his hesitation in writing this (although he has told me that he has spoken about it for thirty or forty years) 'partly because I have great respect for long standing tradition which claims to be a true interpretation of Scripture, and do not lightly set it aside, and partly because the unity of the world-wide evangelical constituency has always meant much to me' (p. 319). He says he prefers to describe himself as 'agnostic' which, he tells me, is how the late F.F. Bruce also described his position. Since in his view Scripture does not come down unequivocally on either side, he pleads 'that the ultimate annihilation of the wicked should at least be accepted as a legitimate, biblically founded alternative to their eternal conscious torment' (p. 320). Hughes, who lectured at that stronghold of Calvinistic orthodoxy Westminster Theological Seminary, Philadelphia, and was one of the editors of *Westminster Theological Journal*, has no such hesitations. He says, 'It would be hard to imagine a concept more confusing than that of death which means existing endlessly without the power of dying. This, however, is the corner into which Augustine (in company with many others) argued himself' (p. 403). Hughes wrote to me that he had 'long been of this judgment and common Christian candour compelled me to state my position.' Gerstner pitches into Hughes, Stott and Fudge for their Revolt against Hell. It is a wonderful example of circular argument. He assumes that the Bible teaches what he

believes about hell and then proceeds to show that they
believe otherwise. He just does not seriously address their
arguments. Not sharing his beliefs about hell is equated
with a rejection of hell itself, which it is absurd to attribute
to such as Stott, Hughes and Fudge.

Packer is in some ways even more disappointing. With all
his capacity for reading and digesting material and with his
gift of lucid exposition, one hoped to see the conditionalist
arguments carefully considered. He had certainly read the
slight treatments of Stott and Hughes and he was aware of
Fudge's work, but he shows no signs of having read Fudge,
Froom or Atkinson and provides no answers to their arguments but gives instead answers to arguments which they
do not use.

Since writing the above I have read Ajith Fernando's
Crucial Questions About Hell published in 1991 by King-
sway with a foreword by Packer. Fernando is a Methodist,
a Youth for Christ worker in Sri Lanka, who in the
mid-seventies wrote a thesis on universalism for his Master
of Theology degree at Fuller Theological Seminary. His
book is an updated, popular version of his thesis, written in
an admirable spirit, with most of which I thoroughly agree.
He pays some attention to conditionalism, referring to
Stott, Travis and Pinnock, but to no major conditionalist
work. From the other side, Michael Green also committed
to print his belief in conditional immortality in 1990
(E.M.B. Green, *Evangelism through the Local Church*,
Hodder, pp. 69f).

While not answering the conditionalist arguments with
any seriousness, these writers do of course state their own
case. They set out certain well known texts and claim that
their meaning is 'obvious'. Of conditionalist interpretations
Packer says: 'I will say as emphatically as I can, that none
of them is natural . . . Conditionalists' attempts to evade the

natural meaning of some dozens of relevant passages impress me as a prime case of avalanche-dodging' (p. 24).

The Biblical Data

I would claim that the natural meaning of the vast majority of relevant texts is quite otherwise. Of course what seems natural and obvious to a person with one set of presuppositions may not seem so to someone with a different set. What we must try to do is to think the way the biblical writers thought and clear our minds of ideas from other cultures. This makes the Old Testament very important, but demands of space make it necessary to pass over the Old Testament, though earlier writers and Fudge quite properly pay it considerable attention. But this is not central to the debate and we will simply make two quotations from Fudge. He says: 'The Old Testament utilizes some fifty Hebrew words and seventy-five figures of speech to describe the ultimate end of the wicked – and every one sounds . . . like total extinction.'

And this is the summary of his chapter 'The End of the Wicked in the Old Testament':

> The Old Testament has very much to say about the end of the wicked. Its poetic books of Job, Psalms and Proverbs repeatedly affirm the principle of divine government. The wicked may thrive now and the righteous suffer, these books tell us, but that picture will not be the final one. These books reassure the godly again and again that those who trust will be vindicated, they will endure forever, they will inherit the earth. The wicked, however proud their boasts today, will one day not be found. Their place will be empty. They will disappear like smoke. Men will search for them and they will not be found. Even their memory

will perish. On these pillars of divine justice the world stands, and by these principles the Lord God governs His eternal kingdom.

The historical books of the Old Testament take us another step. Not only does God declare what He will do to the wicked; on many occasions He has shown us. When the first world became too wicked to exist, God destroyed it completely, wiping every living creature outside the ark from the face of the earth. This is a model of the fiery judgment awaiting the present heavens and earth. When Sodom became too sinful to continue, God rained fire and brimstone from heaven, obliterating the entire population in a moment so terrible it is memorialized throughout Scripture as an example of divine judgment. From this terrible conflagration emerged not a survivor – even the ground was left scorched and barren. Only the lingering smoke remained, a grim reminder of the fate awaiting any man who attempts to quarrel with his Maker. Nations also tasted God's wrath. Edom and Judah, Babylon and Nineveh turn by turn came under His temporal judgments. Some were spared a remnant. Others were not. God described these divine visitations in terms of fire and darkness, anguish and trouble. Unquenchable fire consumed entirely until nothing was left. Again smoke ascended, the prophetic cipher for a ruin accomplished.

The inspired declarations of the prophets combine moral principle with historical fate. The details of actual destruction wrought on earth become symbols for another divine visitation. The prophets speak to their own times, but they also stand on tiptoe and view the distant future. A day is coming, they tell us, when God will bring an end to all He has begun. That judgment will be the last. Good and evil will be gathered alike to see the righteousness of the Lord they have served or spurned. Again there will be fire and storm, tempest and darkness. The slain of God will be many – corpses will lie in the street. Amidst this scene of utter comtempt worms and fire will take their final toll. Nothing will remain of the wicked but ashes – the righteous will tread over them with their feet. God's kingdom will endure forever. The righteous and their children will inherit Mount Zion. Joy and singing will fill the air. All the earth will praise the Lord.

Fudge shows that in the Apocrypha and pseudepigrapha the Old Testament view predominates, although the notion of endless torment is beginning to appear in Jewish literature. A. Edersheim in Appendix 19 of *The Life and Times of Jesus the Messiah* shows that the rabbis were also speculating during this period and teaching that hell meant endless punishment for some. The School of Shammai

arranged all mankind into three classes; the perfectly righteous, who are 'immediately written and sealed to eternal life;' the perfectly wicked, who are 'immediately written and sealed to Gehenna;' and an intermediate class, who, 'go down to Gehinnom, and moan, and come up again.' . . . Substantially the same . . . is the view of the School of Hillel. In regard to sinners of Israel and of the Gentiles it teaches, indeed, that they are tormented in Gehenna twelve months, after which their bodies and souls are burnt up and scattered as dust under the feet of the righteous; but it significantly excepts from this number certain classes of transgressors 'who go down to Gehinnom and are punished there to ages of ages.'

These are patently speculations without any of the authority of the canonical scriptures. They could certainly have influenced the minds of the first Christians, but the ultimate question is, 'What did God the Holy Spirit say in the God-breathed Scriptures?' We must be careful not to import into them alien elements from external sources, however popular or influential they may have been.

When we come to the New Testament the words used in their natural connotation are words of destruction rather than words suggesting continuance in torment or misery. When preparing this paper I found in my files thirty pages of foolscap (dating, I think, from the forties) on which I had attempted to jot down from the Revised Version all passages referring to life after death. This is probably not a complete list but I have worked through it again and the following interesting statistics result.

I found 264 references to the fate of the lost. Ten (that is 4 per cent) call it Gehenna, which conjures up the imagery of the Valley of Hinnom outside Jerusalem, notorious for the hideous rites of Moloch worship, in which children were thrown alive into the red-hot arms of the god – an abomination in the eyes of the Lord (Lv. 18:21; 20:2–5; 2 Ki. 23:10; 2 Ch. 28:3; 33:6; Je. 7:31; 32:35). It is often said to have been the site of the city's rubbish tip in the days of Christ, where bodies of criminals and animals were thrown, but evidence for this is late and unreliable. It is in any case an evil place in which are pictured corpses being consumed by fire and maggots as in Isaiah 66 (Mt. 5:22,29,30; 10:28; 18:9; 23:33; Mk. 9:43,45,47; Lk. 12:5). Two of these call it the Gehenna of fire.

There are twenty-six other references (that is 10 per cent) to burning up, three of which concern the lake of fire of the Apocalypse. Fire naturally suggests destruction and is much used for the destruction of what is worthless or evil.

It is only by a pedantic use of the modern concept of the conservation of mass and energy that it is possible to say that fire destroys nothing. It has a secondary use as a cause of pain, as in the case of the rich man of the Lazarus story.

Fifty-nine (22 per cent) speak of destruction, perdition, utter loss or ruin. Our Lord himself in the Sermon on the Mount uses destruction, which he contrasts with life, as the destination of those who choose the broad road (Mt. 7:13). Paul uses it of 'the objects of his wrath – prepared for destruction' (Rom. 9:22); of 'those who oppose you' who 'will be destroyed' (Phil. 1:28); of the enemies of the cross of Christ whose 'destiny is destruction' (Phil. 3:19). 'The man of lawlessness is . . . doomed to destruction' (2 Thes. 2:3); harmful desires 'plunge men into ruin and destruction' (1 Tim. 6:9). Hebrews 10:39 says 'we are not of those who shrink back to destruction, but of those who believe and are saved.' 2 Peter speaks of 'destructive heresies . . . bringing swift destruction . . . their destruction has not been sleeping' (2:1–3). 'The present heavens and earth are reserved for fire, being kept for the day of judgment and destruction of ungodly men' (3:7). The old order will disappear and 'the elements will be destroyed by fire' (3:10–12). The beast will 'go to his destruction' (Rev. 17:8,11).

The very common word *apollumi* is frequently used of eternal ruin, destruction and loss, as in John 3:16: 'should not perish', but it is also used of the lost sheep, the lost coin and the lost son, who, though metaphorically dead and whose life was in total ruin, was restored (Lk. 15).

Twenty cases (8 per cent) speak of separation from God, which carries no connotation of endlessness unless one presupposes immortality: 'depart from me' (Mt. 7:23); 'cast him into the outer darkness' (Mt. 22:13); he 'shall not enter' the kingdom (Mk. 10:15); 'one will be taken and the other left' (Lk. 17:34); 'he is cast forth as a branch' (Jn. 15:6); 'outside are the dogs', etc. (Rev. 22:15). This concept of banishment from God is a terrifying one. It does not mean escaping from God, since God is everywhere in his creation, every particle of which owes its continuing existence to his sustaining. It means, surely, being utterly cut off from the source and sustainer of life. It is another way of describing destruction.

Twenty-five cases (10 per cent) refer to death in its finality, sometimes called 'the second death'. Without resurrection even 'those who have fallen asleep in Christ have perished' (1 Cor. 15:18). This has been brought out with great force by a number of modern theologians like Oscar Cullmann, Helmut Thielicke and Murray Harris. They show that the teaching of the New Testament is to be sharply contrasted with the Greek notion of the immortality of the soul, which sees death as the release of the soul from the prison of the body. What the Christian looks forward to is not a bodiless entrance 'into the highest heavens' at death but a glorious transformation at the Parousia when he is raised from death. Life is contrasted with death, which is a cessation of life, rather than with a continuance of life in misery.

One hundred and eight cases (41 per cent) refer to what I have called unforgiven sin: adverse judgment, in which the penalty is not specified (e.g. 'they will receive greater condemnation' (Mk. 12:40)); life forfeited, with the wrath of God resting on the unbeliever (Jn. 3:36); being unsaved, without specifying what the saved are delivered from (Mt. 24:13). Other passages show salvation contrasted with lostness (Mt. 16:25), perishing (1 Cor. 1:18), destruction (Jas. 4:12), condemnation (Mk. 16:16), judgment (Jn. 3:17), death (2 Cor. 7:10), never with everlasting misery or pain.

Fifteen cases (6 per cent) refer to anguish – this includes tribulation and distress (Rom. 2:9), deliverance to tormentors (Mt. 18:34), outer darkness (Mt. 22:13), wailing and grinding of teeth (Mt. 25:30), the undying worm (Mk. 9:48), beaten with many stripes (Lk. 12:47), the birth-pains of death (Acts 2:24), sorer punishment (Heb. 10:29).

There is one verse (Rev. 14:11) – this represents less than a half of one per cent – which refers to human beings who have no rest, day or night, the smoke of whose torment goes up for ever and ever, which we shall come back to in a moment.

It is a terrible catalogue, giving most solemn warning, yet in all but one of the 264 references there is not a word about unending torment and very many of them in their natural sense clearly refer to destruction.

Immortality of the Soul

There is thus a great weight of material which *prima facie* suggests destruction as the final end of the lost. The traditional view gains most of its plausibility from a belief that our Lord's teaching about Gehenna has to be wedded to a belief in the immortality of the soul. A fierce fire will destroy any living creature, unless that creature happens to be immortal. If man is made immortal, all our exegesis must change. But is he? From Genesis 3 onwards man looks mortal indeed; we are clearly told that God alone has immortality (1 Tim. 6:16); immortality is something that well-doers seek (Rom. 2:7); immortality for the believer has been brought to light by the gospel (2 Tim. 1:10) – he gains immortality (it would appear) when he gains eternal life and becomes partaker of the divine nature; immortality is finally put on at the last trump (1 Cor. 15:53). No, say the traditionalists, God in making man made him immortal, so that he must live on, not only beyond death but also beyond the second death, for ever and ever. The fires of hell will continue to inflict pain on persons they cannot consume.

Some acknowledge that only God is inherently immortal and that he could if he wished annihilate anything that he has made, including human beings. But he has willed both that all who believe should become partakers of the divine nature and so become immortal; he has also willed that those who refuse the gospel invitation should not die but should remain alive suffering the unending torment which they deserve. So we are not immortal by nature but by divine decree, which in practical terms seems to come to the same thing.

Now the curious thing is that when asked for biblical proof of the immortality of the soul, the answer usually given is that it is nowhere explicitly taught, but that (as we have already quoted from Shedd) 'it is everywhere assumed'. Goulburn similarly says that the doctrine of man's immortality 'seems to be graven on mans heart almost as indelibly as the doctrine of God's existence (p. 68)'. The great Dutch theologian Hermann Bavinck defends it as a biblical doctrine but says that it is better demonstrated by reason than by revelation. That life beyond death is repeatedly taught in Scripture and is instinctively believed by everyone, I readily agree, but of its nature and endurance we know nothing except by revelation. If anything has become pellucidly clear to me over the years it is this: philosophizings about the after-life are worthless; we must stick to Scripture and Scripture alone. Certainly something as important as the immortality of the soul and the endless pain of the lost cannot be assumed!

Passages Relied on for Endlessness of Punishment
What are these 'dozens of relevant passages' which we conditionalists attempt to evade by 'various exegetical expedients' (Packer p. 24)? They seem in fact to be fourteen in number.

There are seven passages which use the word *aionios*: everlasting punishment (Mt. 25:46), everlasting fire (Mt. 18:8; 25:41), an eternal sin (Mk. 3:29), everlasting destruction (2 Thes. 1:9), everlasting judgment (Heb. 6:2), the punishment of everlasting fire (Jude 7). Fudge rightly devotes a chapter early in the book to the meaning of *aionios* and shows (as is well known) that it has two senses. It has a qualitative sense, indicating 'a relationship to the kingdom of God, to the Age to Come, to the eschatological realities which in Jesus have begun already to manifest themselves in the Present Age' (p. 49). This aspect is perhaps best translated 'eternal', since eternity can be thought of as outside time. When I analyse my own thoughts, I find that (rightly or wrongly) everlastingness has virtually no place in my concept of eternal life. Everlasting harp playing or hymn singing or even contemplation is not attractive. What the heart yearns for is deliverance from sin and the bliss of being with God in heaven, knowing that the inexorable march of death has been abolished for ever. *Aionios* can be used also of temporal limitlessness which can be rightly translated 'everlasting'.

It is common to argue that since everlasting punishment is set against everlasting life in Matthew 25:46 and since the life lasts as long as God, so must the punishment. This was the position of Augustine, of which Hughes writes:

> Augustine insisted . . . to say that 'life eternal shall be endless, punishment eternal shall come to an end, is the height of absurdity' (*City of God* 21:23) . . . But, as we have seen, the ultimate contrast is between everlasting life and everlasting death and this clearly shows that it is not simply synonyms but also antonyms with which we have to reckon. There is no more

> radical antithesis than that between life and death, for
> life is the absence of death and death is the absence of
> life. Confronted with this antithesis, the position of
> Augustine cannot avoid involvement in the use of
> contradictory concepts (p. 403).

To this we might add three further considerations: (1) It
would be proper to translate 'punishment of the age to
come' and 'life of the age to come' which would leave open
the question of duration. The Matthean parallel to the
aionios of Mk. 3:29 is indeed 'age to come' (Mt. 12:32). (2)
We have other examples of once-for-all acts which have
unending consequences: eternal redemption (Heb. 9:12),
Sodom's punishment of eternal fire (Jude 7). (3) Just as it is
wrong to treat God and Satan as equal and opposite, so it
is wrong to assume that heaven and hell, eternal life and
eternal punishment, are equal and opposite. Both are real
but who is to say that one is as enduring as the other?

There are three passages which speak of unquenchable
fire, two in the teaching of the Baptist (Mt. 3:12 = Lk. 3:17)
and one from our Lord who speaks of going away 'into
Gehenna into the unquenchable fire' (Mk. 9:43). The chaff
of course is burnt up by the irresistible fire – there is nothing
to suggest that the fire goes on burning after it has destroyed
the rubbish. The same Markan passage (9:48) gives us the
one reference to the undying worm, which (as we have seen)
is a quotation from Isaiah 66:24 which depicts corpses being
consumed by maggots.

There is nothing in any of these ten texts which even
suggests (let alone requires) an interpretation contrary to
the natural interpretation of the great mass of texts which
tell of death, destruction, perishing and consumption by
fire. Nor has the imagery of outer darkness and grinding of
teeth any bearing on the question of endlessness.

This leaves us with one passage in Jude and three passages in the Book of Revelation. Jude has spoken of the people saved from Egypt and the destruction of those who did not believe; and of angels kept in eternal chains in the nether gloom awaiting the day of judgment, when they will suffer as Sodom suffered, undergoing a punishment of eternal fire (v. 5–7); he then goes on to speak of those who defile the Christian love feasts 'for whom the nether gloom of darkness has been reserved for ever' (v. 13). These immoral Christians will suffer the same fate as the fallen angels: nether gloom till the day of judgment, then irreversible destruction like that of Sodom.

In the Book of Revelation two passages speak of the smoke of torment rising for ever and ever. 14:11 says of those with the mark of the beast, tormented with burning sulphur, 'the smoke of their torment goes up for ever and ever; and they have no rest, day or night, these worshippers of the beast.' 19:3 says of the great whore, 'the smoke from her goes up for ever and ever.' Finally, 20:10 speaks of the devil 'thrown into the lake of fire and brimstone where the beast and the false prophet were, and they will be tormented day and night for ever and ever.'

Of these three passages two are concerned with non-human or symbolic figures: the devil, the beast, the false prophet and the great whore, and only one refers to men. But the imagery is the same and they need to be examined together. The mind of John of the Apocalypse is steeped in Holy Scripture and it is to the Old Testament that we must go for enlightenment. After Noah's flood, the second great demonstration of divine judgment is the raining down of burning sulphur on the cities of Sodom and Gomorrah. What is left is total, irreversible desolation and dense smoke rising from the land (Gen. 19:24–28). This fearful example is recalled by Moses (Dt. 29:23), Isaiah (13:19), Jeremiah

(50:40), Lamentations (4:6), Amos (4:11), Zephaniah (2:9), Peter (2 Pet. 2:6), Jude (7) and Jesus himself (Lk. 17:28–32). It seems best to interpret the lake of fire and brimstone, the smoke and the torment of the Apocalypse in the light of this archetypal example. The concept of second death is one of finality; the fire consumes utterly, all that is left is smoke, a reminder of God's complete and just triumph over evil.

The third passage (Revelation 14:11) is the most difficult passage that the conditionalist has to deal with. I freely confess that I have come to no firm conclusions about the proper interpretation of the Book of Revelation. While I would not want to be guilty of undervaluing its symbolism, I am nonetheless chary about basing fundamental doctrine upon its symbolic passages. Certainly, on the face of it, having no rest day or night with smoke of torment going up for ever and ever, sounds like everlasting torment. But, as Stott points out, the torment 'experienced "in the presence of the holy angels and . . . the Lamb," seems to refer to the moment of judgment, not the eternal state' (p. 318). This is the time of which Jesus gave warning (Lk. 12:9) when 'he who denies me before men will be denied before the angels of God'. Final judgment is an experience of unceasing and inescapable pain till all is over; but, as at Sodom, all that is left is the smoke of their torment going up for ever. It is a reminder to all eternity of the marvellous justice and mercy of God.

The proof texts of the Westminster Confession add the passage concerning the rich man and Lazarus (Lk. 16:19–31), which is indeed one of great exegetical difficulty. But the scene with Lazarus in Hades can hardly represent the final state of the lost seeing Hades itself is to be cast into the lake of fire (Rev. 20:14), and in any case there is no reference to the everlastingness of that place of torment. (Further reference to Revelation 14 and Luke 16 will be made in the next chapter.)

So this 'avalanche', these 'dozens', these fourteen passages whose natural meaning we are attempting to evade reduces to perhaps one, and that is far from insuperable, representing less than a half of one per cent of the New Testament passages on the doom of the lost. So both Old and New Testaments taken in their natural sense seem to be almost entirely, if not entirely, on the conditionalist side.

The nub of the whole debate is the question of the natural meaning of the texts but there are other objections to the conditionalist position which should be briefly looked at. These in fact turn out to suggest weighty objections to the traditional position.

Other Objections to Conditionalism

1. Belief in endless torment is said to have been the view of Jesus and the Jews of his day, of the New Testament writers and fathers of the Church, of the Reformers and all Bible-believers, and never seriously questioned till the twentieth century (Packer p.22). I myself, resting largely on the authority of Charles Hodge (*Systematic Theology* III 870), at one time believed this to be true. But it is quite untrue. It was certainly an almost unchallenged view during the middle ages, but it was not so either in first-century Judaism or in the early fathers or at the Reformation and most certainly not in the nineteenth century, which was the heyday of conditionalism among evangelicals.

B.L. Bateson in a private communication says in response to Packer's assertion 'it was never queried with any seriousness (by evangelicals) until the twentieth century' (p. 23): 'The subject was much discussed by evangelicals in the nineteenth century, not only in Britain, but also in the United States and at least fifty books and pamphlets

appeared and many items of correspondence appeared on
both sides in Christian magazines. Here are some of the best
works:

> Edward White, Congregationalist, *Life in Christ*,
> 1878, 3rd edn. 541 pp.
>
> E. Petavel, DD, Swiss pastor, *The Problem of Immor-
> tality*, 1878, 600 pp.
>
> Richard Whately, Protestant Archbishop of Dublin,
> *A View of the Scripture Revelation concerning a Future
> State*. There were nine editions from 1829 of which the
> later ones were conditionalist.
>
> Canon Henry Constable, *The Duration and Nature of
> Future Punishment*. Six editions between 1868 and
> 1886.
>
> W.R. Huntington, DD, Rector of All Saints, Worces-
> ter, USA, *Conditional Immortality*, 1878, 202 pp.
>
> J.H. Pettingell, Congregational minister, *The Life Ev-
> erlasting*, 1882, 761 pp.
>
> Reginald Courtenay, Bishop of Jamaica, *The Future
> States*, 1843.
>
> H.H. Dobney, Baptist minister, *The Scripture Doc-
> trine of Future Punishment*, 1846.
>
> J.M. Denniston, Scottish Presbyterian missionary to
> Jamaica, *The Perishing Soul*, 2nd edn. 1874.
>
> Dr Cameron Mann, Protestant Episcopal Bishop of
> N Dakota, *Five Discourses on Future Punishment*,
> 1888.
>
> Dr Joseph Parker, Congregational minister of the
> City Temple, London from 1874 for 28 years, pro-
> claimed conditionalism in the 25 volumes of *The
> People's Bible*.

Bateson then goes on to mention R.W. Dale, whose book
on the atonement was the most recommended book on the

subject in my student days, and W.H.A. Hay Aitken, who was a well-known mission preacher and Canon of Norwich Cathedral. This is all meticulously documented in Froom's great volumes, and Fudge devoted three chapters to the inter-testamental period and four to the period from post-apostolic times to the present day – something over a quarter of his book – showing that Packer's statement is quite untrue.

2. Belief in annihilation is said to miss out on the awesome dignity of our having been made to last for eternity (Packer p. 24). But how a long period of hopeless, ceaseless pain, 'learning' (in Packer's words) 'the bitterness of the choice' the unbeliever has made, can be said to enhance the dignity of man, I fail to see. Long-term imprisonment is one of the horrors of our supposedly civilized society and long-term prisoners normally gain a hangdog look. What would be the effect of such unending 'learning' which yields no reformation? Certainly not awesome dignity. Or is it the believer who has this dignity? Surely he gains his dignity by grace, rather than by creation with a potential for heaven or hell.

3. Believing in annihilation the Christian 'will miss out on telling the unconverted that their prospects without Christ are as bad as they possibly could be . . . Conditionalism cannot but impoverish a Christian and limit our usefulness' (p. 24). It seems to me to be a complete fallacy to think that the worse you paint the picture of hell the more effective your evangelism will be. I felt a growing distaste as I read through Shedd and a worse distaste as I read through Gerstner. This is not the God that I am trying to present to unbelievers. Shedd quotes Jonathan Edwards: 'Wrath will be executed in the day of judgment without any merciful circumstances . . . in hell there will be no more exercises of divine patience.' Faber likewise says:

> O fearful thought! one act of sin
> Within itself contains
> The power of endless hate of God
> And everlasting pains.

Packer says, 'every moment of the unbeliever's . . . bitterness
. . . furthers the glory of God' (p. 24). But the God whom I
know had compassion on the crowds 'because they were
harassed and helpless, like sheep without a shepherd' (Mt.
9:36). He teaches us to think of him as like a good earthly
father who won't give a snake to the son who asks for a fish
(Lk. 11:11). 'He knows how we are formed, he remembers
that we are dust' (Ps. 103:14). Faber said rightly, there is no
place where kindlier judgment is given than in heaven. I
think that the ordinary decent person who is groping his
way through life, ignorant of God, battered and perplexed
by the sinful world around him, is helped best by introduc-
ing him or her to the Jesus of the gospels in his gentleness,
truthfulness and power. As we talk, while not hiding the
seriousness of sin, we must see that the love of God gets
through. To present God as the one whose 'divinely executed retributive process' (Packer p. 24) will bring him into
everlasting torment unless he believes, is hardly likely to
help. To any normal way of thinking (and Jesus has told us
when we think about God to think how the best of human
fathers act), this depicts God as a terrible sadist, not as a
loving Father.

Whether in practice the adoption of conditionalism
makes our evangelism less effective, it is impossible to say.
Many preachers of endless torment have been greatly used
by God but it is doubtful whether that part of the message
effected the conviction. Equally I have no reason to think
that the adoption of conditionalism impairs a man's evangelism. Basil Atkinson was always on the look-out to put in

a word for Jesus. I was very touched when one day I heard that he, a man whose mind lived in academia and Christian theology, had gone up to a group of lads lounging around in the Cambridge market-place and told them that Jesus loved them. I haven't noticed that John Stott's or Michael Green's conditionalism has made them any less of evangelists. In personal talks I often find myself explaining the self-destructive power of sin and of its ultimate power to destroy absolutely. I explain that that is how God has made the world. Judgment expresses his wrath against the abominable thing which he hates.

The Glory of Divine Justice
4.   We are said to miss out on the glory of divine justice, and, in our worship, on praise for God's judgments (Packer p. 21). We should have 'a passionate gladness' that God's 'adorable justice' should be done for the glory of our Creator (p. 21). I cannot see that this is true. In my book *The Enigma of Evil* I try to grapple with all the moral difficulties of the Bible and many of the difficulties of Providence. My main theme is to show how God's judgments reflect the goodness of the God we adore. The one point at which I am so seriously perplexed that I have to devote a whole chapter to it is the subject of hell. My problem is, not that God punishes, but that the punishment traditionally ascribed to God seems neither to square with Scripture nor to be just. Many stress that on the cross Jesus suffered the pains which we deserve. But, though he suffered physical torture, the utter dereliction of separation from the Father, and death, he did not suffer endless pain. I know that no sinner is competent to judge of the heinousness of sin but I cannot see that endless punishment is either loving or just.

C.S. Lewis was brought up in Northern Ireland where that extraordinary hell-fire preacher W.P. Nicholson had exerted so great an influence. In one of his early books, *The Pilgrim's Regress* he tells of his spiritual pilgrimage in allegory.

Chapter one starts in Puritania, where he dreams of a boy who is frustrated by the prohibitions of his elders. He is told that they are the rules of the Steward, who has been appointed by the Landlord who owns the land. One day his parents take him to see the Steward:

> When John came into the room, there was an old man with a red, round face, who was very kind and full of jokes, so that John quite got over his fears, and they had a good talk about fishing tackle and bicycles. But just when the talk was at its best, the Steward got up and cleared his throat. He then took down a mask from the wall with a long white beard attached to it and suddenly clapped it on his face, so that his appearance was awful. And he said, 'Now I am going to talk to you about the Landlord. The Landlord owns all the country, and it is very, very kind of him to allow us to live on it at all – very, very kind.' He went on repeating 'very kind' in a queer sing-song voice so long that John would have laughed, but that now he was beginning to become frightened again. The Steward then took down from a peg a big card with small print all over it, and said, 'Here is a list of all the things the Landlord says you must not do. You'd better look at it.' So John took the card: but half the rules seemed to forbid things he had never heard of, and the other half forbade things he was doing every day and could not imagine not doing: and the number of rules was so enormous that he felt he could never remember them

all. 'I hope,' said the Steward, 'that you have not already broken any of the rules?' John's heart began to thump, and his eyes bulged more and more, and he was at his wit's end when the Steward took off the mask and looked at John with his real face and said, 'Better tell a lie, old chap, better tell a lie. Easiest for all concerned,' and popped the mask on his face all in a flash. John gulped and said quickly, 'Oh, no, sir.' 'That is just as well,' said the Steward through the mask. 'Because, you know, if you did break any of them and the Landlord got to know of it, do you know what he'd do to you?' 'No, sir,' said John: and the Steward's eyes seemed to be twinkling dreadfully through the holes of the mask. 'He'd take you and shut you up for ever and ever in a black hole full of snakes and scorpions as large as lobsters – for ever and ever. And besides that, he is such a kind, good man, so very, very kind, that I am sure you would never want to displease him.' 'No, sir,' said John. 'But, please, sir . . .' 'Well,' said the Steward. 'Please, sir, supposing I did break one, one little one, just by accident, you know. Could nothing stop the snakes and lobsters?' 'Ah! . . .' said the Steward; and then he sat down and talked for a long time, but John could not understand a single syllable. However, it all ended with pointing out that the Landlord was quite extraordinarily kind and good to his tenants, and would certainly torture most of them to death the moment he had the slightest pretext. 'And you can't blame him,' said the Steward. 'For after all it is his land, and it is so very good of him to let us live here at all – people like us, you know.' Then the Steward took off the mask and had a nice, sensible chat with John again, and gave him a cake and brought him out to his father and mother. But just as they were going he bent down and whispered in John's ear, 'I shouldn't bother about it all too much if I were you.' At the same time he slipped the card of the rules into John's hand and told him he could keep it for his own use.

Unending torment speaks to me of sadism, not justice. It is a doctrine which I do not know how to preach without negating the loveliness and glory of God. From the days of Tertullian it has frequently been the emphasis of fanatics. It is a doctrine which makes the Inquisition look reasonable. It all seems a flight from reality and common sense.

I have a suspicion (though I may well be wrong) that many of the sincere Christians who hold this doctrine don't quite believe it themselves. They are tempted to whittle down some of the Bible's teaching. Jesus speaks of the many on the broad road to destruction in contrast to the few on the road to life but Charles Hodge says (III p. 870), 'We have reason to believe . . . that the number of the finally lost in comparison with the whole number of the saved will be very inconsiderable.' (Shocking adjective!) B.B. Warfield (p. 63) speaks of them as 'a relatively insignificant body'. Goulburn says (p. 164), 'no one to whom the offer of grace and salvation is fully and fairly made, can possibly perish except by the wilful, deliberate, open-eyed rejection of the offer'. But what of the multitudes who have heard the offer imperfectly presented and what of the multitudes who have simply neglected their great salvation? Goulburn seems to suggest that there are few on the road to destruction. Salmond (p. 674) sets great hope on deathbed repentances, however faint and feeble. As does Pusey (pp. 11–17).

Packer says that hell is 'unimaginably dreadful' (p. 20), 'far, far worse than the symbols' (p. 25), and he recommends that we 'do not attempt to imagine what it is like'. But is it not the preacher's duty to exercise his imagination in a disciplined way to bring home to his hearers the dread truth, whatever it is? It seems to me that Fudge is a most unwavering preacher of hell, not tempted to whittle down what the Bible actually says. Its solemn teaching appears to be that our destiny is sealed at death, and this gives great urgency to our preaching. (See Heb. 9:27, 'It is appointed for men to die once, and after that comes judgment.' 2 Cor. 5:10, 'We must all appear before the judgment seat of Christ, so that each one may receive good or bad, according to what he has done in the body.' Rom. 2:5–8, 'On the day of wrath . . . he will render to every man according to his works: to those who by patience and well doing seek glory and honour and immortality, he will give eternal life; but for those who are factious and do not obey the truth, but obey wickedness, there will be wrath and fury.' John 3:36, 'He who does not obey the Son shall not see life, but the wrath of God rests upon him.' John 8:24, 'I told you that you would die in your sins, for you will die in your sins unless you believe that I am he.')

Some argue that destruction is no punishment, since many an unbeliever wants to die, so mere death would be a denial of justice. This assumes that the first death is the end and that there is no Day of Judgment and that we are not judged according to our works. This is plainly unscriptural and not the view of any conditionalist that I know. The very wicked who have suffered little in this life will clearly get what they deserve. Perhaps a major part of the punishment will be a realization of the true awfulness of their sin, in its crucifixion of the Son of God and in its effects on others. The horror (particularly of the latter) would be greater for some than for others.

5. Conditionalists, we are told, 'appear to back into' their doctrine 'in horrified recoil from the thought of millions in

endless distress, rather than move into it because the obvious meaning of Scripture beckons them' (Packer p. 24). As I have already shown, I was drawn to conditionalism by Scripture, rather than by a horrified recoil from the other doctrine. But I do plead guilty to a growing horror at the thought of millions in endless distress, which I find exceedingly difficult to reconcile not only with the goodness of God, but also with the final supremacy of Christ. If there are human beings alive suffering endless punishment, it would seem to mean that they are in endless opposition to God, that is to say, we have a doctrine of endless sinning as well as of suffering. How can this be if Christ is all in all? I plead guilty also to failing to see how God and the saints could be in perfect bliss with human beings hopelessly sinning and suffering. Packer's answer to this (p. 24) is that Gods joy will not be marred by the continuance in being of the damned, so that the Christian's joy will not be either.

These speculations don't look to me like the beckonings of Scripture's obvious meaning. I have thought about this subject for more than fifty years and for more than fifty years I have believed the Bible to teach the ultimate destruction of the lost, but I have hesitated to declare myself in print. I regard with utmost horror the possibility of being wrong. We are all to be judged by our words (Mt. 12:37) and teachers with greater strictness (Jas. 3:1). Whichever side you are on, it is a dreadful thing to be on the wrong side in this issue. Now I feel that the time has come when I must declare my mind honestly. I believe that endless torment is a hideous and unscriptural doctrine which has been a terrible burden on the mind of the church for many centuries and a terrible blot on her presentation of the gospel. I should indeed be happy if, before I die, I could help in sweeping it away. Most of all I should rejoice to see a number of theologians (including some of the very first water) joining Fudge in researching this great topic in all its ramifications.

Bibliographical Note regarding some publications referred to in this chapter:

Froom, L.E., *The Conditionalist Faith of Our Fathers* (Washington, DC: Review and Herald, 1966)

Atkinson, B.F.C., *Life and Immortality* (privately printed, no date, still obtainable from the Rev B.L. Bateson, 26 Summershard, S Petherton, Somerset TA13 5DP for £1 post free).

Guillebaud, H.E., *The Righteous Judge* (privately printed, 1964; photocopies obtainable also from Bateson for £2 post free)

Packer, J.I., Leon Morris lecture 'The Problem of Eternal Punishment' in *Crux*, the journal of Regent College, Vancouver, Sept 1990, from which all quotations have been taken. A shorter version has been published in booklet form in the *Orthos* series by the Fellowship of Word and Spirit, 37 Martlet Avenue, Disley, Cheshire SK12 2JH.

Edwards, D.L., and Stott, J.R.W., *Essentials* (London: Hodder & Stoughton, 1990)

Hughes, P.E., *The True Image* (Grand Rapids: Eerdmans/Leicester, Inter-Varsity Press, 1989)

Goulburn, E.M., *Everlasting Punishment* (London: Rivingtons, 1880)

Warfield, B.B., 'Predestination' in Hastings', *Dictionary of the Bible* Vol 4.

Salmond, S.D.F., *The Christian Doctrine of Immortality* (Edinburgh: T & T Clark, 1897)

Pusey, E.B., *What is Of Faith as to Everlasting Punishment?* (Oxford: Parker, 3rd edn., 1881)

Fudge, E.W., *The Fire That Consumes: The Biblical Case for Conditional Immortality*, Revised Edn. (Carlisle: Paternoster, 1994)

Twenty-Eight

Rutherford House — The Debate Develops

Of the ten papers read at the conference I can only mention four. Henri Blocher's was a devout and difficult paper which I was anxious to see in print. He attempted a renewed understanding of the traditional dogma, saying 'we dare not disregard the authority of the greatest doctors in Christian, especially evangelical, history'. (p. 286) He stressed in particular that 'the main fact about everlasting punishment, the fate of reprobates, is this: sin shall be no more'. The damned will agree with God's just judgment and suffer 'remorse-in-agreement with God.' 'What comes next? Nothing . . . (It is) total death, absolute fixity . . . What remains is the corpse of a sinful life together with the lucid consciousness of that truth' (pp. 304–8). This is all very paradoxical and seems to me to owe more to the doctors of the church than to Holy Scripture.

Paul Helm read a characteristically lucid paper 'Are They Few That Be Saved?' in which he argues that there is nothing unscriptural in believing that a person with no knowledge of Christ who sincerely prays, 'O most merciful one, have mercy on me' will be saved. It is Christ alone who saves, not the knowledge of Christ.

David Powys read a paper on 'The Nineteenth and Twentieth Century Debates about Hell and Universalism' which was material from a large thesis (580 pages) since submitted to The Australian College of Theology for the degree of Doctor of Theology under the title 'The Hermeneutics of Hell: the fate of the un-righteous in New Testament thought.' He is widely read in the English literature and he writes without making assumptions concerning scriptural inspiration and so should reach some of those who might not take Fudge seriously. His position is that New Testament thought is consistently conditionalist. His inter-pretation of the rich man and Lazarus story is particularly inter-esting. His main points are: (1) It is addressed to Pharisees as the context shows (Lk. 16:14 – and Pharisees are mentioned in every chapter from 11 to 19). (2) The Pharisees had come to replace the concept of resurrection by the belief that at death souls passed either to heavenly bliss or to torment depending on their degree of faithfulness to God's law as interpreted by their tradition. (3) In doing this they forgot the real teaching of the Law, e.g. care for the poor. (4) The view of the after-life presented in the story has nothing Christian in it, it is simply that of current Pharisaic thought, except that the rich man finds himself in the wrong place beyond all help, while the unclean beggar is now comforted. (5) It is a chilling attack on Pharisaic piety by the use of satire.

His treatment of the Book of Revelation is also interesting. It has 'very little that touches on the fate of the unrighteous. Its purpose was pastoral, to promote steadfast faith amongst the persecuted. While it has eschatological content, its purpose was not to function as a programme guide to the eschaton.' The threat of torture to those who apostatize is not literal but figurative – far worse than the terror of the human torturer is the terror of denying God in the presence of the Lamb and the holy angels. Powys' treatment does not carry immediate conviction but the whole work is a most valuable contribution to the debate, which (perhaps in a more condensed form) merits publication and careful study.

The most immediately relevant paper at the conference as far as I was concerned was that of Kendall Harmon, 'The Case Against Conditionalism: A Response to Edward William Fudge.'

Kendall is a young American trained under Dr Packer at Regent College, Vancouver, and at The Episcopal School of Ministry, Pittsburgh. He had found himself continually troubled by the neglect of hell in the modern church and had come to Oxford to research the subject under Dr Geoffrey Rowell of Keble College. He says that conditionalists (he mentions me by name) show 'an inadequate appreciation for the role of tradition in Christian thinking'. I doubt whether this is true. Both Stott and I have been very reluctant to commit ourselves to this view precisely because we respect the weight of tradition, though the unanimity of that tradition is not nearly so complete as the traditionalists commonly suppose. Fudge and Froom go to a lot of trouble in examining Augustine, Calvin and other doctors of the church.

He then goes on to suggest three respects in which Fudge's work is flawed. It is flawed in methodology. He says that Fudge 'over-emphasises the Old Testament background at the expense of the intertestamental literature (maintaining that) the New Testament language shares the background of apocalyptic writings, but not its ideas' (p. 206). This he regards as unscholarly. But Fudge does in fact believe both that some New Testament ideas and some New Testament language (for instance, the imagery of the Valley of Hinnom to represent hell) originated in the intertestamental period but that none of it negates the consistent teaching of the Old Testament. Secondly, it is flawed exegetically, since Fudge, he says, often sees a gap between the Day of Judgement and the final extinction which the New Testament never mentions. Fudge replies that he does not overtly use this schema as a principle of interpretation. It seems to me that the New Testament stresses that the judgment is (a) dreadful, (b) final. Nowhere does it say that it is instantaneous. Thirdly, it is said to be flawed hermeneutically. Fudge is said not to treat parallel images as parallel. There are three images of hell: punishment, destruction and exclusion – exclusion (he says) 'is hardly discussed'. The latter point is simply not true – Fudge gives considerable space to this element. Harmon is very keen on the imagery of exclusion, for if man is immortal it means that the lost will suffer pain everlastingly. However, he nowhere argues the case for human immortality. Harmon seems to join the great crowd of exegetes who think that immortality is assumed in the Bible, though not specifically taught. Sad to say Harmon's paper did not seem to me a really serious attempt to answer Fudge. It looked like another case of the doctors of the church taking precedence over the natural meaning of Scripture.

From subsequent discussion, Harmon's objection to my view and that of Fudge appears to be that our definition of death is unsatisfactory. We describe death as the absence of life and then go on to describe the unbeliever's resurrection, judgment and final end. Admittedly the Bible does not give a clear picture of the intermediate state between death and resurrection. But the difficulty of defining that state, which to Harmon is a grave theological difficulty, should in no way be allowed to undermine what is exegetically clear. Physical death, both in ordinary experience and in the Bible, is the cessation of life which is complete and final. It is also an exegetical fact that finally God will be all in all. Good theology must be based on sound exegesis but a theological difficulty (there are many of them!) must not be allowed to overturn good exegesis. It still seems to me that he is assuming a universal immortality without attempting to prove it.

Incidentally Harmon has criticized my use of C.S. Lewis. The long quotation in the previous chapter is not of course to claim his support for conditional immortality; he clearly believed in some continuance of the damned, as can be seen in *The Great Divorce* and at the end of *The Pilgrim's Regress* (Book 10, chapter 4). I do, however, apologize, for it is treatment from which I have myself suffered and which I find very irritating: I state the case which I am about to answer and this is taken up by an opponent to refute me without tackling my own answer! Lewis, though still believing in the Black Hole, has turned it into a very different (and somewhat elusive!) concept. Nevertheless I find his Steward a telling caricature of those I have been criticizing.

Since Edinburgh Kendall has done a great deal more work and has gained the DPhil for a thesis 'Finally Excluded from God? Some Twentieth Century Theological Explorations of the Problem of Hell and Universalism with Reference to the Historical Development of These Doctrines'. The thesis is in two sections: A. The Understanding of Hell in Christian History, which leads up to The Collision Between the Traditional Hell and Enlightenment Humanitarianism. Section B deals with Twentieth Century Explorations: firstly with Universalism in the Thought of J.A.T. Robinson; secondly with Theories of Hell as Destruction. Here he has three examples, one from mainstream theology (J.M. Shaw), one from evangelical theology (here he cites Clark Pinnock – I understand he has done this for reasons of space. He regards Fudge as a stronger representative of this school of thought but considers that his earlier critique of Fudge in Universalism and the Doctrine of Hell is sufficient refutation); and one from Roman Catholic theology (Schillebeeck). As a representative of the traditional doctrine he takes C.S. Lewis, discussing his theological work in *The Problem of Pain* and his imaginative work in *The Pilgrim's Regress, The Screwtape Letters* and *The Great Divorce*. It is good to have this thoughtful and even-tempered discussion of the whole subject, even though it does not seem to me to grapple seriously with Fudge's argument.

The next important step for me after Edinburgh came in the summer of 1992. A publisher said to me, 'We badly need a book on hell from your point of view; the traditionalists are pouring out books and pamphlets; if you will write a short book on the subject I will most certainly publish it.' As I have believed in conditional immortality for more than fifty years and feel strongly about it, I thought perhaps that I should drop other things and have a go at it. But I realized that this is a subject which cannot be isolated and judged simply on its merits – it is interwoven with other things. A common reaction in some quarters is: 'He takes that line because he is a woolly liberal who wants to water down the plain teaching of Christ', or, 'He is an Anglican who cannot stomach either the true doctrine of hell or an honest universalism, so he is attempting a typical compromise.' But I am not a woolly liberal – my whole life has been an attempt to bring Christians back to the Bible and to taking the Bible at its face value. And I am not a compromising Anglican – I am a Reformation Anglican, who stands by the doctrines so carefully worked out in the sixteenth century, unmoved by the blandishments of the eighteenth-century Enlightenment or the nineteenth-century rise of scientific criticism. It seemed necessary if I was to be read by evangelicals that I should establish my credentials.

Then I slightly misremembered something that C.S. Lewis had written. In *The Pilgrim's Regress* he traces his spiritual and intellectual pilgrimage in a somewhat obscure allegory. In later editions he apologizes for the obscurity, since he greatly disliked unnecessary obscurity in other people. Then he goes on to explain that good allegory exists not to hide but to reveal; it makes the inner world more palpable by giving it an (imagined) concrete embodiment. I interpreted this to mean that it conveys a position which can be felt without having to spell out that position in detail. Suddenly the idea came to me: Wouldn't this also apply to autobiography? I could show my outlook at various points without having to justify it by spelling it all out.

This idea came to me just before setting out on holiday in Wales with Michael and his family. It turned out to be a most extraordinary holiday. I found myself waking up at about 2 a.m. each morning with fifty new ideas for the book, which I promptly jotted down. Concurrently with this unwonted activity in my brain came an unwonted sluggishness in my bowel! I had been suffering a little from constipation before the holiday began and had taken the usual precautions, all to no avail. The remedy from the pharmacist did no better, and when more than a fortnight had passed I thought I should call for the elders of the church. As the only elder available was Michael, he anointed me and we prayed, still to no avail. As I was next going on to Nottingham to stay with Peter's family, we reported the trouble to him and he got a consultant friend to sort me out. I returned home with a great sheaf of autobiographical notes and the recognition that a change is as good as a rest! Since when I have been writing away.

Twenty-Nine

The Unfinished Task

As I look back over the years I have a feeling that my whole life has been a preparation for the writing of this book. The purpose of the book is twofold: (1) to reaffirm the importance for the whole Christian Church of coming back to trust in and to obey the revelation which God has given us in Holy Scripture; and (2) to attempt to set right the interpretation of one important feature in that revelation. But the book is set in the context of a life which has been governed by two convictions: (1) that Jesus Christ is an authoritative and entirely trustworthy teacher; and (2) that he taught us to regard the Holy Scriptures as the word of the Living God. And the life is set in the context of a world vision: it is God's intention to call out a people from every nation and tribe and tongue to worship him through Christ before the final overthrow of evil and the establishment of the perfect reign of righteousness. The task is evangelism based on a sound theology of Christ and the Word.

The battle has swayed backwards and forwards with sad disappointments and wonderful gains and it will continue to do so until the End. It has been wonderful to see closed lands opening up to the gospel. In our student days we prayed for Nepal, where Christianity was totally prohibited; now it has a flourishing church. The same is true of many lands. With the help of linguistics, of radio and of aircraft there are now few peoples entirely without gospel witness. The great bastions of atheism have given way – Communism has collapsed in the Soviet Empire and a deep Christian revival is taking place in China. Within Christendom there have been huge numerical losses but considerable spiritual gains with the revival of Bible-based Christianity in all the churches.

But there have been sad disappointments. The zeal of youth naturally hoped for quick results, for sustained and unimpeded progress, forgetting that 'the mills of God grind slowly'. If a work is to be deep and lasting, it needs to be assailed again and again. The fact is that the battle with liberalism is far from having been won either academically or ecclesiastically. I wrote in 1972: 'My *cri de coeur* is that liberals would take conservative theology seriously. It will be a great day when someone settles down to write a closely argued, honest refutation of the conservative position' (*The Renewal and Unity of the Church in England*, p. 24). James Barr in *Fundamentalism* (1977) and David Edwards in *Essentials* (1988) both had some sort of a try at it but neither of them (it seemed to me) really took the conservative position seriously. This was partly because the conservatives had largely abandoned their role as an opposition to the current liberal criticism of the Bible and had become part of the establishment. Barr and Edwards could therefore assume that a liberal approach to the Bible was fundamentally right and that a remobilizing of the old arguments was all that was required. This left the unsuspecting theological student ill-prepared to face the assaults on his faith. So the heart-breaking spectacle has continued of students who had come to faith in Bible-believing communities either losing their faith or gradually losing the sharpness and clarity of their faith and with it their warmth of devotion and their zeal for evangelism. If all who had owed their faith to such communities had adhered to the fundamentals while seeking to deepen their faith, the church would have been a vastly greater spiritual force than it is today.

So what are my hopes for the future? For evangelicals I hope three things. I hope that they will work for clarity of expression. An ideology is the most powerful thing in the world, and Christianity which purports to offer good news cannot afford obscurity. In Oxford there is a good deal of obscure theology but the simple fact is that if the gospel is not understood it is not good news to the hearer. Of course we do not want over-simplification since that too distorts the good news, but there are certain habits in academic circles which militate against clarity and which need to be carefully watched. For instance, some theologians present everyone else's views and conceal their own, supposedly in the interests of scholarly objectivity. But the best teachers are those who passionately believe what they teach and are not afraid to provoke dissent. Another tendency is to encourage much quick reading to keep up with the latest theological fashions, rather than careful reading of a comparatively small amount of material of real importance. This means that a great variety of options are left open and undecided. But progress in truth requires the making of decisions – not of course irrevocable decisions but at least tentative decisions – on which further explorations can be built and the jungle of possible hypotheses tamed. The purpose of theology for the Christian is that he may know how to communicate the faith with integrity. John Wesley, the Oxford don, was right in trying out his sermons on his illiterate charwoman.

My hope, secondly, is that they will go back to the centre to check their foundations. There is always a danger among us of succumbing to anti-intellectualism in one form or another, or of drifting into liberalism. Our foundation is faith in Christ witnessed to inwardly by the Holy Spirit and outwardly by Holy Scripture. The one unchanging objective element in this witness of God is the Christ made known to us in the canonical gospels. It is these four little books to which we must return and reaffirm the greatest of all theological decisions: The Jesus who said, 'Heaven and earth will pass away, but my words will not pass away,' is to be our teacher whom we will follow in everything, including his view of Scripture.

My hope, thirdly, is that they will develop the habit of continually going back to the centre to check against the primary sources the conclusions which they build on these foundations. This does not mean flouting church traditions. It is exceedingly unlikely, as C.H. Spurgeon pointed out, that genuinely new interpretations of biblical doctrine will be true, but theologians over the centuries have propounded views and systems some of which are highly esteemed in certain circles, which need to be examined with care lest they should be reading into Scripture more than is really there. On the other hand, the post-Enlightenment church, with its policy of rigorously questioning everything is (as I argued in *Redating Matthew, Mark and Luke*) more likely to undervalue what tradition can teach us than to overvalue it. Evangelicals should ask themselves in all seriousness when considering questions of dogmatic theology or of biblical criticism whether a view squares with that of Jesus. To a liberal this is an irrelevant question but to an orthodox Christian it is all-important.

What are my hopes for the future of the Church of England? It is certainly not that the three main streams in the church should be strengthened; it is rather that Catholics, liberals and evangelicals should all be reformed and the church brought nearer to the pattern of a self-propagating, self-supporting and self-governing body as envisaged by that great missionary statesman, Roland Allen. If Catholics be thought to embody traditions of beauty and dignity in worship and a sense of continuity with the historic church, then that is what the whole church should strive for. If the liberals be thought to embody freedom and honesty of thought and a care for the social needs of our time, then that is what we should all strive for. If evangelicals are thought to embody zeal for evangelism and biblical preaching and a concern for world mission, then that too is the call of the whole church.

But if Catholic 'truth' means the unchurching of the Noncon-formists and the artificial denial of the sacrament to those who have no episcopally ordained priest, then we must oppose it. It is intolerable that a clergyman should be converted into a commun-ion-taking machine who dashes from congregation to congrega-tion taking services and preaching sermonettes, not at times convenient to the people but at the only times possible to him. If the liberal conception of freedom of thought means a denial of the primacy of revelation or if social action becomes a substitute for gospel preaching, then we must declare it false. Where there is no gospel, there is no church. The idea (favoured by some) that the whole church should squeeze out Catholic and evangelical 'extremists' and adopt a middle-of-the-road liberalism is suicidal madness.

Evangelicals have many weaknesses and some serious divi-sions, two of the most obvious of which are the question of establishment and the question of women's ministry. Some think that it is high time the church was disestablished and was seen neither to support or to be supported by a patently unchristian state. Others think that establishment still provides some witness to the gospel. There is no absolute principle at stake here. The church prospered for its first three hundred years with no state support and could obviously do so again. On the other hand, God is Sovereign over the nation, which should be subservient to him. Neutrality is impossible for states as for individuals and it may be wrong to press for disestablishment as long as the people still desire this slight acknowledgement of God to remain. I am not inclined to campaign on either side.

On the question of women's ministry, I acknowledge that the feminists have had good grounds for accusing men of either deliberate or thoughtless oppression of the other sex. This, however, was not the result of following the principles of biblical Christianity. As far back as the Victorian era, before feminism had become a force, it was noted that one of the effects of

Christianity had been to raise the status of women in society. But the New Testament does teach that God has given a certain hierarchical structure to society: the man is head of the wife and children are to be obedient to parents. The ignoring of this, together with the breakdown of the monogamous ideal, has plunged western society into chaos and it is of first importance that the church should recover this doctrine – and with it the true glory of motherhood. There is difference of opinion as to how this should work out in the church. Few would wish to deny to women opportunities for theological education and active work in the congregation, but the exercise of authority over men seems to be definitely discouraged. I hope that the role of deaconess will be restored to full honour.

In all these matters the theological colleges hold the key position. The day of the learned country parson has gone and it is a struggle for the ordinary parochial minister to keep up his reading; therefore the brief years spent as a student are strategically important. I hope that a succession of good teachers will be raised up to ground the future leaders of the Church of England in the biblical faith, and indeed the future leaders of all the churches. There is a great ferment at work in all the churches, Protestant, Roman Catholic and the ancient Eastern churches. O that God would drive us all back to our foundations to find our unity at the centre in Christ himself.

And what of my personal hopes? I have no desire to live to be a burden to those I love but I shall count it a great privilege if I am allowed to continue to pray a little longer. In a world of such great need where one can apparently do nothing to help, it is wonderful to know that feeble prayers in the name of our mighty Lord do help; they help those suffering torment, they help those in the front line of the gospel battle. I hope too that my mental powers may be spared to enable me to write a little more and to complete some of my unfinished business on The Christian View of the Bible. I hope also to continue to bear witness to those without faith, especially to my elderly friends who as yet do not know Christ. Not to 'win Christ' is the greatest loss imaginable. It is terrible to lose all one's possessions, to lose one's husband or wife or one's only child, but it is as nothing to the loss of the Saviour who gave his life for us. My prayer with and for them is:

Lord, grant that we may so pass through things temporal that we finally lose not the things eternal.

Postscript

John Wenham died on 13th February 1996, aged 82. He was best known as the author of *The Elements of New Testament Greek*, the Greek textbook used most widely in the English-speaking world. However he himself regarded his most important works to be those exploring the authority and truth of the Bible. And it is probably true that his influence has been greatest as a twentieth-century defender of the grounds of historic Christianity. His has not been a headline-grabbing style – which is why he described himself as a nobody, in his subtitle for this his latest and last book. Yet, as his story demonstrates, he was in fact a remarkable man, playing a crucial role in the survival and resurgence of Biblical orthodoxy in the Church in England.

Although he reckoned himself fearful, he was never afraid to be unconventional, as he was not afraid to be honest. In films they have the ugly term 'biopic'. This book, completed before severe strokes in 1994 ended his active life, might be termed 'biotheology', theology emerging from and examined in a particular life. His intention has been to demonstrate the provenance of his creed and the integrity of his answer to one of the hardest theological questions of every age: How can the great God of love, whom he came to know as a young man, tolerate, indeed create, a place of unending torment and consign to it creatures whom He loves?

Theoretical theology can be quite comfortable – playing with ideas rather like shuffling images on a computer screen; but it can easily be deceptive, a disguise for a personal agenda which is never revealed. By sleight of hand the theologian conceals the presupposition on which his *oeuvres* are built and the life-circumstances out of which they grew. Theological theories must argue for themselves in the market-place of ideas; but true theology is about real life. It applies to life; it emerges from life and is finally verified, or falsified, in experience. This frank account of the development of his faith and ideas in the crucible of an ordinary life provides a wealth of detail about the formative period of the post-war evangelical revival in England – and for many people this will be fascinating in itself. But it is also the platform for a plea to examine seriously the urgent question of hell.

The final paragraph of this book was not a pious hope. Yet, when thoroughly disabled by strokes, he became progressively and painfully more dependent on others, primarily on David and Clare who nursed him to the end. The depths of enfeebled prayer and frustration through which he then went seemed to be for him the final experience of the cross he had gladly shouldered 66 years before.

The publication of this book was delayed at that time, but he died in the certainty that it would see the light of day. It has been a privilege to prepare it for press, and I am glad it goes out under the imprint of Paternoster Press, publishers of his *Easter Enigma*. I am grateful for their encouragement.

Michael Wenham
1997

Index of Names

F02